Lecture Notes in Computer Science 2492

Edited by G. Goos, J. Hartmanis, and J. van Leeuwen

T0226288

Springer
Berlin
Heidelberg
New York
Barcelona
Hong Kong
London
Milan
Paris
Tokyo

Francisco José Perales
Edwin R. Hancock (Eds.)

Articulated Motion and Deformable Objects

Second International Workshop, AMDO 2002
Palma de Mallorca, Spain, November 21-23, 2002
Proceedings

 Springer

Series Editors

Gerhard Goos, Karlsruhe University, Germany
Juris Hartmanis, Cornell University, NY, USA
Jan van Leeuwen, Utrecht University, The Netherlands

Volume Editors

Francisco José Perales
Director, Computer Graphics and Vision Group
Sub-Director Computer Science Engineering School (EPS-UIB)
Department of Computer Science and Maths
C/Valldemossa km 7.5, PC 07071, Palma de Mallorca, Baleares, Spain
E-mail: paco.perales@uib.es

Edwin R. Hancock
Department of Computer Science, University of York
YO1 5DD York, UK
E-mail: erh@minster.york.ac.uk

Cataloging-in-Publication Data applied for

A catalog record for this book is available from the Library of Congress.

Bibliographic information published by Die Deutsche Bibliothek
Die Deutsche Bibliothek lists this publication in the Deutsche Nationalbibliografie;
detailed bibliographic data is available in the Internet at http://dnb.ddb.de

CR Subject Classification (1998): I.4, I.2.10, I.6, I.5, I.3

ISSN 0302-9743
ISBN 3-540-00149-2 Springer-Verlag Berlin Heidelberg New York

Springer-Verlag Berlin Heidelberg New York
a member of BertelsmannSpringer Science+Business Media GmbH

http://www.springer.de

© Springer-Verlag Berlin Heidelberg 2002
Printed in Germany

Typesetting: Camera-ready by author, data conversion by Olgun Computergrafik
Printed on acid-free paper   SPIN: 10870677   06/3142   5 4 3 2 1 0

Preface

The AMDO 2002 workshop took place at the Universitat de les Illes Balears (UIB) on 21 23 November, 2002, sponsored by the International Association for Pattern Recognition (IAPR), AERFAI (Spanish Association for Pattern Recognition and Image Analysis), the CICYT (Comision Interministerial de Ciencia y Tecnologia, Spanish Government), the European Commission (Human Potential Programme: High Level Scienti c Conferences), and the Mathematics and Computer Science Department of the UIB. In addition, Egse (Eurographics Spanish Chapter) helped with dissemination and promotion. The subject of the workshop was ongoing research in articulated motion on a sequence of images and sophisticated models for deformable objects. The goals of these areas are to understand and interpret the motion of complex objects that can be found in sequences of images in the real world. These topics (geometric and physically deformable models, motion analysis, articulated models and animation, visualization of deformable models, 3D recovery from motion, single or multiple human motion analysis and synthesis, applications of deformable models and motion analysis, face tracking, recovering and recognition models, etc.) are actually very interesting ways of organizing important research to solve more general problems. Another objective of this workshop was to relate elds using computer graphics, computer animation, or applications in several disciplines combining synthetic and analytical images. In this regard it is of particular interest to encourage links between researchers in areas of computer vision and computer graphics who have common problems and frequently use similar techniques.

The workshop included ve sessions of presented papers and two tutorials. Invited talks treating various aspects of the topics were: Haptic-based Deformable Solid of Arbitrary Topology, by Prof. H. Qin from the State University of New York at Stony Brook (USA); Passive 3D Human Motion Capture: Vision-Based Tracking Meets Computer Animation, by Prof. I. Kakadiaris from Houston University (USA); and Recovering Non-rigid 3D Shape Using a Plane+Parallax Approach, by Prof. N. Perez de la Blanca from the University of Granada (Spain).

November 2002

F.J. Perales, E.R. Hancock
Program Co-Chairs

Organization

AMDO 2002 was organized by the Department of Mathematics and Computer Science, Universitat de les Illes Balears (UIB) in cooperation with IAPR (International Association for Pattern Recognition) and AERFAI (Spanish Association for Pattern Recognition and Image Analysis).

Program Committee

General Workshop Co-Chairs: F.J. Perales, Mathematics and Computer Science Department, UIB (Spain)

E.R. Hancock, Department of Computer Science, University of York (UK)

Organizing Chairs: M. Gonzalez, A. Igelmo , R. Mas, P.M. Mascaro, A. Mir, P. Palmer, F.J. Perales, J.M. Buades, UIB (Spain)

Tutorial Chairs: M. Gonzalez, R. Mas, A. Mir, F.J. Perales, UIB (Spain)

Programme Committee

Aloimonos, Y.	University of Maryland, USA
Aggarwal, J.K.	University of Texas, USA
Ayache, N.	INRIA, Sophia-Antipolis, France
Badler, N.I.	University of Pennsylvania, USA
Boulic, R.	EPFL, Switzerland
Brunet, P.	University Polytechnic Catalonia, Spain
Cipolla, R.	University of Cambrige, UK
Cohen, I.	University of Southern California, USA
Davis, L.S.	University of Maryland, USA
Del Bimbo, A.	University di Firenze, Italy
Gong, S.	Queen Mary and West eld Coll., UK
Kakadiaris, I.A.	University of Houston, USA
Kittler, J.	University of Surrey, UK
Kunii, T.L.	University of Hosei, Japan
Huang, T.S.	University of Urbana-Champaign, USA
Jain, A.	Michigan State University, USA
Medioni, G.	University of Southern California, USA
Metaxas, D.	University of Pennsylvania, USA
Nagel, H.-H.	Institut für Algorithmen und Kognitive Systeme, Germany
Nastar, C.	LUV, France
Pentland, A.	Media Lab, MIT, USA
Perez de la Blanca, N.	University of Granada, Spain
Qin, H.	Stony Brook University, New York, USA
Sanfeliu, A.	IRI, CSIC-UPC, Spain
Seron, F.	University of Zaragoza, Spain
Shirai, Y.	University of Osaka, Japan
Susin, A.	University Polytechnic Catalonia, Spain
Terzopoulos, D.	University of Toronto, Canada
Teixeira, J.C.	FCTUC, Portugal
Thalmann, D.	EPFL, Switzerland
Villanueva, J.	UAB-CVC, Spain

Sponsoring Institutions

IAPR (International Association for Pattern Recognition)
European Commission (Human Potential Programme)
MCyT (Ministerio de Ciencia y Tecnologia, Spanish Government)
TIC2001-5233-E
Mathematics and Computer Science Department, Universitat de les Illes Balears (UIB)
Conselleria d Innovaciọ i Energia (Govern de les Illes Balears)
AERFAI (Spanish Association for Pattern Recognition and Image Analysis)

Table of Contents

Articulated Motion and Deformable Objects AMDO 2002

Virtual Clay: Haptics-Based Deformable Solids of Arbitrary Topology

Kevin T. McDonnell and Hong Qin

Department of Computer Science
State University of New York at Stony Brook
Stony Brook, NY 11794–4400
{ktm,qin}@cs.sunysb.edu

Abstract. This paper presents Virtual Clay as a novel, interactive, dynamic, haptics-based deformable solid of arbitrary topology. Our Virtual Clay methodology is a unique, powerful visual modeling paradigm which is founded upon the integration of (1) deformable models, (2) free-form, spline-based solids, (3) procedural subdivision solids of arbitrary topology, and (4) dynamic objects governed by physical laws. Solid geometry exhibits much greater modeling potential and superior advantages to popular surface-based techniques in visual computing. This is primarily because a CAD-based solid representation of a real-world physical object is both geometrically accurate and topologically unambiguous. We first introduce the concept of Virtual Clay based on dynamic subdivision solids. Then, we formulate the mathematics of Virtual Clay through the integration of the geometry of subdivision solids with the principle of physics-based CAGD. Our Virtual Clay models respond to applied forces in a natural and predictive manner and offer the user the illusion of manipulating semi-elastic clay in the real world. We showcase example sculptures created with our Virtual Clay sculpting environment, which is equipped with a large variety of real-time, intuitive sculpting toolkits. The versatility of our Virtual Clay techniques allows users to modify the topology of sculpted objects easily, while the inherent physical properties are exploited to provide a natural interface for direct, force-based deformation. More importantly, our sculpting system supports natural haptic interaction to provide the user with a realistic sculpting experience. It is our hope that our Virtual Clay graphics system can become a powerful tool in graphics, computer vision, animation, computer art, interactive techniques, and virtual environments.

1 Introduction and Rationale

Existing solid modeling techniques are oftentimes based on one or several of the following geometric foundations: implicit surfaces, including Constructive Solid Geometry (CSG) and blobby models; Boundary representations (B-reps), such as subdivision surfaces and general polygonal meshes; spline-based solids, including Bézier and B-spline solids; and cell decompositions, such as voxel-based models. Although these approaches are ideal for certain applications, each tends

F.J. Perales and E.R. Hancock (Eds.): AMDO 2002, LNCS 2492, pp. 1–20, 2002.
© Springer-Verlag Berlin Heidelberg 2002

to fall short in o ering a exible and uni ed representation that can be used to manipulate deformable solid objects of inhomogeneous material distributions. In this work we attempt to overcome some of the di culties associated with existing modeling approaches by developing a physics-based, deformable, volumetric model founded upon *subdivision solids*. Our new model serves as the basis for a virtual sculpting system that features haptic interaction and a suite of intuitive sculpting tools.

Solid modeling approaches are inherently complex due to the great number of degrees of freedom that are required to represent real-world objects. In principle, such freedom is necessary in order to design complex mechanical parts and to model more organic or natural-looking objects. When interacting with spline-based solids, certain geometric quantities, such as the knot vectors in the formulation of Non-Uniform Rational B-splines (NURBS), have little intuitive or physical meaning. Users are typically forced to manipulate a large number of geometric parameters in order to make small changes to solid objects. This problem is especially severe when the modeled object consists of both complex interior structure and boundary information. The inclusion of interior information for solid modeling inevitably increases the number of degrees of freedom by at least one order of magnitude. Furthermore, most geometry-based interfaces permit only *indirect* interaction through control point manipulation, which is usually tedious and very time-consuming.

Physics-based modeling techniques can alleviate many of these problems by augmenting geometric objects with physical attributes such as mass, damping and sti ness distributions. Geometric parameters can be hidden from the user by providing natural, force-based interfaces that facilitate *direct* manipulation of solid objects through virtual sculpting tools. The system synchronizes the geometric and physical representations of objects in order to maintain the underlying geometric structures of sculpted solids. Such dynamic and interactive approaches can provide inexperienced users with a natural, force-based interface, while at the same time provide expert users with the familiar geometric interface if desired.

In this paper we use a physics-based approach to conceal from users the inherent topological and geometric complexity of subdivision solids. Physical attributes are assigned both on the boundary and in the interior of deformable subdivision solid objects. Meanwhile, we propose and develop a number of haptics-based tools that assist users during 3D interaction with force-feedback. In this manner users can use haptic exploration to gain a better understanding of the physical attributes of virtual sculptures. Haptics can enhance the functionality of physics-based models in a natural and intuitive way. Note that both physics-based modeling and haptic interaction are founded upon real-world physical laws. Therefore, their integration o ers numerous new modeling, manipulation, and visualization advantages. For example, the haptic interface fundamentally improves understanding by permitting direct interaction with virtual objects and by enhancing the sense of realism through computer communication. Our deformable model is very general and should nd application not only in virtual sculpting, but also in education, surgical simulation, virtual reality, and entertainment.

2   Contributions

Our novel deformable model is based on a new type of subdivision model pioneered by MacCracken and Joy [10]. Whereas, their algorithm was conceived only as a new mechanism for free-form deformation (FFD), we employ their subdivision rules to systematically formulate free-form subdivision solids for physics-based volumetric sculpting. It may be noted that the new subdivision solids naturally include free-form volumetric splines such as B-spline solids as their special cases [12].

In comparison with existing modeling techniques associated with subdivision surfaces, subdivision solid formulations transcend surface-based approaches by de ning geometry and topology both in the interior and on the boundary of solid objects. In our approach, we augment subdivision solids with physical properties that permit users to manipulate solids directly through a haptic interface and through physical forces. The inherent geometric parameters of the solid maintain the subdivision structure, while the physical attributes support direct manipulation. The geometric and topological complexities of subdivision solids are concealed by both our physics-based formulation and by an intuitive user interface. Our sculpting system provides users with many virtual tools that let them directly manipulate solid objects. The user can quickly and easily make topological, geometric and physical changes to sculpted objects without the need to understand the complicated mathematics of subdivision solids.

Our system o ers both an explicit and an implicit solver. The former is e cient and is easy to implement, while the latter guarantees numerical stability. In addition, our physical model incorporates diverse types of elastic behavior that can produce structurally stable objects that exhibit great shape variation. Furthermore, we have devised and implemented a local, adaptive subdivision algorithm that can be employed to create re ned features in any region(s) of interest. Additionally, our novel sculpting system provides the user with a suite of powerful, haptics-based tools that interact directly with our deformable modeling framework.

3   Background Review

3.1   Deformable Models

Our deformable subdivision solid model is based on well-established techniques and algorithms from deformable and physics-based modeling. Physically-based solid models were introduced to the graphics and vision communities by Terzopoulos and colleagues [14,22,23,24]. In essence, the geometry of their models is discretized from continuous surfaces and solids and is attached to mass-spring meshes. Others have used modal dynamics [17] and other nite element approaches [5] in order to improve the stability and accuracy of dynamic models. Bara , Witkin, Kass and others [2,3,27] have developed techniques for animating and constraining non-penetrating dynamic surfaces. Qin and colleagues [11,19,20] derived dynamic models for direct manipulation of spline- and subdivision-based surfaces. James and Pai [9] developed a dynamic surface model based on the Boundary Element Method (BEM).

3.2   Subdivision Solids

Subdivision solids [10] have recently emerged as a generalization of tri-cubic B-spline solids to free-form solid models of arbitrary topologies. In general, B-spline solids and other spline-based solid representations are cumbersome to use in sculpting applications since many separate solids must be carefully patched together to create simple features such as handles and holes. Subdivision solids, in contrast, can represent a topologically complex, deformable object with a single *control lattice*. In contrast to the *control mesh* that de nes a typical sub-division surface, which consists of points, edges and polygons, the control lattice of a subdivision solid consists of points, edges, polygons and closed polyhedra (which we call cells). Note that the use of cells results in the complete subdi-vision of the volumetric space occupied by the control lattice. In this manner it allows users to represent a volumetric object without any geometric ambiguity or topological inconsistency. The geometric construction of our deformable solid model is based on [10]. Since the original subdivision rules do not de ne the sur-face structure, we use the Catmull-Clark subdivision surfaces rules [4] to obtain smooth boundaries.

Because of their unique advantages [12,13], subdivision solids can provide a very general framework for representing volumetric objects. While subdivision surfaces are very convenient and general for creating models in which only the boundary is important, subdivision solids can o er users additional exibility whenever necessary or appropriate. Like subdivision surfaces, subdivision solids are natural candidates for multiresolution analysis and level-of-detail (LOD) con-trol since one can subdivide a given model until the desired amount of detail is achieved. Subdivision solids depend solely on the use of simple subdivision algo-rithms that are similar to those found in most subdivision surface approaches. Thus, the solid subdivision algorithm is relatively easy to implement and does not require very sophisticated data structures.

3.3   Haptic Interfaces

Our sculpting system o ers a number of haptics-based sculpting tools that at-tempt to enhance the sense of realism experienced by the user. A good review of haptics literature can be found in [21]. Thompson *et al.* [25] derived e cient intersection techniques that permit direct haptic rendering of NURBS surfaces. Miller and Zeleznik [15] de ned a set of robust haptic principles and techniques that can be applied to nearly any type of haptic interface. Dachille *et al.* [6] developed a haptic interface that permits direct manipulation of dynamic sur-faces. Balakrishnan *et al.* [1] developed *ShapeTape*, a curve and surface manipulation technique that can sense user-steering bending and twisting motions of the rubber tape. To date, haptics has been an active area of research that has demonstrated great potential for the development of natural and intuitive human-computer interfaces.

4   Deformable Subdivision Solids

Our deformable subdivision solid model marries the geometric information and topological structure of subdivision solids with physical attributes and other relevant material quantities. Figure 1 shows a cubical control lattice after one level of subdivision. The complex cell structure in the interior of the solid is highlighted in Figure 1b. The di erence in complexity between the subdivision solid wireframe (Figure 1c) and subdivision surface wireframe (Figure 1d) can also be easily observed. The second wireframe is that of a Catmull-Clark surface which coincides with the boundary of the solid. The rst wireframe clearly demonstrates the topological and geometric complexity introduced by the cells of the solid. In order to manage the complex non-manifold topological nature of subdivision solids, we employ the radial-edge data structure invented by Weiler [26]. This data structure can be viewed as a generalization of the winged-edge data structure for polygonal surfaces to non-manifold objects. Note that, in the interest of clarity and convenience, we render only the boundary surfaces of solid sculptures for most of the examples in this paper. Nevertheless, a large amount of topological, geometric, physical and material information is employed for the interior description and is therefore hidden.

After a user-speci ed number of subdivisions of the control lattice, the resulting subdivision solid is assigned physical properties such as mass, damping, and sti ness. To avoid ambiguity, we use the term subdivided lattice to describe the control lattice after one or more applications of the subdivision algorithm. Material properties are assigned both in the inside and on the boundary of the subdivided solid. Note that a subdivision surface (or any other pure surface model) could not represent heterogeneous interior attributes because the interior of a subdivision surface is empty. The control lattice is retained but is not assigned any physical parameters. That is, material properties are associated only with the limit shape of subdivision solids and not with the initial control lattice. The control structure is required to maintain the geometric smoothness and continuity of the subdivided model.

Using our approach, each point in the subdivided solid is assigned an initial mass by the application. To avoid confusion with points in the control lattice, these points will henceforth be called mass points. Vertices in the control lattice shall be called control points. Each edge between mass points is assigned an initial spring sti ness. Such edges are termed normal springs, while edges in the control lattice shall be called control edges. Each face in the subdivided lattice is also assigned a set of angular springs, which we describe in detail later. These faces in the subdivided solid are called subdivided faces, while faces in the control lattice are termed control faces. Similarly, cells in the

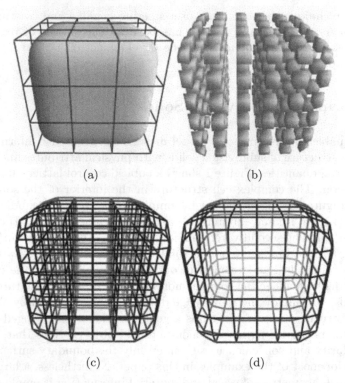

Fig. 1. (a) A subdivision solid after one level of subdivision along with its control lattice. (b) After scaling the cells, the complex interior structure becomes visible. (c) A wireframe rendering of the subdivided solid. (d) A wireframe of a Catmull-Clark subdivision surface that coincides with the boundary. The difference in geometric and topological complexity of the solid and surface is significant.

subdivided lattice are subdivided cells, and cells in the control lattice are control cells. In summary, the initial control lattice is subdivided and is then used to de ne a mass-spring lattice containing mass points and two types of springs.

Like virtually all procedural subdivision algorithms, the subdivision solid representation can be expressed as a global matrix multiplication:

$$\mathbf{d} = \mathbf{A}\mathbf{p}. \tag{1}$$

The $\mathbf{p}$ is a column vector of the control point positions; the matrix $\mathbf{A}$ is a sparse, rectangular matrix that contains weights given by the subdivision rules; and the column vector $\mathbf{d}$ gives the positions of the mass points. Note that matrix $\mathbf{A}$ is a global subdivision matrix and that local changes to the subdivision rules can be expressed by changing a few rows of the matrix. Due to the sparsity of $\mathbf{A}$, we employ a sparse matrix storage scheme to improve time performance and to save memory.

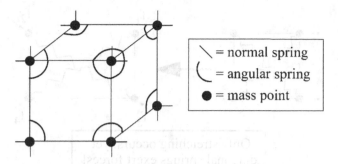

Fig. 2. A typical cell in the subdivided lattice. Normal springs (straight lines) resist stretching forces, while angular springs (arcs) resist shearing forces. Each subdivided edge is assigned a normal spring, and each vertex in each face is assigned an angular spring.

Figure 2 shows a typical hexahedral cell from a subdivided solid along with its mass points, normal springs, and angular springs. Normal springs are traditional linear springs found in many other deformable models and in introductory physics textbooks. Their end-points are mass points that appear in the subdivided lattice. The force exerted on each end-point is given by Hooke s law: $\mathbf{f} = -k(\mathbf{x} - \mathbf{x}^0)$, where k is the spring s sti ness, $\mathbf{x}$ is the current position of the end-point, and $\mathbf{x}^0$ is the rest position of the end-point. In our solid model, each normal spring can have a di erent sti ness and rest length, which permits the de nition of a wide variety of physical behaviors.

Traditional mass-spring lattices often su er from structural instability since they do not attempt to maintain internal angles (*i.e.*, to avoid shearing). Some other deformable models rely on diagonal springs to avoid these problems, but these types of springs can exert forces even when shearing is not occurring (see Figure 3). In order to better characterize an object s resistance to shearing forces, we employ angular springs instead. The system assigns one angular spring per mass point per subdivided face. An angular spring exerts forces on points only when its associated angle deviates from its initial value. The angular spring pushes its end-points away from (or towards) each other in order to regain the original angle. In this way the model attempts to enforce a soft curvature constraint on faces.

Figure 4 shows the arrangement of angular springs in a subdivided face. For each mass point in each subdivided face, we compute the initial rest angle of the two normal springs that coincide at that mass point. When the face undergoes forces as a result of shearing deformation, the angular springs respond by exerting forces on the two end-points to bring the angle back to its initial value (see Figure 5). The initial angle (θ^0) and current angle (θ) can be computed directly using the dot product of the two incident edges ($\mathbf{s}_1$ and $\mathbf{s}_2$): $\theta = \cos^{-1} \frac{\mathbf{s}_1 \cdot \mathbf{s}_2}{|\mathbf{s}_1||\mathbf{s}_2|}$.
To compute the forces that should be applied to each end-point of $\mathbf{s}_1$ and $\mathbf{s}_2$ (indicated by $\mathbf{e}_1$ and $\mathbf{e}_2$ in Figure 5), we calculate where the end-points would be

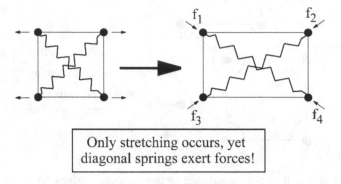

Only stretching occurs, yet
diagonal springs exert forces!

Fig. 3. Diagonal springs exhibit incorrect behavior when stretching occurs but not shearing, as this figure demonstrates. In this special case, diagonal springs erroneously exert forces to resist stretching. Angular springs (Figures 4 and 5) should be used instead in order to correctly characterize an object's resistance to shearing forces.

if the current angle equaled the rest angle (*i.e.*, $\theta = \theta^0$). This requires computing two rotations around the mass point. The axis of rotation is computed using the cross product of $\mathbf{s}_1$ and $\mathbf{s}_2$: $\mathbf{s}_1 \times \mathbf{s}_2$. The rotations provide two new *virtual* points, $\mathbf{e}'_1$ and $\mathbf{e}'_2$, from which we compute displacements $\mathbf{d}_1 = \mathbf{e}'_1 - \mathbf{e}_1$ and $\mathbf{d}_2 = \mathbf{e}'_2 - \mathbf{e}_2$. Using Hooke s law, linear spring forces are applied to $\mathbf{e}_1$ and $\mathbf{e}_2$ in the directions of $\mathbf{d}_1$ and $\mathbf{d}_2$ to help bring the angle back to its rest value.

It should be noted that our unique formulation of deformable subdivision solids and its aforementioned sti ness distribution (especially the structure of its angular springs) are founded upon concepts and their rigorous analysis from di erential geometry [22]. Consider a 3×3 metric tensor function $\mathbf{G}(\mathbf{s})$:

$$
\mathbf{G} = \begin{array}{ccc}
\frac{\partial \mathbf{s}}{\partial u} \cdot \frac{\partial \mathbf{s}}{\partial u} & \frac{\partial \mathbf{s}}{\partial u} \cdot \frac{\partial \mathbf{s}}{\partial v} & \frac{\partial \mathbf{s}}{\partial u} \cdot \frac{\partial \mathbf{s}}{\partial w} \\[2mm]
\frac{\partial \mathbf{s}}{\partial v} \cdot \frac{\partial \mathbf{s}}{\partial u} & \frac{\partial \mathbf{s}}{\partial v} \cdot \frac{\partial \mathbf{s}}{\partial v} & \frac{\partial \mathbf{s}}{\partial v} \cdot \frac{\partial \mathbf{s}}{\partial w} \\[2mm]
\frac{\partial \mathbf{s}}{\partial w} \cdot \frac{\partial \mathbf{s}}{\partial u} & \frac{\partial \mathbf{s}}{\partial w} \cdot \frac{\partial \mathbf{s}}{\partial v} & \frac{\partial \mathbf{s}}{\partial w} \cdot \frac{\partial \mathbf{s}}{\partial w}
\end{array}, \tag{2}
$$

where (u, v, w) is a local parameterization for $\mathbf{s}(\mathbf{x})$. One important result is that the above matrix tensor remains unchanged if there is no solid deformation for any solid object $\mathbf{s}(\mathbf{x})$ (*i.e.*, rigid-body motion does not modify the tensor function $\mathbf{G}(\mathbf{s})$). The amount of deformation of a given object is therefore de ned by a function of $G_{ij}^0 - G_{ij}^n$, which is the di erence between the metric tensors of the initial and current states of the object, where the superscript denotes time, and the subscripts indicate matrix entries. Therefore, in the context of deformable subdivision solids, normal springs attempt to minimize the change for the diagonal terms of $\mathbf{G}(\mathbf{s})$, while the angular springs attempt to minimize the variation of the o -diagonal terms.

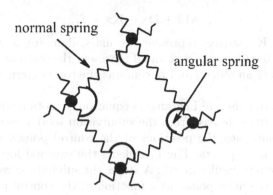

Fig. 4. To help maintain the structural stability of a dynamic subdivision solid, the system employs angular springs to help maintain internal angles and to counteract shearing forces. Traditional springs, indicated by jagged lines, are used to resist stretching forces.

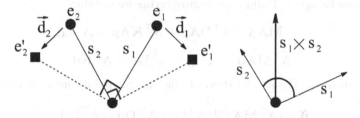

Fig. 5. To compute the forces exerted by an angular spring, we begin by computing where end-points e_1 and e_2 would be if there were no shearing (given by e'_1 and e'_2). The points are rotated about the mass point using the axis of rotation (given by the cross product $s_1 \times s_2$). Using these virtual positions we compute a pair of displacements (d_1 and d_2). The displacements are used to provide the spring forces we apply to the end-points to help bring the angle back to its rest configuration. In this example we assume the rest angle is 90 degrees.

5 Numerical Algorithms for Physics-Based Simulation

We have implemented both an explicit numerical solver for time integration and an implicit one. When extensive user interaction is required, the explicit solver is used to provide real-time update rates. The implicit solver can be invoked when numerical stability is more of a concern or when one is performing o ine simulations.

5.1 Explicit Time Integration

Our dynamic model is founded upon the energy-based Lagrangian equation of motion, which has the following continuous and discrete forms, respectively:

$$\mu \ddot{s} + \gamma s + \frac{\partial E(s)}{\partial s} = f, \tag{3}$$

$$M\hat{x} + Dx + Kx = f_x. \qquad (4)$$

The M, D and K matrices represent the mass, damping and internal energy distributions of an object; the x, x and $\hat{x}$ represent the discrete position, velocity and acceleration of an object; and f_x contains the total external forces acting an object.

We augment the discrete Lagrangian equation of motion with geometric and topological quantities derived from the subdivision solid algorithm. Recall that p is a vector containing the positions of the control points, and d stores the positions of the mass points. The f_d collects the external forces acting on the mass points. The rectangular matrix A stores the subdivision weights that de ne the positions of the mass points as a function of the control points. Subject to the constraints de ned by Equation 1, we augment the Lagrangian equation of motion as follows. First we substitute d for the generic x and multiply each side by A^T:

$$A^T M\hat{d} + A^T Dd + A^T Kd = A^T f_d.$$

By applying Equation 1 and rearranging terms we obtain:

$$A^T MA\hat{p} + A^T DAp + A^T KAp = A^T f_d,$$

$$A^T MA\hat{p} = A^T f_d - A^T Dd - A^T Kd.$$

Then we solve for the acceleration of the control points using a least-squares approach:

$$\hat{p} = (A^T MA)^{-1}(A^T f_d - A^T Dd - A^T Kd). \qquad (5)$$

Note that Equation 5 essentially states that the external forces acting on the mass points are mapped to the control points (which are purely geometric objects) using the subdivision matrix. Once the accelerations of the control points are computed, the model s position and velocity are computed using a forward Euler method to drive the simulation:

$$p_{i+1} = p_i + \hat{p}_i \Delta t,$$

$$p_{i+1} = p_i + p_i \Delta t.$$

5.2   Implicit Time Integration

While the explicit numerical solver derived above is easy to implement and is very e cient, it tends to su er from numerical instability when large time-steps are taken or when spring sti nesses are very high. To ameliorate this problem we derived and implemented an implicit solver based on backward Euler integration. Discrete derivatives are computed using backward di erences:

$$\hat{p}_{i+1} = \frac{(p_{i+1} - 2p_i + p_{i-1})}{\Delta t^2},$$

$$p_{i+1} = \frac{(p_{i+1} - p_{i-1})}{2\Delta t}.$$

Fig. 6. The user interface consists of a PHANToM haptic device, a standard 2D mouse, and on-screen GUI controls.

We obtain the time integration formula

$$2\mathbf{M_p} + \Delta t \mathbf{D_p} + 2\Delta t^2 \mathbf{K_p}\ \mathbf{p}_{i+1} =$$
$$2\Delta t^2 \mathbf{f_p} + 4\mathbf{M_p}\mathbf{p}_i - (2\mathbf{M_p} - \Delta t \mathbf{D_p})\mathbf{p}_{i-1}, \qquad (6)$$

where

$$\mathbf{M_p} = \mathbf{A}^\top \mathbf{M}\mathbf{A},$$
$$\mathbf{D_p} = \mathbf{A}^\top \mathbf{D}\mathbf{A},$$
$$\mathbf{K_p} = \mathbf{A}^\top \mathbf{K}\mathbf{A},$$

and the subscripts denote evaluation of the quantities at the indicated time-steps. It is straightforward to employ the conjugate gradient method [18] to obtain an iterative solution for $\mathbf{p}_{i+1}$. To achieve interactive simulation rates, we limit the number of conjugate gradient iterations per time-step to 10. We have observed that two iterations typically su ce to converge the system to a residual error of less than 10^{-4}. More than two iterations tend to be necessary when the physical parameters are changed dramatically during interactive sculpting.

6   Sculpting System and Toolkits

6.1   Architecture and Interface

The user interface (see Figure 6) of our sculpting system consists of a Sensable Technologies PHANToM 1.0 3D haptic input/output device, a standard 2D mouse, and on-screen GUI controls. The PHANToM features a thimble for the user s index nger and can exert a real-world force in any 3D direction. The mouse is used in conjunction with the PHANToM to activate or enable over a dozen sculpting tools. Forces are exerted on the user s nger only when a haptics-based sculpting tool is active. The entire system runs on a generic Microsoft Windows NT PC with an Intel Pentium III 550 Mhz CPU and 512 MB RAM. Experimental results and system performance data are provided towards the end of the paper.

An overview of the physical simulation and design process is shown in Figure 7. After an initialization step in which data structures are assembled, the system runs in an in nite loop that continuously updates the physical state of a sculpture. The system traverses all springs and computes the total internal forces acting on the mass points. External forces are queried from the input devices and added to the system. The aggregate forces acting on the mass points are then mapped to the control vertices (see Section 5). The acceleration and velocity of the control lattice are then computed in order to move the control lattice to its new position. The subdivision matrix is applied to the control vertices to obtain the new positions of the mass points. This step is required to maintain the geometric and subdivision structure of the subdivided lattice. At any time during the simulation, the user may pause the execution and invoke a tool that causes a change in topology (for instance, to create a protrusion). This type of action requires re-subdivision of the geometry and the re-assembly of certain data structures.

A second thread is required to control the haptic interaction and to accept 3D input from the user. When any haptic tool is in use, this thread computes the haptic force to be felt by the user. Without a second thread of execution, the haptic device is not able to send real-time forces to the user s nger. This causes the PHANToM to buzz and vibrate, which is very distracting during sculpting.

Regarding data structures, most geometric quantities and matrices are stored in one- and two-dimensional arrays. The sophisticated topological structure of subdivision solids is represented using a simpli ed version of Weiler s radial-edge data structure [16,26]. By storing adjacency information, this data structure allows our system to e ciently query and update topological information. Fast accesses are critical to make topological changes as e ciently as possible.

The remainder of this section brie y covers the sculpting functionality of our system. The interested reader is directed to [12,13] for a full description of each sculpting tool.

6.2   Haptic Tools

Through our non-compressive rope tool (Figure 8a) the user can select any of the mass points, both on the boundary and in the interior, and exert a linear spring force on the point. This tool is employed to deform a shape much in the same way that an artist might mold a piece of clay with his ngers. The PHANToM exerts a real force on the user s hand that is a linear function of the mass of the attached point, the distance of the cursor to the point, and the strength of the rope tool (whose sti ness can be changed in the GUI). The user

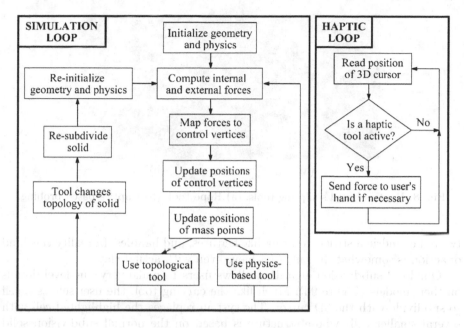

Fig. 7. An overview of the physical simulation and design process featured in our sculpting system. The application requires two separate execution threads in order to generate real-time haptic feedback.

also has the ability to study an object s sti ness both graphically and haptically through our probing tool (Figure 8b). When active, the probing tool exerts a force on the user s hand proportional to the local sti nesses of those springs within a given radius of the tool. In addition, the user can run the cursor over the surface of a solid to examine the boundary tactilely. In this way a designer can feel how smooth the surface is at the current subdivision level and also look for any surface anomalies that might be hard to detect visually.

6.3   Geometric and Topological Tools

Our geometric and topological tools operate directly on the control lattice. For instance, using the 3D cursor provided by the PHANToM, the user can carve material from a sculpture (Figure 9a). As with all of the tools that modify the topology of the sculpted object, the radial-edge data structure and certain matrices need to be re-computed to e ect the change. Second, the extrusion tool (Figure 9b) can be employed to extrude new material from the face on the surface nearest the 3D cursor. When the user activates the tool, a new control cell is created and attached to the face. It grows in the direction of the surface normal, and its size is computed based on the size of the control cell to which it is attached. Third, two cells near the surface of a sculpture can be joined together by using our joining tool (Figure 9c). This tool is very useful for making loops,

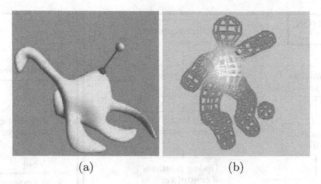

(a)   (b)

Fig. 8. Haptics-based sculpting tools. (a) Rope tool. (b) Haptics-based probing.

twisted cylindrical structures, ring-like features, and handles. In reality this kind of action is somewhat di cult to achieve even with actual clay.

Our local subdivision algorithm allows users to make very ne-level details on their models (Figure 9d). Much like the carving tool, the user selects a cell to subdivide with the 3D cursor. The system replaces the highlighted cell with several smaller cells whose structure is based on the normal subdivision solid rules. Faces and edges in adjacent cells are also subdivided in order to avoid T-shapes and other topological anomalies (such as a vertex in the middle of a face). This process is illustrated in Figure 10. Although this procedure complicates the local topological structure, the resulting control lattice is still valid and can be treated and manipulated like any other subdivision control lattice.

Sharp features (Figure 9e) such as corners and creases can be created by tagging faces, edges, or points as sharp . In our implementation, sharp features are created by using di erent subdivision rules for tagged geometric elements. Note that since we use a Catmull-Clark surface to represent the boundary, one can use other special rules, such as those found in [7,8,10].

6.4 Deformation Tools

Our sculpting system features a number of tools that use physics to interact with a model. The use of physical tools frees the user from the need to deal with the multitude of control vertices inherent in subdivision solid objects. In addition, the user can interact with deformable subdivision solids directly, rather than through indirect and often non-intuitive control point manipulation.

For example, our B-spline manipulation tool (Figure 11a) lets the user select mass points from a sculpture, build a cubic B-spline curve that interpolates the points, and then manipulate the spline using its control points. In this way the user can use a B-spline to quickly design curved regions as well as make large, well-controlled deformations. It is straightforward to generalize this tool to B-spline surfaces and other types of curve and surface representations.

Since our model de nes geometric and physical properties on both the boundary and interior, the user has the option of modifying the mass and sti ness

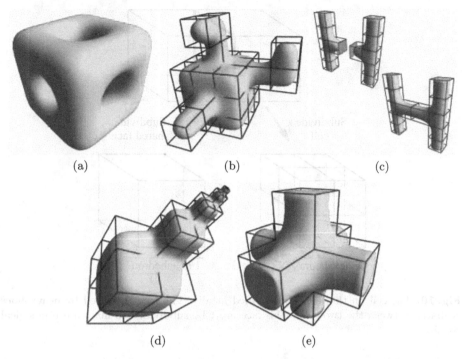

(a)   (b)   (c)

(d)   (e)

Fig. 9. Geometry-based and topology-based sculpting tools. (a) Carving. (b) Extrusion. (c) Joining. (d) Detail editing. (e) Sharp feature creation.

distributions both in the inside and on the boundary (Figure 11b). Our virtual sculpting material is more general than real clay since it can actually have different physical properties throughout the sculpture. This o ers extra exibility and advantages to the user. For instance, the user can use such functionality to localize the e ects of certain physics-based tools, especially the rope tool.

The in ation and de ation tools (Figures 11c and 11d) allow the user to grow and shrink local portions of the model, respectively. The rest lengths of springs are increased or decreased, depending on whether in ation or de ation is taking place. The in ation tool is typically used to create bumps and rounded features, while the de ation tool is useful for shrinking and tapering parts of sculptures.

The physical trimming tool (Figure 11e) allows users to e ectively turn o cells in the subdivided lattice. Unlike the cell-deletion tool, which modi es the topology of a sculpture, this tool directly operates on the physical representation. It enables the user to prevent portions of a model from participating in the physical simulation.

Sometimes the user may wish to deform only a local region of a sculpture. This action can be facilitated by using our physical window feature (Figure 11f) that constrains the physical simulation to occur in a local region of interest. In addition to localizing the e ect of deformation, the physical window speeds up the simulation and improves frame rates by reducing the amount of

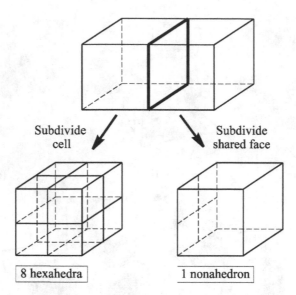

Fig. 10. The cell on the left is subdivided locally. The face indicated by heavy lines is shared between the two cells. This face must be subdivided to maintain topological consistency.

data that needs to be processed by the system. For instance, the subdivision matrix $\mathbf{A}$ as well as the vectors $\mathbf{d}$ and $\mathbf{p}$ can be partitioned into free $(\mathbf{A}_1, \mathbf{p}_1, \mathbf{d}_1)$ and xed $(\mathbf{A}_2, \mathbf{p}_2)$ matrices:

$$\mathbf{d} = \mathbf{Ap} \quad \rightarrow \quad \mathbf{d}_1 = \mathbf{A}_1\mathbf{p}_1 + \mathbf{A}_2\mathbf{p}_2.$$

The xed portions can be computed once and stored for look-up later. Other matrices such as $\mathbf{M}$, $\mathbf{D}$ and $\mathbf{K}$ can be modi ed in a similar manner.

6.5   Additional GUI Controls

In addition to the sculpting tools, our GUI contains several widgets that allow the user to change the global state of the model and various simulation parameters, such as the time-step, damping coe cient, spring sti ness values, etc. The user can also change the sti ness (or strength) of the rope tool using a slider in the GUI. High values of this sti ness allow the user to made large, sweeping deformations in a short amount of time. Also, the user can press the Reset Rest Shape button in order to rede ne the rest shape of a sculpture to its current shape. Without this functionality a sculpted object would always revert to its initial physical state due to the elasticity of the springs.

7   Experimental Results and Time Performance

Table 1 details the data sizes and run-time statistics for the sculptures featured in this paper. This table contains the running times only for the simulation loop.

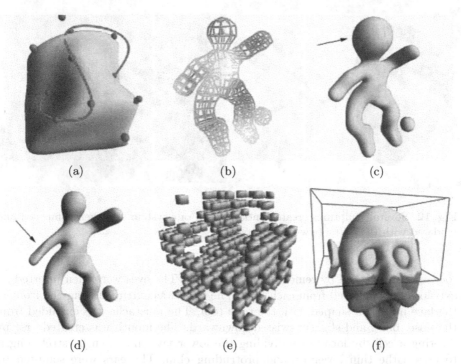

(a)   (b)   (c)

(d)   (e)   (f)

Fig. 11. Physics-based sculpting tools. (a) B-spline curve manipulation. (b) Stiffness painting. (c) Deflation. (d) Inflation. (e) Physical trimming. (f) Physical window.

Table 1. Data-set sizes and simulation timing information for some of the models described in this paper. All statistics are for one level of subdivision, except for the soccer player, which was subdivided twice.

Model	Control Cells	Subdivided Cells	Update Time (ms)
Man's head	123	1069	114.7
Soccer player	24	1536	85.0
Chair with holes	76	744	82.5
Chair without holes	62	552	50.6
Mug	102	816	80.9

Note that in order to generate nal images, we subdivided the models several additional times to produce smooth boundary surfaces seen in the gures.

7.1   Example Sculpture: Human Head

We shall use the sculpted cartoon head in Figure 12 to describe how our sculpting tools can be used in practice. The sculpting of the head required the use of almost every design tool, and so it serves as a good example of how to use our sculpting system. We began with a $5 \times 5 \times 5$ block containing 125 control cells. Cells on the underside and back were carved out to give the head its general shape. The eye

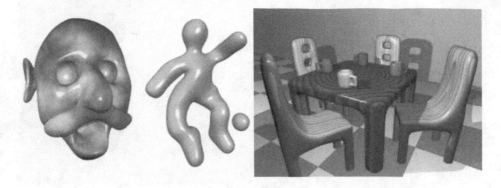

Fig. 12. Several sculptures created entirely with our system and then composed and rendered with POV-Ray (www.povray.org).

sockets were created by removing one cell each. The eyes were then inserted by extruding a single cell from each hole. The nose was extruded from the front of the face and then shaped with the rope tool. The mustache was extruded from the nose, bent, and slightly twisted downward. The mouth was created rst by deleting a cell, by locally subdividing the lower jaw, and then by stretching it to create the thin lower lip and protruding chin. The ears were sculpted by extruding a few cells on either side of the head, locally subdividing them, and then stretching and denting them to make them thin and oval. The deformation and in ation tools were employed to give the top of the head a more rounded appearance. Then the de ation tool was used to smooth out bumps and pits. For certain features the physical window was activated to constrain the in uence of the rope tool on the model. Finally, the surface of the solid was extracted and ray-traced o ine.

8   Conclusions

We have developed a novel deformable solid modeling framework along with its intuitive, natural haptic interface based on the unique integration of subdivision solids and physics-based techniques. Our system for shape design and sculpting permits the user to create real-world, complicated models in real-time using an extensive suite of geometry-based, topology-based, physics-based, and haptics-based tools. Within our modeling environment, the virtual clay responds to direct, user-applied forces in a predictable and intuitive manner while the haptic feedback can signi cantly enhance the sense of realism. Our physical formulation of topologically complex subdivision solids frees users from the need to deal with abstract geometric quantities and esoteric mathematical structures that often hinder the extensive use of sophisticated solid models on a large scale. To verify the applicability of our sculpting system on virtual clay and its powerful toolkits, we have conducted many sculpting sessions which have resulted in numerous interesting sculptures. The gallery of our virtual sculptures in Figure 12 (see [12,13] for more examples) should appeal to a wide spectrum of users including researchers, designers, animators, artists and even non-professionals.

Acknowledgments

This research was supported in part by the NSF CAREER award CCR-9896123, the NSF grant DMI-9896170, the NSF ITR grant IIS-0082035, the NSF grant IIS-0097646, Alfred P. Sloan Fellowship, and Honda Initiation Award.

References

1. R. Balakrishnan, G. Fitzmaurice, G. Kurtenbach, and K. Singh. Exploring interactive curve and surface manipulation using a bend and twist sensitive input strip. In *Proceedings of the 1999 ACM Symposium on Interactive 3D Graphics*, pages 111–118, 1999.
2. D. Baraff and A. Witkin. Dynamic simulation of non-penetrating flexible bodies. In *Computer Graphics (SIGGRAPH 92 Proceedings)*, volume 26, pages 303–308, July 1992.
3. D. Baraff and A. Witkin. Large steps in cloth simulation. In *Computer Graphics (SIGGRAPH 98 Proceedings)*, pages 43–54, July 1998.
4. E. Catmull and J. Clark. Recursively generated B-spline surfaces on arbitrary topological meshes. *Computer Aided Design*, 10:350–355, Sept. 1978.
5. G. Celniker and D. Gossard. Deformable curve and surface finite elements for free-form shape design. In *Computer Graphics (SIGGRAPH 91 Proceedings)*, pages 257–266, July 1991.
6. F. Dachille IX, H. Qin, A. Kaufman, and J. El-Sana. Haptic sculpting of dynamic surfaces. In *Proceedings of the 1999 Symposium on Interactive 3D Graphics*, pages 103–110, 1999.
7. T. DeRose, M. Kass, and T. Truong. Subdivision surfaces in character animation. In *Computer Graphics (SIGGRAPH 98 Proceedings)*, pages 85–94, July 1998.
8. H. Hoppe, T. DeRose, T. Duchamp, M. Halstead, H. Jin, J. McDonald, J. Schweitzer, and W. Stuetzle. Piecewise smooth surface reconstruction. In *Computer Graphics (SIGGRAPH 94 Proceedings)*, pages 295–302, July 1994.
9. D. L. James and D. K. Pai. ARTDEFO: Accurate Real Time Deformable Objects. In *Computer Graphics (SIGGRAPH 99 Proceedings)*, pages 65–72, Aug. 1999.
10. R. MacCracken and K. I. Joy. Free-form deformations with lattices of arbitrary topology. In *Computer Graphics (SIGGRAPH 96 Proceedings)*, pages 181–188, August 1996.
11. C. Mandal, H. Qin, and B. C. Vemuri. A novel FEM-based dynamic framework for subdivision surfaces. In *Proceedings of Solid Modeling '99*, pages 191–202, 1999.
12. K. T. McDonnell and H. Qin. Dynamic sculpting and animation of free-form subdivision solids. *The Visual Computer*, 18(2):81–96, 2002.
13. K. T. McDonnell, H. Qin, and R. A. Wlodarczyk. Virtual Clay: A real-time sculpting system with haptic toolkits. In *Proceedings of the 2001 ACM Symposium on Interactive 3D Graphics*, pages 179–190, March 2001.
14. D. Metaxas and D. Terzopoulos. Dynamic deformation of solid primitives with constraints. In *Computer Graphics (SIGGRAPH 92 Proceedings)*, pages 309–312, July 1992.

15. T. Miller and R. C. Zeleznik. The design of 3D haptic widgets. In *Proceedings of the 1999 Symposium on Interactive 3D Graphics*, pages 97–102, 1999.
16. M. J. Muuss and L. A. Butler. Combinatorial solid geometry, boundary representations, and n-manifold geometry. In D. F. Rogers and R. A. Earnshaw, editors, *State of the Art in Computer Graphics: Visualization and Modeling*, pages 185–223. Springer-Verlag, 1991.
17. A. Pentland and J. Williams. Good vibrations: Modal dynamics for graphics and animation. In *Computer Graphics (SIGGRAPH 89 Proceedings)*, pages 215–222, July 1989.
18. W. H. Press, S. A. Teukolsky, W. T. Vetterling, and B. P. Flannery. *Numerical Recipes in C: The Art of Scientific Computing*. Cambridge University Press, Cambridge, second edition, 1992.
19. H. Qin, C. Mandal, and B. C. Vemuri. Dynamic Catmull-Clark subdivision surfaces. *IEEE Transactions on Visualization and Computer Graphics*, 4(3):215–229, July 1998.
20. H. Qin and D. Terzopoulos. D-NURBS: a physics-based framework for geometric design. *IEEE Transactions on Visualization and Computer Graphics*, 2(1):85–96, Mar. 1996.
21. M. A. Srinivasan and C. Basdogan. Haptics in virtual environments: taxonomy, research status, and challenges. *Computers & Graphics*, 21(4):393–404, July 1997.
22. D. Terzopoulos and K. Fleischer. Deformable models. *The Visual Computer*, 4(6):306–331, Dec. 1988.
23. D. Terzopoulos and K. Fleischer. Modeling inelastic deformation: viscoelasticity, plasticity, fracture. In *Computer Graphics (SIGGRAPH 88 Proceedings)*, pages 269–278, August 1988.
24. D. Terzopoulos, J. Platt, A. Barr, and K. Fleischer. Elastically deformable models. In *Computer Graphics (SIGGRAPH 87 Proceedings)*, pages 205–214, July 1987.
25. T. V. Thompson, D. E. Johnson, and E. Cohen. Direct haptic rendering of sculptured models. In *Proceedings of the 1997 Symposium on Interactive 3D Graphics*, pages 167–176, 1997.
26. K. J. Weiler. *Topological Structures for Geometric Modeling*. PhD thesis, Rensselaer Polytechnic Institute, August 1986.
27. A. Witkin and M. Kass. Spacetime constraints. In *Computer Graphics (SIGGRAPH 88 Proceedings)*, volume 22, pages 159–168, Aug. 1988.

g-HDAF Multiresolution Deformable Models

Ioannis A. Kakadiaris[1], Emmanuel Papadakis[2], Lixin Shen[1],
Donald Kouri[3], and David Ho man[4]

[1] Visual Computing Lab, Department of Computer Science
University of Houston, Houston, TX 77204-3010
ioannisk@uh.edu
http://www.cs.uh.edu/~ioannisk
[2] Department of Mathematics, University of Houston, Houston, TX 77204
[3] Department of Physics, University of Houston, Houston, TX 77204
[4] Department of Chemistry and Ames Laboratory
Iowa State University, Ames, IS 50011

Abstract. In this paper, we construct a new class of deformable models
using a new family of biorthogonal wavelets, named generalized Hermite
Distributed Approximating Functional (g-HDAF) Wavelets. The scaling functions of this new family are symmetric and the corresponding
wavelets optimize their smoothness for a given number of vanishing moments. In addition, we embed these multiresolution deformable models
to the physics-based deformable model framework and use them for fitting 3D range data. We have performed a number of experiments with
both synthetic and real data with very encouraging results.

1 Introduction

Modeling shapes is an integral part of computer vision driven by the need for
shape reconstruction from sampled data and shape recognition. The deformable
superquadrics introduced by Terzopoulos and Metaxas [12] represent the physics-
based uni cation of the parameterized and free-form modeling paradigms. The
geometric structure of the models supports both global deformation parameters,
which e ciently represent the gross shape features of an object and local deformation parameters, which capture shape details. An important bene t of this
global/local descriptive power, in the context of computer vision, is that it can
potentially satisfy the often con icting requirements of shape reconstruction and
shape recognition. However, these models do not exhibit a smooth transition in
the number of parameters required by the range of generated shapes.

To overcome this shortcoming, Vemuri and Radisavljevic [14] introduced a
multiresolution hybrid modeling scheme that used an orthonormal wavelet basis [9]. By virtue of the multiresolution wavelet representation, their hybrid models have the unique property of being able to scale smoothly from global to local
deformations depending on the number of the coe cients used to represent them.

* This work was supported in part by the following grants: NSF CAREER award CISE
9985482, NSF CHE-0074311, DMA-0070376, and R.A. Welch Foundation E-0608.

F.J. Perales and E.R. Hancock (Eds.): AMDO 2002, LNCS 2492, pp. 21–31, 2002.
© Springer-Verlag Berlin Heidelberg 2002

Thus, one may choose a set of wavelet coe cients at a particular decomposition level from the multiresolution representation of the hybrid model to augment the global parameters of the model.

In this paper, we construct a new class of multiresolution deformable superquadrics with respect to new biorthogonal wavelets, named Generalized Hermite Distributed Approximating Functional (g-HDAF) Wavelets. The scaling functions of this new family are symmetric, and the corresponding wavelets exhibit enhanced smoothness for a given number of vanishing moments. In addition, we embed these multiresolution deformable models into the physics-based deformable model framework and use them for tting 2D and 3D data. Our contributions are the following: 1) the development of a new class of linear phase wavelets (note that their associated scaling functions are symmetric with respect to the origin), 2) the development of a new class of deformable models using this new biorthogonal wavelet basis, and 3) a comparative study of the wavelet transform of a deformable model s displacement map with respect to various commonly used wavelets. The multiresolution wavelet basis that we have developed allows us to construct compact and diverse shape representations.

Our motivation to develop a new class of linear-phase wavelets stems from the fact that there are no known classes of well-localized (in the time domain) symmetric multiresolution lters. In fact, it is known that orthonormal compactly supported scaling functions cannot be symmetric (with the exception of the Haar scaling function) [2]. An important property of the newly developed g-HDAF wavelets is their enhanced smoothness as compared with the smoothness of the most commonly utilized classes of compactly supported orthonormal wavelets. This higher degree of smoothness together with their symmetry will increase the sparsity of the wavelet representation of the local deformations of the deformable models.

2   Methods

2.1   g-HDAF Multiresolution Deformable Models for Shape Modeling

The models used in this work are three-dimensional surface shape models. The material coordinates $\mathbf{u} = (u, v)$ of a point on these models are speci ed over a domain Ω [10,12]. The position of a point (with material coordinates $\mathbf{u}$) on a deformable model at time t with respect to an inertial reference frame Φ is given by: $^{\Phi}\mathbf{x}(\mathbf{u}, t) = {}^{\Phi}\mathbf{t}(t) + {}^{\Phi}_{\phi}\mathbf{R}(t) {}^{\phi}\mathbf{p}(\mathbf{u}, t)$, where $^{\Phi}\mathbf{t}$ is the position of the origin O of the model frame ϕ with respect to the frame Φ (the model s translation), and $^{\Phi}_{\phi}\mathbf{R}$ is the matrix that determines the orientation of ϕ with respect to Φ. $^{\phi}\mathbf{p}(\mathbf{u}, t)$ denotes the position of a model point with material coordinates $\mathbf{u}$ w.r.t. the model frame. It can be expressed as the sum of a reference shape $^{\phi}\mathbf{s}(\mathbf{u}, t)$ and a local displacement $^{\phi}\mathbf{d}(\mathbf{u}, t)$: $^{\phi}\mathbf{p}(\mathbf{u}, t) = {}^{\phi}\mathbf{s}(\mathbf{u}, t) + {}^{\phi}\mathbf{d}(\mathbf{u}, t)$. The reference shape, $\mathbf{s}$, captures the salient shape features of the model, and it is the result of applying global deformations, $\mathbf{T}$, to a geometric primitive $\mathbf{e} = [e_x, e_y, e_z]^{\top}$. The geometric primitive $\mathbf{e}$ is de ned parametrically in $\mathbf{u} \in \Omega$ and has global shape parameters $\mathbf{q_e}$. For the purposes of this research, we employ a superquadric $\mathbf{e}(u, v) [-\frac{\pi}{2}, \frac{\pi}{2}) \times [-\pi, \pi) \to \mathbb{R}^3$, whose global shape parameters are $\mathbf{q_e} = [a_1, a_2, a_3, \epsilon_1, \epsilon_2]^\top$. A superquadric surface is de ned by a vector sweeping a closed surface in space by varying the material coordinates u and v. The parametric equation of a superquadric is given by [1]:

$$\mathbf{e}(\mathbf{u}) = [a_1 C_u{}^{\epsilon_1} C_v{}^{\epsilon_2}, a_2 C_u{}^{\epsilon_1} S_v{}^{\epsilon_2}, a_3 S_u{}^{\epsilon_1}]^\top,$$

where $-\frac{\pi}{2} \leq u \leq \frac{\pi}{2}$, $-\pi \leq v \leq \pi$, $S_u = \operatorname{sgn}(\sin u)|\sin u|^\epsilon$, $C_u = \operatorname{sgn}(\cos u)|\cos u|^\epsilon$, and $a_1, a_2, a_3 \geq 0$ are the parameters that de ne the superquadric size, and ϵ_1 and ϵ_2 are the squareness parameters in the latitudinal and longitudinal planes, respectively. Local displacements $\mathbf{d}$ are computed using nite elements. Associated with every nite element node i is a nodal vector variable $\mathbf{q}_{d,i}$. We collect all the nodal variables into a vector of local degrees of freedom $\mathbf{q}_d = (\ldots, \mathbf{q}_{d,i}^\top, \ldots)^\top$. If we denote the original nodal discretization at resolution $j = 0$ by the vector α_0, then $\alpha_0 = \mathbf{H}\mathbf{q}_d$ (analysis) and $\mathbf{q}_d = \mathbf{H}^\top \alpha_0$ (reconstruction), where the matrix $\mathbf{H}$ corresponds to the g-HDAFs and the vector $\mathbf{q}_d$ is hierarchically expressed to the new biorthonormal basis. We compute the local displacement $\mathbf{d}$ based on the nite element theory as $\mathbf{d}(u, v) = \mathbf{S}\mathbf{q}_d(u, v)$. Here, $\mathbf{S}$ is the shape matrix whose entries are the nite element shape functions. In the next subsection, we present our construction of the g-HDAFs.

2.2   Biorthogonal g-HDAF Wavelets

For the purposes of this paper, we construct a new class of Quadrature Mirror Filters (QMF), which we name *generalized HDAF biorthogonal filters*. Hermite Distributed Approximating Functionals (HDAFs) were introduced by Ho man and Kouri in [4,5]. Nonetheless HDAFs are not periodic functions so they are not QMFs [8]. Several classes of wavelets have been generated, inspired by the original HDAFs with varying degrees of success (e.g., [6]).

In previous work, we presented how to use HDAFs to construct low pass lters for orthonormal univariate scaling functions (which we called *modified HDAF scaling functions*), which have produced results that improved previous constructions [8]. An HDAF $h_{N,\sigma}$ is de ned in the Fourier domain by:

$$h_{N,\sigma}(\xi) = e^{-\frac{4\pi^2 \xi^2 \sigma^2}{2}} \sum_{n=0}^{N} \frac{4\pi^2 \xi^2 \sigma^2}{2^n n!}^n, \qquad (1)$$

where $N \in \mathbb{Z}^+$ and $\sigma \in \mathbb{R}^+$. We modi ed the HDAF as follows [8]:

$$m_0(\xi) := \begin{cases} h_{N,\sigma}(\xi) & \text{if } |\xi| \leq \frac{1}{4} \\ 1 - h_{N,\sigma}(\xi - \frac{1}{2})^2 & \text{if } \frac{1}{4} \leq \xi \leq \frac{1}{2} \\ 1 - h_{N,\sigma}(\xi + \frac{1}{2})^2 & \text{if } -\frac{1}{2} \leq \xi \leq -\frac{1}{4}, \end{cases}$$

and we extended m_0 1-periodically. Under the condition $m_0(\frac{1}{4}) = h_{N,\sigma}(\frac{1}{4}) = \frac{\sqrt{2}}{2}$, $m_0(\xi)$ satis es the orthogonality condition $|m_0(\xi)|^2 + m_0(\xi + \frac{1}{2})^2 = 1$, $\xi \in \mathbb{R}$, and $\phi(\xi) := \prod_{j=1}^{\infty} m_0\left(\frac{\xi}{2^j}\right)$, $\xi \in \mathbb{R}$ is an orthogonal scaling function, which we called modied HDAF scaling function (m-HDAF).

In this paper, we introduce a new family of biorthogonal inite impulse response (IIR) wavelet lters based on the HDAFs, which we name *generalized HDAF wavelets*. Let us dene the auto-correlation of a function ϕ as:

$$\Phi(x) = \int \phi(y)\phi(y+x)\,dy.$$

Now denote $M_0(\xi) = m_0^2(\xi)$. Clearly, $\Phi(\xi) = \phi^2(\xi)$, so $\Phi(2\xi) = m_0^2(\xi)\Phi(\xi)$. Since Φ is absolutely integrable and ϕ is in $L^2(\mathbb{R})$, one can assert that Φ can be replaced by a uniformly continuous function. With this remark in mind, we consider Φ to be continuous.

One can also verify that $\Phi(k) = \delta_{k,0}$, for all $k \in \mathbb{Z}$, and

$$M_0(\xi) + M_0(\xi + \frac{1}{2}) = 1. \qquad (2)$$

We refer to lters that satisfy Eq. (2) as interpolating lters, and to such Φ as *interpolating scaling functions*.

Proposition 1.   *The following are true: 1) $\Phi(x)$ almost everywhere equals to a continuous and $\Phi(k) = \delta_k$, $k \in \mathbb{Z}$; 2) $\Phi \in L^2(\mathbb{R})$, and the integer translates of $\Phi(x)$ form a Riesz basis for their closed linear span, i.e., there exist two constants $0 < c \le C < \infty$, such that*

$$c \le \sum_{k \in \mathbb{Z}} |\Phi(\xi + k)|^2 \le C$$

where $c = e^{-\frac{2\pi^2\sigma^2}{3}}$ and $C = 1$.

Proof: 1) This follows immediately from the fact $\Phi = \phi^2 \in L^1(\mathbb{R})$. 2) For all $\xi \in \mathbb{R}$, $\Phi(\xi) = \prod_{k=1}^{\infty} M_0(\xi/2^k)$ and $M_0^2(\xi) + M_0^2(\xi + \frac{1}{2}) \le [M_0(\xi) + M_0(\xi + \frac{1}{2})]^2 = 1$. Thus, with a similar discussion as presented in [9], we know that $\Phi \in L^2(\mathbb{R})$. Since $\sum_{k \in \mathbb{Z}} |\phi(\xi + k)|^2 = 1$, then

$$\sum_{k \in \mathbb{Z}} |\Phi(\xi + k)|^2 = \sum_{k \in \mathbb{Z}} |\phi(\xi + k)|^4 \le \sum_{k \in \mathbb{Z}} |\phi(\xi + k)|^2 = 1.$$

In addition, we can assume that $\xi \in [-\frac{1}{2}, \frac{1}{2}]$ because $|\Phi(\xi + k)|^2$ is an 1-periodic function. Hence, $-\frac{1}{2} \le \frac{\xi}{2^k} \le \frac{1}{2}$ for every non-negative integer k. Therefore, $M_0(\frac{\xi}{2^k}) = h^2(\frac{\xi}{2^k})$. Further,

$$\Phi(\xi) = \prod_{k=1}^{\infty} e^{-\left(\frac{2\pi\xi\sigma}{2^k}\right)^2} \left[\sum_{n=0}^{N} \frac{\left(\frac{2\pi\xi\sigma}{2^k}\right)^{2n}}{2^n n!}\right]^2$$

$$= \prod_{k=1}^{\infty} e^{-\left(\frac{2\pi\xi\sigma}{2^k}\right)^2} \prod_{k=1}^{\infty}\left[\sum_{n=0}^{N} \frac{\left(\frac{2\pi\xi\sigma}{2^k}\right)^{2n}}{2^n n!}\right]^2$$

$$= e^{-\frac{4\pi^2\xi^2\sigma^2}{3}} \prod_{k=1}^{\infty}\left[\sum_{n=0}^{N} \frac{\left(\frac{2\pi\xi\sigma}{2^k}\right)^{2n}}{2^n n!}\right]^2 \geq e^{-\frac{\pi^2\sigma^2}{3}}.$$

This leads to $\sum_{k\in\mathbb{Z}} |\Phi(\xi + k)|^2 \geq \Phi^2(\xi) \geq e^{\frac{-2\pi^2\sigma^2}{3}}.$ □

Proposition 1 implies that Φ is an interpolatory Riesz scaling function associated with an MRA.

A function Φ is stable, if Φ and its integer translates form a Riesz basis of their closed linear span. To obtain a numerically stable decomposition and reconstruction algorithm, the integer translates of Φ and Φ^d must form a pair of dual Riesz bases. In other words, Φ and Φ^d must be stable and satisfy the following biorthogonal conditions:

$$\langle \Phi, \Phi^d(\cdot - k)\rangle = \delta_{k,0}, \quad k \in \mathbb{Z}, \tag{3}$$

and in this case we say that Φ^d is a dual scaling function of Φ. In the following, we present two di erent methods for constructing the dual re nable function Φ^d. The rst method is used to construct Φ^d directly from Φ. The second method is used to design a dual lter M_0^d of the lter M_0 and then construct Φ^d using the in nite product formula where instead of M_0 we use M_0^d. The lter M_0^d, which is a 1-periodic function, is a dual lter of lter M_0, if

$$M_0(\xi)\overline{M_0^d(\xi)} + M_0(\xi + \tfrac{1}{2})\overline{M_0^d(\xi + \tfrac{1}{2})} = 1 \tag{4}$$

for all ξ in $[-\frac{1}{2}, \frac{1}{2}]$. Note that M_0 may have more than one dual lter. It is well known that if Φ and Φ^d are stable and the corresponding lowpass lters satisfy Eq. (4), then they are dual functions. However, Eq. (4) is only a necessary condition for Φ and Φ^d to be a dual pair.

Method 1: Using a standard technique, the dual scaling function Φ^d can be de ned as follows:

$$\Phi^d(\xi) = \frac{\Phi(\xi)}{\sum_{k\in\mathbb{Z}} |\Phi(\xi + k)|^2}.$$

Clearly, the functions Φ and Φ^d are biorthonormal, i.e., $\langle \Phi, \Phi^d(\cdot - k)\rangle = \delta_k$. Let c and C be the lower and upper bound of the stable function Φ, respectively. Then Φ^d is also stable with lower bound C^{-1} and upper bound c^{-1}, respectively. This is due to the fact that $\sum_{k\in\mathbb{Z}} |\Phi(\xi + k)|^2$ is 1-periodic and $\sum_{k\in\mathbb{Z}} |\Phi^d(\xi + k)|^2 = (\sum_{k\in\mathbb{Z}} |\Phi(\xi + k)|^2)^{-1}$. Thus, Φ and Φ^d are dual functions. The dual frequency response is given by

$$M_0^d(\xi) = \frac{\phi^d(2\xi)}{\phi^d(\xi)} = \frac{M_0(\xi)}{M_0^2(\xi) + M_0^2(\xi + \frac{1}{2})}. \tag{5}$$

Method 2: Given an interpolatory FIR filter, the construction of its dual filters is provided in a number of papers [7,11]. In this paper, we extend the work of [7] from FIR to IIR.

Proposition 2. *Let M_0 be a lowpass filter satisfying Eq. (2). Then, for each $J \in \mathbb{Z}^+$ the filter,*

$$M_0^d = \binom{2J}{J} M_0^J (1 - M_0)^J + \sum_{j=0}^{J-1} \binom{2J}{j} M_0^{2J-1-j}(1 - M_0)^j$$

is a dual filter of M_0 with $M_0^d(0) = 1$.

Proof: Using Eq. (2) and $\binom{2J}{j} = \binom{2J}{2J-j}$, we have

$$M_0^d(\xi + \frac{1}{2}) = \binom{2J}{J} M_0^J(\xi + \frac{1}{2})[1 - M_0(\xi + \frac{1}{2})]^J$$

$$+ \sum_{j=0}^{J-1} \binom{2J}{j} M_0^{2J-1-j}(\xi + \frac{1}{2})[1 - M_0(\xi + \frac{1}{2})]^j$$

$$= \binom{2J}{J} M_0^J(\xi)[1 - M_0(\xi)]^J + \sum_{j=0}^{J-1} \binom{2J}{2J-j} [1 - M_0(\xi)]^{2J-1-j} M_0^j(\xi).$$

Hence, we have that

$$M_0(\xi)\overline{M_0^d(\xi)} + M_0(\xi + \frac{1}{2})\overline{M_0^d(\xi + \frac{1}{2})} = [M_0(\xi) + (1 - M_0(\xi))]^{2J} = 1.$$

Finally, since $M_0(0) = 1$, we conclude that $M_0^d(0) = 1$ by the definition of M_0^d. □

Let M_0^d be given by Eq. (6). Then, the dual filter M_0^d satisfies $M_0^d(\xi) = 1 + O(|\xi|)$. Since the infinite product $\Phi^d(\xi) = \prod_{k=1}^{\infty} M_0^d(\frac{\xi}{2^k})$ converges uniformly on every compact set, it is continuous. This implies that Φ^d is well defined. Therefore, if the function Φ^d is in $L^2(\mathbb{R})$ and Φ^d and its integer shifts form a Riesz basis, then Φ^d will be the dual scaling function of Φ.

The advantages of each method are now obvious. Using Method 1, we can directly construct a dual scaling function Φ^d of the scaling function Φ. Using Method 2, one can easily obtain a dual filter M_0^d. In our work, we always use Method 2 to get the dual filter M_0^d of M_0 with $J = 1$, i.e., $M_0^d = M_0(\xi)[3 - 2M_0(\xi)]$. The main reason is that for any N, the maximum values of frequency response of M_0^d obtained from Eq. (5) and Eq. (6) are $\frac{1}{2}(1 + \sqrt{2})$ and 1.125, respectively. These values are attained at the same point $\xi_0 \in [0, \frac{1}{2}]$ with $M_0(\xi_0) = \frac{3}{4}$.

Finally, if M_0^d is obtained using Method 2, it is not difficult to show that: 1) M_0 and M_0^d are C^1 functions at the points $k \pm \frac{1}{4}$ for all $k \in \mathbb{Z}$, 2) at the points $k \pm \frac{1}{2}$, M_0 and M_0^d are C^∞ functions for odd N and C^N functions for even N; 3) the decay of the filter taps of M_0 and M_0^d are of the order of n^{-3}; and 4) the resulting biorthogonal wavelets have $2N + 2$ vanishing moments.

2.3   Shape Reconstruction

Through the application of Lagrangian mechanics, the geometric parameters of the deformable model, the global (parameterized) and local (free-form) deformation parameters, and the six degrees of freedom of rigid-body motion are systematically converted into generalized coordinates or dynamic degrees of freedom as described in [10]. The resulting Lagrangian equations for shape estimation are of the form $\mathbf{q} + \mathbf{Kq} = \mathbf{f}_q$, where $\mathbf{K}$ is the stiffness matrix, $\mathbf{f}_q$ are the generalized external forces that act on the model, and $\mathbf{q}$ are the model's generalized coordinates. The damping and the stiffness matrices determine the viscoelastic properties of the deformable model. Expressing the stiffness matrix in the g-HDAF wavelet basis is explained in detail in [8]. In physics-based shape estimation techniques, data points apply forces to the deformable model. These forces are converted to generalized 3D forces. Based on these forces the model will deform to minimize the discrepancy between the model and the data.

3   Experimental Results

We have applied the new multiresolution shape models for recovering the 3D surface shape from synthetic and real range data. We have assessed the accuracy, limitations, and advantages of the g-HDAF deformable models by comparing the performance of the multiresolution deformable models constructed using g-HDAFs (Gn), m-HDAFs (Hn), Daubechies (Dn), Symlets (Sn) [2], the Butterworth filter (Bn) [3], orthogonal spline filter (M) [9], orthogonal fractional splines (Fn) [13] with X vanishing moments, Coiflets (Cn) with 2X vanishing moments, and the orthogonal spline with 4 vanishing moments. Due to space restrictions, we present only selected results. Complete results for a variety of data and the complete set of the wavelet bases we examined can be found at [8].

In the first experiment, we applied our technique to fitting synthetic data obtained from a graphical model of a chess piece. Fig. 1(a) depicts the data, Fig. 1(b) depicts the estimated shape model, while Figs. 1(c-e) depict the estimated (by the fitting process) displacement maps $\mathbf{q}_{d_x}(u, v)$, $\mathbf{q}_{d_y}(u, v)$ and $\mathbf{q}_{d_z}(u, v)$, respectively. In the second experiment, we applied our technique to fitting female breast surface data. Fig. 1(f) depicts the breast range data obtained from a subject, Fig. 1(g) depicts the estimated shape model, while Figs. 1(h-j) depict the estimated displacement maps $\mathbf{q}_{d_x}(u, v)$, $\mathbf{q}_{d_y}(u, v)$ and $\mathbf{q}_{d_z}(u, v)$, respectively.

Table 1 depicts the RMSE of the reconstructed maps using the LL subband only for the g-HDAF and m-HDAF filters. To evaluate the efficiency of the

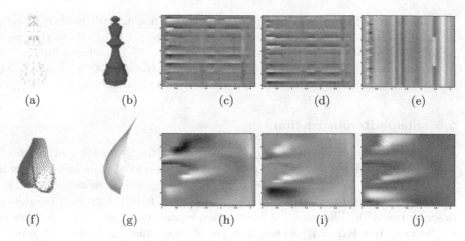

Fig. 1. (a,f) Synthetic data from a graphics model of a chess piece and real range data from a female patient's breast. (b,g) The estimated deformable models, and (c-e,h-j) depiction of $\mathbf{q}_{d_x}(u,v)$, $\mathbf{q}_{d_y}(u,v)$ and $\mathbf{q}_{d_z}(u,v)$, respectively.

Table 1. The estimated (by the fitting process) displacement maps $\mathbf{q}_{d_x}$, $\mathbf{q}_{d_y}$, $\mathbf{q}_{d_z}$ are decomposed one level by interpolating g-HDAF filters (Gn) and m-HDAF filters (Hn). The table shows the RMSE (R) of the reconstructed maps for the data in Fig. 1(g) if all the detail subbands are suppressed.

	$\mathbf{q}_{d_x}$	$\mathbf{q}_{d_y}$	$\mathbf{q}_{d_z}$		$\mathbf{q}_{d_x}$	$\mathbf{q}_{d_y}$	$\mathbf{q}_{d_z}$
W	R	R	R	W	R	R	R
G2	1.1625	1.3390	2.5604	H2	1.5623	1.8138	3.3715
G3	1.1118	1.2789	2.4434	H3	1.3706	1.5867	2.9955
G4	1.0826	1.2440	2.3740	H4	1.2737	1.4732	2.7961
G5	1.0631	1.2205	2.3269	H5	1.2160	1.4055	2.6732
G6	1.0489	1.2033	2.2922	H6	1.1776	1.3602	2.5894
G7	1.0380	1.1900	2.2653	H7	1.1501	1.3276	2.5281
G8	1.0292	1.1794	2.2436	H8	1.1293	1.3028	2.4809
G9	1.0220	1.1705	2.2257	H9	1.1128	1.2831	2.4432
G10	1.0158	1.1631	2.2104	H10	1.0995	1.2671	2.4122
G11	1.0106	1.1566	2.1973	H11	1.0884	1.2537	2.3861
G12	1.0060	1.1510	2.1858	H12	1.0789	1.2423	2.3639
G13	1.0019	1.1461	2.1757	H13	1.0708	1.2324	2.3445
G14	0.9982	1.1417	2.1666	H14	1.0636	1.2238	2.3275
G15	0.9949	1.1377	2.1585	H15	1.0574	1.2161	2.3124

g-HDAF lter, Table 2 presents the RMSE performance (R) of a variety of lters applied to a number of datasets if all highpass subbands are suppressed. Table 3 contains the number of transform coe cients of one level decomposition which can be ignored if we require the RMSE of the reconstructed $\mathbf{q}_{d_x}(u,v)$, $\mathbf{q}_{d_y}(u,v)$ and $\mathbf{q}_{d_z}(u,v)$ to be 0.0001. Applying this procedure to a sequence of the

Table 2. The estimated (by the fitting process) displacement maps are decomposed one level by g-HDAF filters (Gn), m-HDAF filters (Hn), Daubechies' orthogonal filter (Dn), least symmetric orthogonal filters (Sn), Coiflets (Cn), orthogonal spline filter (M), Butterworth filters (Bn), and fractional spline filters (Fn). Depicted are the mean and variance of the reconstruction error if all the detail subbands are suppressed.

W	(Mean,Var)$\times 10^{-4}$	W	(Mean,Var)$\times 10^{-4}$	W	(Mean,Var)$\times 10^{-4}$	W	(Mean,Var)$\times 10^{-4}$
G2	(19, 36)	H2	(30,59)	D4	(42,78)	C4	(32,58)
G4	(17, 33)	H4	(21,41)	D8	(30,55)	M	(17,32)
G6	(17, 32)	H6	(19,37)	D12	(34,64)	B5	(35,65)
G8	(17, 32)	H8	(18,35)	S4	(34,62)	B9	(33,61)
G10	(16 31)	H10	(17,34)	S8	(31,56)	B13	(32,59)
G12	(16 31)	H12	(17,33)	S12	(31,58)	F4	(33,62)
G14	(16 31)	H14	(17,32)	S14	(31,58)	F12	(32,59)

Table 3. The table depicts the percentage (%) of the coefficients for the data in Fig. 1(g) that can be ignored if the RMSE of the reconstructed maps is 0.0001.

	q_{d_x}	q_{d_y}	q_{d_z}		q_{d_x}	q_{d_y}	q_{d_z}		q_{d_x}	q_{d_y}	q_{d_z}
W	%	%	%	W	%	%	%	W	%	%	%
G2	77.05	76.73	77.52	H2	76.87	76.48	77.40	D8	76.89	76.60	77.60
G4	77.06	76.75	77.51	H4	76.99	76.65	77.58	S4	76.92	76.55	77.58
G6	77.06	76.76	77.49	H6	77.01	76.67	77.60	S8	76.89	76.60	77.60
G8	77.06	76.76	77.48	H8	77.01	76.70	77.58	C4	76.94	76.62	77.58
G10	77.06	76.76	77.48	H10	77.01	76.70	77.58	M	77.04	76.72	77.55
G12	77.06	76.76	77.47	H12	77.04	76.72	77.55	B9	77.82	77.87	79.46
G14	77.06	76.76	77.47	H14	77.04	76.72	77.55	F8	78.16	78.09	79.55

Table 4. The table depicts the mean and variance of the percentage of the coefficients that can be ignored if the RMSE of the reconstructed maps is 0.0001.

W	(Mean,Var)(%)	W	(Mean,Var)(%)	W	(Mean,Var)(%)	W	(Mean,Var)(%)
G2	(80.83 5.36)	H2	(80.35,5.23)	D4	(70.50,21.07)	C4	(70.66,20.88)
G4	(80.83 5.37)	H4	(80.50,5.19)	D8	(70.72,20.71)	M	(80.52,5.20)
G6	(80.83 5.37)	H6	(80.51,5.19)	D12	(70.08,21.69)	B5	(75.94,13.70)
G8	(80.83 5.37)	H8	(80.52,5.20)	S4	(70.58,20.99)	B9	(75.36,14.60)
G10	(80.83 5.37)	H10	(80.52,5.20)	S8	(70.57,21.04)	B13	(75.12,14.95)
G12	(80.83 5.37)	H12	(80.52,5.20)	S12	(71.50,19.03)	F4	(76.22,13.16)
G14	(80.82 5.37)	H14	(80.52,5.20)	S14	(71.43,19.18)	F12	(75.40,14.62)

estimated displacement maps, Table 4 depicts the percentage of the insigni cant coe cients when the RMSE of the reconstructed maps is 0.0001. Again, for comparison, other lters are included in this table. From above four tables, we can see that the g-HDAF lters perform best among all the lters examined in this paper. Since our lters are symmetric, we use the symmetric extension of the functions $\mathbf{q}_{d_x}(u,v)$, $\mathbf{q}_{d_y}(u,v)$ and $\mathbf{q}_{d_z}(u,v)$, and the most favorable extension for the other families.

An inspection of the table reveals the following. The main reasons for obtaining an overall improved performance using the proposed lters are the following. First, all g-HDAF biorthonormal wavelets are literally linear phase wavelets. The linear phase, which is the result of symmetry of the corresponding low pass lters, enhances the sparsity of wavelet decompositions, especially if the input matrix is symmetrically padded. Second, g-HDAFs appear to be smoother than their Daubechies / Symlets / Coi ets counterparts with the same number of vanishing moments. In addition, the symmetry of the low pass lters reduces the computational complexity. However, one possible drawback could be the sig-ni cant length of g-HDAF lters (in this paper, we used lters with 23 lter taps for M_0 and 45 taps for M_0^d). Although, g-HDAFs have in nite length only a small portion of their lter taps, located around the origin, plays a signi cant role in the wavelet transform. This is due to the very good localization of the g-HDAF scaling functions and wavelets in the time domain, which, in turn, is due to the optimal localization of HDAFs in the time domain. Note also that the length of the signi cant part of the low pass lters remains almost the same for any number of vanishing moments.

4   Concluding Remarks

In this paper, we presented the construction of a new class of linear phase wavelets (g-HDAFs) and the development of a new class of deformable models using this new biorthogonal wavelet basis. Experimental results indicate that the g-HDAF multiresolution deformable models achieve higher energy compaction than those based on conventional wavelets. This attribute makes them useful for shape reconstruction, shape recognition, and geometry compression.

References

1. A. Barr. Global and local deformations of solid primitives. *Computer Graphics*, 18(3):21–30, 1984.
2. I. Daubechies. *Ten Lectures on Wavelets*. SIAM, 1992.
3. C. Herley and M. Vetterli. Wavelets and recursive filter banks. *IEEE Transactions on Signal Processing*, 41(8):2536–2556, 1993.
4. D. Hoffman and D. Kouri. Distributed approximating functional theory for an arbitrary number of particles in a coordinate system independent formalism. *Journal of Physical Chemistry*, 97:4984–4988, 1993.
5. D. Hoffman, N. Nayar, O. A. Sharafeddin, and D. Kouri. On an analytic banded approximation for the discretized free propagator. *Journal of Physical Chemistry*, 95:8299, 1991.
6. D. Hoffman, G. W. Wei, D. S. Zhang, and D. Kouri. Shannon-Gabor wavelet distributed approximating functional. *Chemical Physics Letters*, 287:119–124, 1998.
7. H. Ji and Z. Shen. Compactly supported (bi)orthogonal wavelets generated by interpolatory refinable functions. *Advances in Computational Mathematics*, pages 81–104, 1999.

8. I. Kakadiaris, E. Papadakis, L. Shen, D. Kouri, and D. Hoffman. HDAF-based multiresolution deformable models for shape modeling and reconstruction. Technical Report 02-70, Department of Computer Science, University of Houston, Houston, TX, February 2002.
9. S. G. Mallat. A theory for multi-resolution signal decomposition: The wavelet representation. *IEEE Trans. Pattern Analysis and Machine Intelligence*, 11(7):674–693, 1989.
10. D. Metaxas and D. Terzopoulos. Shape and nonrigid motion estimation through physics-based synthesis. *IEEE Transactions on Pattern Analysis and Machine Intelligence*, 15(6):580 – 591, June 1993.
11. W. Swelden. The lifting scheme: A custom-designed construction of biorthogonal wavelets. *Applied and Computational Harmonic Analysis*, 3:186–200, 1996.
12. D. Terzopoulos and D. Metaxas. Dynamic 3D models with local and global deformations: Deformable superquadrics. *IEEE Transactions on Pattern Analysis and Machine Intelligence*, 13(7):703 – 714, 1991.
13. M. Unser and T. Blu. Fractional splines and wavelets. *SIAM Review*, 42(1):43–67, March 2000.
14. B. Vemuri and A. Radisavljevic. Multiresolution stochastic hybrid shape models with fractal priors. *ACM Transactions on Graphics*, 13(2):177–207, April 1994. Special Issue on Interactive Sculpting.

Muscle-Driven Motion Simulation
Based on Deformable Human Model
Constructed from Real Anatomical Slice Data

Hiroshi Inaba, Shin-ya Miyazaki, and Jun-ichi Hasegawa

Graduate School of Computer and Cognitive Sciences, Chukyo University
101 Tokodachi, Kaizu-cho, Toyota-city, Aichi, 470-0393 Japan
{inaba,miyazaki,hasegawa}@sccs.chukyo-u.ac.jp
Tel. +81-565-45-0971(ext.6781), Fax. +81-565-46-1299

1 Introduction

Recently, much research has been reported on human motion simulation which is applicable to sports medicine, rehabilitation, plastic surgery and so on. Digital human body is a general term for those synthesized models and is expected to analyze and evaluate real human s behaviors. It enables us to experiment various kinds of cases safely without giving patients any pain. However, for the time being, those models do not have enough capability to be applied to practical use.

Not only deformed shapes but also motion features are important for practical use. Therefore, the model has to be dynamic, motion should be driven by muscle force, and the deformed shape should be decided as a result of elastic object s interaction.

Several kinds of digital human body projects have been done. Reference [1,2,3] have developed motion generation driven by muscle force, although models are simpli ed in the eld of physiology. Ref. [4,5] have constructed a human body model based on captured motions, in which motion is given beforehand, and its purpose is to obtain deformed shapes rather than motion generation.

In this paper, we propose a digital human body model which is constructed from anatomical slice data and driven by muscle force. The model is composed of rigid bones and deformable tissues such as skeletal muscle and fatty tissue, which generates both motion and deformation of the human body at the same time. In the simulation process, contraction force is given rst to some skeletal muscles, then corresponding bones are moved. After that, muscles are not only moved but are also deformed depending on the relative positions of the bones. At that time, fatty tissues connected with muscles are also moved and deformed. By iterating the above process in short time intervals, body motion with shape deformation can be generated. In the next experiment, this method is applied to motion simulation of the lower limbs and the results are visualized in animation.

The remaining part of this paper is constructed as follows: Section 2 explains the procedure of human body construction from Visible Human anatomical slice data. Sections 3 and 4 show motion generation and tissue deformation, respec-

F.J. Perales and E.R. Hancock (Eds.): AMDO 2002, LNCS 2492, pp. 32–42, 2002.

tively. In section 5, the appropriateness of synthesized deformation is discussed with experimental results.

2 Human Body Model

2.1 Basic Structure

Our digital human body consists of three components: bone, muscle and fatty tissue. The bone builds the base for posture. The muscles move the skeleton by contracting themselves and construct the inner shape of the human body model. The fatty tissue forms the body surface being deformed by the movement of skeleton and muscle deformation.

2.2 Model Components and Construction

The shape of each component is represented as a 3D polygonal pillar. It can be constructed by using slice images obtained from a real human body (Fig. 1(a)). If two or more regions of the same component are included in a slice, the procedure is applied to each of them. The detail procedure for construction is as follows.

Reduction in the number of slices

Polygonal representation After the border of each component region is extracted from each slice. Intersectional points of the border with several lines outgoing radically from the center point of the region is obtained (Fig. 1(c)). These points become vertices of the polygon, and a set of lines between two adjoining points makes a simpli ed border (Fig. 1(d)).

3D Construction A 3D shape is constructed by connecting every pair of corresponding vertices between two adjoining slices.

The shapes of bone and muscle decide the inner of fatty tissue (Fig. 2(a)). The detail procedure is as follows.

Reference point selection The center point of the major bone region is used as the reference point in each slice.

Setting of inner points Using lines outgoing radically from the reference point, the following points are obtained sequentially:

Intersection points of the bone border with the radial lines

Intersection points of the muscle border with the radial lines

These points are regarded as polygon vertices representing the inner surface of the fatty tissue (Fig. 2(b)). If two or more points exist on a single radial line, only the nearest one to the reference point is kept (Fig. 2(c)).

3D Construction A polygonal pillar is constructed in the same way for other components mentioned above.

The whole shape of fatty tissue is obtained as shown in Fig. 2(d) by combining the inner surface as in Fig. 2(c) and the other as in Fig. 1(c). An example of constructed body components is shown in Fig. 3.

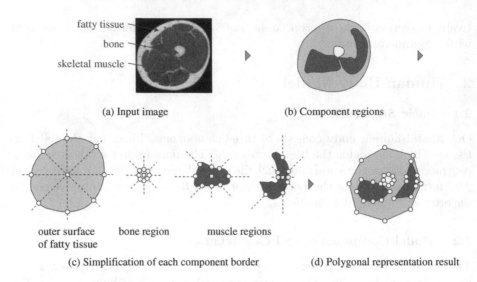

fatty tissue
bone
skeletal muscle

(a) Input image

(b) Component regions

outer surface
of fatty tissue

bone region

muscle regions

(c) Simplification of each component border

(d) Polygonal representation result

Fig. 1. Construction of components

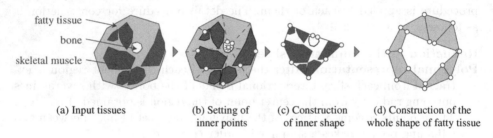

fatty tissue
bone
skeletal muscle

(a) Input tissues

(b) Setting of
inner points

(c) Construction
of inner shape

(d) Construction of the
whole shape of fatty tissue

Fig. 2. Construction of fatty tissue shape

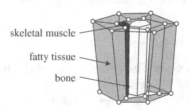

skeletal muscle
fatty tissue
bone

Fig. 3. An example of constructed body parts

3 Motion Generation

3.1 Outline of Motion Generation

Each muscle can generate force by contracting itself. This force is transformed to a joint torque to rotate and move the skeleton connected to the muscle. Shapes of muscle and fatty tissue are deformed according to the postural change of the skeleton. By performing this process repeatedly, human motion is generated. The results are visualized in the form of animation (Fig. 4).

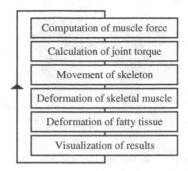

Fig. 4. Procedures of motion generation

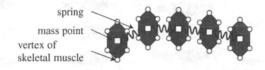

Fig. 5. Arrangement of mass points and springs

3.2 Muscle Contraction

An active human motion is basically generated by muscle contractions. Extra force for contracting muscles is called contraction force , and is applied to each of the speci ed muscles. This force is applied for shortening muscle length.

Fig. 5 shows an example of mass point and spring arrangement. Sequentially arranged mass points and springs are placed on the center axis of the muscle. The contraction force $\mathbf{F}_i$ applied to mass point i is given by Eq. (1). m_i, k, L, and D represent mass point, spring constant, natural length and damping ratio of springs, respectively. $\mathbf{r}_{ij}$ is a relative vector from point i to point j, and $\mathbf{v}_{ij}$ is the relative velocity. Con guration of mass points is determined under the e ect of contraction force. Muscle is attached to skeleton only by mass points, called muscle end point, which is placed on the muscle end. So, only the force on the muscle end point operates the skeleton directly. Therefore, using force on the position of the muscle end point can calculate joint torque.

$$\mathbf{F}_i = m_i \cdot \mathbf{g} \sum_j k \cdot 1 - \frac{L}{|\mathbf{r}_{ij}|} \cdot \mathbf{r}_{ij} + D \cdot \mathbf{v}_{ij} + M \cdot \frac{L}{|\mathbf{r}_{ij}|} \qquad (1)$$

4   Tissue Deformation

4.1   Muscle Deformation

Skeletal muscles are deformed according to the movement of the skeleton. The deformation is performed on movement of mass points arranged on the centerline of the skeletal muscle. The detail procedures are as follows.

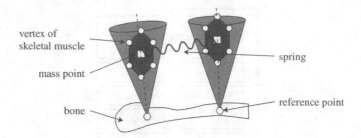

Fig. 6. Conic areas for restricting mass point movement

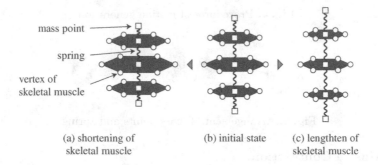

| (a) shortening of skeletal muscle | (b) initial state | (c) lengthten of skeletal muscle |

Fig. 7. Illustration of skeletal muscle deformation

Restriction of mass point movement to restrict the area of mass point movement, mass points are anchored onto the bone s surface. At rst, the closest polygon to each mass point is found. Then, the center of the polygon is decided as the anchor point. Mass point movement is restricted in a conic region according to the anchor point as shown in Fig. 6. The top of the cone is located on the anchor point, and the center axis goes through the anchor and mass points in their initial state.

Restriction of constant volume The whole shape of each muscle is deformed to keep its volume constant. This is real muscle s volume is almost unchanged even if it deforms strongly. Sectional areas of the muscle increase contrastly depending on muscle shrinkage (Fig. 7).

4.2   Fatty Tissue Deformation

Elastic Model of Fatty Tissue. To obtain a deformed shape of fatty tissue, an elastic object model developed by our group [6] is employed. In this model, the whole shape is represented by a set of volume elements. Each volume element should be a polyhedron. This model generates proper stress for restoring the initial shape even if the object is extremely deformed. This means that, an elastic object constructed by this model is more robust for large-scale deformation than mass-and-spring model.

Displacements of mass points in each local element are obtained as $\mathbf{r}_i - \mathbf{R}i$ to satisfy the Eq. 2. Here $\mathbf{R}_i$ shows the relative vector of the vertex i in the equilibrium shape with respect to the center of the element. Also $\mathbf{r}_i$ shows the relative vector of the vertex i in the deformed shape. k is the elastic constant which decides exibility of deformation. In fact, $\mathbf{R}_i$ is obtained to solve Eqs. 3 and 4, where $\mathbf{Ro}_i$ is the initial position of $\mathbf{R}_i$. The unit vector of the rotation axis $u = (u_x, u_y, u_z)$ and θ shows the rotation angle.

$$\mathbf{r}_i \times (\mathbf{R}_i - \mathbf{r}_i) = K \qquad \mathbf{r}_i \times \mathbf{R}_i = \vec{0} \qquad (2)$$

$$\mathbf{R}_i = \mathbf{M} \cdot \mathbf{Ro}_i \qquad (3)$$

$$\mathbf{M} = \mathbf{uu}^{\mathrm{T}} + \cos\theta \, (\mathbf{I} - \mathbf{uu}^{\mathrm{T}}) + \sin\theta \begin{array}{ccc} 0 & -u_z & u_y \\ u_z & 0 & -u_x \\ -u_y & u_x & 0 \end{array} \qquad (4)$$

Deformation. Deformation of the fatty tissue is de ned globally by changes in posture and local deformation by changes in muscle shapes. The detail procedure is as follows (Fig. 8).

Reference points As shown in Fig. 8(a), for vertex p of fatty tissue, the closest vertex g of the skeletal muscle is selected. g is called the reference point of p.

De nition of moving vector When the shape of the skeletal muscle is mod- i ed by change in posture, the movement of each vertex is represented by a moving vector (Fig. 8(b)).

Inner shape deformation of fatty tissue If a vertex of the skeletal muscle is a reference point, and its moving vector is $\mathbf{v}$, the corresponding vector of the fatty tissue is also moved by $\mathbf{v}$ (Fig. 8(c)).

Whole shape deformation of body surface After the above process, the shape of each volume element is changed based on elastic calculation. This results in the deformation of the whole shape of fatty tissue. This also means that the body surface (the outer shape of fatty tissue) is obtained (Fig. 8(d)).

If a vertex that is arranged to the inside of the fatty tissue touches a bone, it is moved on the bone surface. The above process is not performed.

5 Experiments and Discussion

5.1 Experiments

Outline of Muscle Behavior. In the following experiment, our method is applied to a human leg model. The lower limb is composed of 16 muscles and exion motion at the knee joint is generated. Some muscle s role is to generate a exion motion, others simply deform and form the outline around the pelvis.

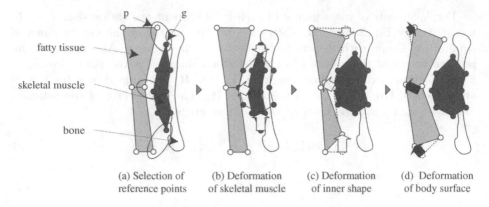

fatty tissue

skeletal muscle

bone

(a) Selection of reference points

(b) Deformation of skeletal muscle

(c) Deformation of inner shape

(d) Deformation of body surface

Fig. 8. Illustration of fatty tissue deformation

Table 1. Specification of images

	Original image	Input image
image size(pixel)	2048×1216	290×337
pixel size(mm)	0.33×0.33	1×1
number of images	1179	236
image interval(mm)	1	5

Construction of Human Body Model. We extracted bone shape, muscle and fatty tissue from axial photographs of the Visible Human Dataset [8] (slice no. 1700-2878). Table 1 shows a speci cation of original images and input images. We used clipping images to calculate an elastic equation quickly and selected images at 5 slice intervals to obtain a rough shape of tissue. Each tissue component is extracted semi automatically. The model is simpli ed in resolution for fast computation, and the degree of simpli cation is decided by comparing original shape to the nal shape. As a result, the number of polygons in the constructed model is about 0.5 percent compared with the model constructed using ordinal Marching cubes method. In our current model, the knee joint has a mechanism to rotate around an identical point and it s limited in rotation angle. For the mass and moment of inertia of bone, we used the parameter values in ref. [7].

The nal results are visualized as a 3D animation. We can see the behavior of both bone and muscle transparently.

5.2   Results

Fig. 9-11 show experimental results. In these   gures, fatty tissue and muscle deformation are demonstrated well. Fig. 9 shows the results of motion simulation for the lower limb. In the   gures, the body surface at a knee joint can be observed in motion. Fig. 10 and 11 magnify the knee joint part and the femur part, respectively, in the same simulation. Motion animation was generated in real time by using a standard PC (Spec; Pentium III 1GHz×2, 1GB Memory, GeForce3, OS; Windows 2000).

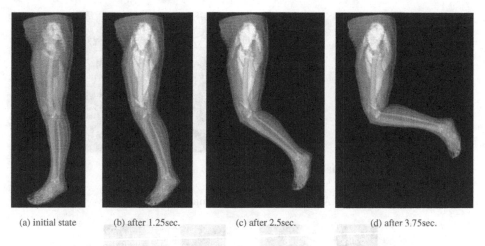

(a) initial state   (b) after 1.25sec.   (c) after 2.5sec.   (d) after 3.75sec.

Fig. 9. Results of motion generation

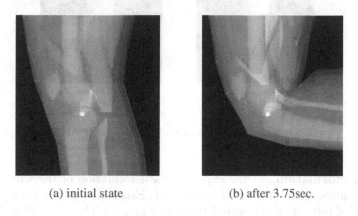

(a) initial state   (b) after 3.75sec.

Fig. 10. A result of body surface deformation at a knee joint

5.3   Discussion

Motion Generation. From the experimental results, it is con rmed that exion motion at the knee joint could be generated by contracting skeletal muscles
located on the femur. However, the property of contraction force used in our
skeletal muscle model is di erent from that of real human s behavior, employing
a simple spring-based model for skeletal muscles. Although, we presented only
simulation results for a single motion in this paper, our method can generate
various motion by modifying the timing and parameters of muscle contractions.
Our skeletal muscle model cannot be expanded on cooperative works with plural
muscles at the present. To solve this problem, a biomechanics model of skeletal
muscle must be introduced (e.g. ref. [9]). If such a higher performance model is
constructed, it will become possible to generate more complicated and continuous motion, such as a stand-up and kick motion.

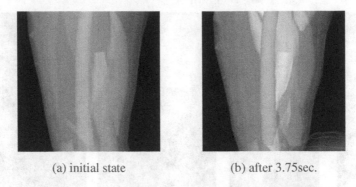

(a) initial state　　　　　　　　　　(b) after 3.75sec.

Fig. 11. A result of tissue deformation of the femur

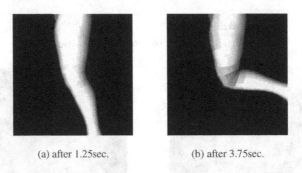

(a) after 1.25sec.　　　　　　　　　(b) after 3.75sec.

Fig. 12. Visualization of body surface deformation

Tissue Deformation. In the experiments deformation of the whole shape of the lower limbs in motion can be observed. Especially, in the knee joint part, the shape of fatty tissue is subject to change greatly. The result of body surface deformation at the front of the knee joint was very natural, but at the back of the knee joint, the result had some heavy curves inside of the human body. This tendency was con rmed independently of the degree of body shape simpli cation. Also, unexpected phenomenon was discovered that the shape of fatty tissue was broken when the degree of deformation became heavy or the joint angle became too large. The main reason for this is a failure of elastic calculation due to heavy deformation.

Visualization of Results. For a motion simulation system with deformable body model proposed here, it is very important and useful to develop a function for visualizing the deformation results in detail. Therefore, the degree of deformation is visualized by classifying them with colors. Fig. 12 shows change in the degree of deformation on the body surface area in a motion. Each volume element on the surface of fatty tissue is calculated, and color intensity shows the degree of deformation. In Fig. 12, white means no deformation was made, and blue and red mean increases and decreases of deformation, respectively.

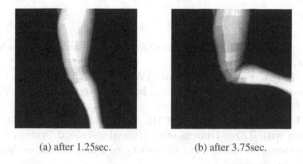

(a) after 1.25sec.   (b) after 3.75sec.

Fig. 13. Visualization of change of fatty tissue shape

Fig. 13 shows changes in the fatty tissue shape from the initial state. The degree of fatty tissue deformation for each volume element of fatty tissue is calculated by Eq. (5). $\mathbf{Ro}_i$ and $\mathbf{r}_i$ are the same as de ned by Eq. 2. N is the number of vertices in a fatty tissue volume element. The colors are assigned in the same manner as mentioned above.

$$\frac{\sum_{i=1}^{N} |\mathbf{Ro}_i - \mathbf{r}_i|}{N} \tag{5}$$

These visualization results make it easy to understand a change of the tissue shape in a special situation such as a loss of tissue function and a change to the internal structure of human body. These results can give informed consent in the medical   eld, especially in the   eld of cosmetic surgery.

6   Conclusions

In this paper, a digital human model with movable and deformable body parts was proposed. This model consists of skeleton, muscle and fatty tissue, and could be used for motion generation with body shape deformation. In the experiments, the model was applied to the motion generation of human lower limbs. The results were promising. Our future works include evaluation of the reality of motion and shape generation, cooperative work generation by plural muscles, muscle deformation based on elasticity of muscle itself, and application to other parts of the human body.

Acknowledgments

We would like to thank the colleagues of the Hasegawa laboratory for its insightful discussions. We would also like to thank Marvin Lenoar for his unconditional assistance. This work was supported in part by the grant-in-aid for Private University High-Tech Research Center, Ministry of Education, Culture, Sports, Science and Technology, Japan.

References

1. MusculoGraphics Inc.: SIMM (Software for Interactive Musculoskeletal Modeling). http://www.musculographics.com
2. Taku KOUMURA, Yoshihisa SHINAGAWA, Tosiyasu L. KUNII: Creating and retargeting motion by the musculoskeletal human body model. The Visual Computer 16:254-270 (2000)
3. Kazunori HASE, Junya NISHIGUCHI, Nobutoshi YAMAZAKI: Model of Human Walking with Three-Dimensional Musculo-Skeletal System and Hierarchical Neuronal System. Biomechanism 15,Society of Biomechanisms Japan ,pp.187-198 (June 2000) (in japanese)
4. Kenichi YAMAZAKI, Naoki SUZUKI, Asaki HATTORI, Akihiko TAKAMATSU, Akihiko UCHIYAMA: The Development of 4D Muscle Model for 4D Quantitative Movement Analysis. Journal of JSCAS, Vol. 2, No. 1, pp.22-29 (May 2000) (in japanese)
5. Luciana Porcher Nedel, Daniel Thalmann: Anatomic modeling of deformable human bodies. The Visual Computer 16:306-321 (2000)
6. Shin-ya MIYAZAKI, Shunsuke YOSHIDA, Takami YASUDA, Shigeki YOKOI: Proposal to Model Elastic Objects Based on Maintaining Local Shapes. The Transactions of IEICE, Vol. J82-A, No. 7, pp.1138-1155 (1999) (in japanese)
7. Dempster WT.: Space requirements of the seated operator. WADC Technical Report, Wright-Patterson Air Force Base, pp.55-159 (1955)
8. Michael J. Ackerman: The Visible Human Project. Proceedings of IEEE, Vol. 86, No. 3 (March 1998)
9. Felix E.Zajac: Muscle and Tendon: Properties, Models, Scaling, and Application to Biomechanics and Motor Control. Critical Reviews in Biomedical Engineering, Vol. 17 Issue 4, (1989)

Model Acquisition Using Shape-from-Shading

Antonio Robles-Kelly* and Edwin R. Hancock

Department of Computer Science
University of York, York YO1 5DD, UK
{arobkell,erh}@cs.york.ac.uk

Abstract. In this paper we show how the Mumford-Shah functional can be used to derive diffusion kernels that can be employed in the recovery of surface height in shape-from-shading. We commence from an initial field of surface normals which are constrained to fall on the Lambertian reflectance cone and to point in the direction of the local Canny edge gradient. We aim to find a path through this field of surface normals which can be used for surface height reconstruction. We demonstrate that the Mumford-Shah functional leads to a diffusion process which is a Markov chain on the field of surface normals. We find the steady state of the Markov chain using the leading eigenvector for the transition probability matrix computed from the diffusion kernels. We show how the steady state path can be used for height recovery and also for smoothing the initial field of surface normals.

1 Introduction

Computer vision provides several routes to automatic object and scene modelling which are of potential practical use to the graphics community. Broadly speaking these may be divided into those that are geometrically based and those that are based on photometric models. Turning our attention first to the geometric methods, the main contribution here has been to exploit projective geometry to develop algorithms for 3D object reconstruction from points, lines and curves [1,2]. When calibration data are at hand, then provided correspondence information is available, then both planar and curved surfaces may be reconstructed from multiple views. For curved surfaces there has been considerable success in using turntable sequences for surface reconstruction from both detected feature points [3] and occluding contour [4]. Photometric methods, on the other hand, aim to recover surface information from shading or texture variations. This is a classical problem in computer vision, which has lead to a considerable literature on the development of algorithms for shape-from-shading [5,6], photometric stereo [7,8] and shape-from-texture [9,10]. However, until recently these methods have been relatively neglected in comparison with their geometric counterparts. One of the reasons for this is that there are a number of well documented problems with shape-from-shading. These mainly stem from the fact that it is an underconstrained problem that must be augemented with constraints on local surface smoothness and initial surface normal direction to be rendered tractable. The resulting algorithms have a tendency to oversmooth surface detail and also to be numerically unstable. Moreover, the method relies on a very simple photometric model, which is confined to situations of Lambertian reflectance from a constant albedo surface illuminated by a single point light-source of known direction. Nonetheless, there

---

* Supported by CONACYT, under grant No. 146475/151752.

F.J. Perales and E.R. Hancock (Eds.): AMDO 2002, LNCS 2492, pp. 43–55, 2002.
© Springer-Verlag Berlin Heidelberg 2002

has recently been significant progress in overcoming some of the perceived limitations of the process. For instance, in the remote sensing community the method is used to infer terrain structure from radar images of Mars and Venus [11].

The original work on shape-from-shading adopted a variational approach and aimed to recover surface normal directions by applying Euler's method to a regularised energy function [5,12]. The energy function contained distinct terms to encourage data-closeness. The resulting iterative scheme had a tendency to oversmooth fine surface detail and to locate solutions that were dominated by the smoothness constraint rather than the data-closeness constraint. There have since been a multitude of papers attempting to improve the method and render it useful for practical shape-analysis tasks (for a good recent review, see the comprehensive comparative study of Zhang et al [13]). However, recently there has a consolidated effort in the literature aimed at overcoming the well documented problems with shape-from-shading. One of the most important of these is the method of Dupuis Oliensis [14] which does not use regularisation and has been proved to reconstruct height information correctly from intensity data. Bichsel and Pentland [15] have developed a fast variant of the method. One of the more successful recent advances in the field has been to use the apparatus of level-set theory to solve the image irradiance equation as a boundary value problem [16,17]. Related work by Rouy and Tourin [18] has proved the correctness and uniqueness of the solutions to shape-from-shading for the case when the light source and viewing directions are co-incident. In this work the problem is cast in a viscosity setting using the Hamilton-Jacobi-Bellman equations. In an effort to overcome the problems of poor data-closeness and over-smoothing, Worthington and Hancock have developed a new framework for shape-from-shading [6] in which the image irradiance equation is treated as a hard constraint [6] and curvature consistency constraints can be used to recover meaningful topographic surface structure [6]. However, the method only delivers fields of surface normals (Gauss maps) and height recovery requires a surface integration algorithm to be applied as a post-processing step.

The aims in this paper are twofold. First, we aim to show how the idea of imposing data-closeness using by constraining the surface normals to reside on the irradiance cone may be combined with ideas from spectral graph theory [19] to recover surface height data directly. Second, we aim to demonstrate that the resulting surfaces provide detailed and accurate models of the viewed object.

Our method draws on spectral graph theory [19] to develop a means of reconstructing a surface from its 2D field of surface normals, or Gauss map. The Gauss map is characterised using an affinity or transition probability matrix. The matrix elements are computed using the sectional curvature between locations in the Gauss map. We make use of the result that the steady state random walk on a graph is given by the leading eigenvector of the associated transition probability matrix [20,21]. With our characterisation, this steady state random walk is a curvature minimising path through the Gauss map. Local smoothing is then performed by fitting a quadric patch to the height estimates for the sites contained within each block. From the updated surface normal directions a new transition probability matrix may be estimated. The processes of height estimation and surface normal adjustment are interleaved and iterated until a stable height function is recovered.

2   Lambertian Reflectance

In the case of Lambertian reflectance from a matte surface of constant albedo illuminated with a single point light-source, the observed intensity is independent of the viewing direction. The observed intensity depends only on the quantity of absorbed light, and this in turn is proportional to the cosine of the incidence angle. Suppose that L is the unit-vector in the direction of the light source and that N_i is the unit-vector in the surface normal direction at the pixel i. According to Lambert's law, the observed image intensity at the pixel indexed i is $E_i = N_i \cdot L$.

Lambert's equation provides insufficient information to uniquely determine the surface normal direction. However, as recently observed by Worthington and Hancock [22], the equation does have a simple geometric interpretation which can be used to constrain the direction of the surface normal. The equation specifies that the surface normal must fall on the surface of a right-cone whose axis is aligned in the light-source direction L and whose apex angle is $\arccos(E)$.

Worthington and Hancock [22] exploit this property to develop a two-step iterative process for SFS. The process commences from a configuration in which the surface normals are placed on the position on the irradiance cone where their projections onto the image plane are aligned in the direction of the local (Canny) image gradient.

3   Diffusion Kernels

Stated formally, our goal is the recovery of height information from the field of surface normals. From a computational standpoint the aim is to find a path along which simple trigonometry may be applied to increment the estimated height function. To be more formal suppose that the surface under study is S and that the field of surface normals is sampled on the plane Π. Our aim here is to find a curve Γ across the plane Π that can be used as an integration path to reconstruct the height-function of the surface S. The projection of the curve Γ onto the surface S is denoted by Γ_S. Further, suppose that $\kappa(s)$ is the sectional curvature of the curve Γ_S at the point Q with parametric co-ordinate s. We seek the path Γ_S that minimises the Mumford-Shah [23] functional

$$\mathcal{E}(\Gamma_S) = \int_{\Gamma_S} \alpha + \beta\kappa(s)^2 \ ds \tag{1}$$

where α and β are constants. The probability of the path can be written as $P_{\Gamma_S} = \exp[-\mathcal{E}(\Gamma_S)]$.

The field of unit surface normals for the surface S on the plane Π is denoted by N. Accordingly, and following do Carmo [24], we let $T_Q(S)$ represent the tangent plane to the surface S at the point Q which belongs to the curve Γ_S. To compute the sectional curvature $\kappa(s)$ we require the differential of the surface or Hessian matrix $dN_Q : T_Q(S) \to T_Q(S)$. The maximum and minimum eigenvalues λ_1 and λ_2 of dN_Q are the principal curvatures at the point Q. The corresponding eigenvectors $e_1 \in T_Q(S)$ and $e_2 \in T_Q(S)$ form an orthogonal basis on the tangent plane $T_Q(S)$. At the point Q the unit normal vector to the curve Γ is n_Γ and the unit tangent vector is $t_Q \in T_Q(S)$. The sectional curvature of Γ at Q is given by

$$\kappa(s) = \frac{(t_Q.e_1)^2(\lambda_1 - \lambda_2) + \lambda_2}{n_\Gamma.N_Q} \tag{2}$$

where $(t_Q.e_1)^2(\lambda_1 - \lambda_2) + \lambda_2$ is the normal curvature and $\psi = \arccos n_\Gamma.N_Q$ is the angle between the curve normal and the surface normal.

In practice, we will be dealing with points which are positioned at discrete positions on the pixel lattice. Suppose that i and j are the pixel indices of neighbouring points sampled on the pixel lattice along the path Γ_S. With this discrete notation, the path energy and its probability are given by

$$\mathcal{E}(\Gamma_S) = \sum_{(i,j)\in\Gamma_S} \alpha + \beta\kappa_{i,j}^2 \ s_{i,j} \text{ and } P_{\Gamma_S} = \prod_{(i,j)\in\Gamma_S} \exp - \alpha + \beta\kappa_{i,j}^2 \ s_{i,j} \tag{3}$$

where $\kappa_{i,j}$ is an estimate of the curvature based on the surface normal directions at the pixel locations i and j, and $s_{i,j}$ is the path distance between these points. Hence, we can view the integration path Γ as Markov chain across the field of surface normals. The diffusion kernel for the process, i.e. probability of migrating between sites i and j is

$$K = \exp[-\mathcal{E}_{i,j}] = \exp - \alpha + \beta\kappa_{i,j}^2 \ s_{i,j} \tag{4}$$

In order to compute the path curvature appearing in the diffusion kernel, we make use of the surface normal directions. To commence, we note that $|\kappa_{i,j}| = \frac{1}{R_{i,j}}$ where $R_{i,j}$ is the radius of the local circular approximation to the integration curve on the surface. Suppose that the surface normal directions at the pixel locations i and j are respectively N_i and N_j. The approximating circle connects the points i and j, and has the path segment $s_{i,j}$ as the connecting chord. The change in direction of the radius vector of the circle is $\theta_{i,j} = \arccos N_i.N_j$ and hence $\cos\theta_{i,j} = N_i.N_j$. If the angle $\theta_{i,j}$ is small, then we can make the Maclaurin approximation $\cos\theta_{i,j} \simeq 1 - \frac{\theta_{i,j}^2}{2} = N_i.N_j$. Moreover, the small angle approximation to the radius of curvature of the circle is $R_{i,j} = \frac{s_{i,j}}{\theta_{i,j}}$. Hence, $\kappa_{i,j}^2 = \frac{2(1-N_i.N_j)}{s_{i,j}^2}$. As a result, we find that the cost associated with the step from the pixel i to the pixel j is $\mathcal{E}_{i,j} = \alpha s_{i,j} + \frac{2\beta}{s_{i,j}}(1 - N_i.N_j)$. The total cost associated with the integration path Γ_S is hence

$$\mathcal{E}_{\Gamma_S} = \alpha L_{\Gamma_S} + \sum_{(i,j)\in\Gamma_S} \frac{2\beta}{s_{i,j}}(1 - N_i.N_j) \tag{5}$$

where L_{Γ_S} is the length of the path. Hence, the integration path is a form of elastica which attempts to find an energy minimising path through the surface normals. The energy function is a variant of the Mumford-Shah functional. It has two terms. The first encourages the integration path to be one of minimum length. The second term encourages a path which minimises the total change in surface normal direction. There are clearly a number of ways in which the energy can be minimised. However, here we choose to make use of the fact that from Equation 6 it is clear that the energy function specifies a Markov chain on the sites of the Gauss map. In other words, the path can be viewed as a diffusion on the Gauss map. The steady state random walk for this diffusion can be found by locating the leading eigenvector of the transition probability matrix for the Markov chain.

To pursue the graph-spectral analysis of the Gauss map, we require a transition probability matrix. For the pixels indexed i and j we commence by computing the weight

$$w_{i,j} = \begin{array}{ll} \exp[-\mathcal{E}_{i,j}] & \text{if } j \in \mathcal{N}_i \\ 0 & \text{otherwise} \end{array} \qquad (6)$$

where $\mathcal{N}_i$ is the set of pixels-neighbours of the pixel i. Hence, the curvature weight is only non-zero if pixels abut one-another.

From the curvature dependant weights, we construct a transition probability matrix in which the upper diagonal elements sum to unity. The element in the row indexed i and column indexed j is

$$P(j,i) = P(i,j) = \frac{w_{i,j}}{\sum_{l=1;l\in V}^{|V\times V|} \sum_{k=l;k\in V}^{|V\times V|} w_{k,l}} \qquad (7)$$

In next section, we describe how the leading eigenvector of this matrix can be used to determine steady state random walk for the Markov chain and how this path may be used for the purposes of surface integration.

4 Random Walks and Markov Random Chains

The set of pixel sites can be viewed as a weighted graph $G = (V, E, P)$ with index-set V and edge-set $E = \{(i,j)|(i,j) \in V \times V, i \neq j\}$. The off-diagonal elements of the transition probability matrix P are the weights associated with the edges. In this paper, we exploit a graph-spectral property of the transition matrix P to develop a surface height recovery method. This requires that we have the eigenvalues and eigenvectors of the matrix P to hand. To find the eigenvectors of the transition probability matrix, P, we first solve polynomial equation $|P - \lambda I| = 0$. The unit eigenvector ϕ_i associated with the eigenvalue λ_i is found by solving the system of linear equations $P \phi_i = \lambda_i \phi_i$ and satisfies the condition $\phi_i^T \phi_i = 1$.

Consider a random walk on the graph G. The walk commences at the node j_1 and proceeds via the sequence of edge-connected nodes $\Gamma = \{j_1, j_2, j_3, ...\}$ where $(j_i, j_{i-1}) \in E$. Suppose that the transition probability associated with the move between the nodes j_l and j_m is $P(l, m)$. If the random walk can be represented by a Markov chain, then the probability of visiting the nodes in the sequence above is $P_{\Gamma_S} = P(j_1) \prod_{l=1}^{|V|} P(j_{l+1}, j_l)$. This Markov chain can be represented using the transition probability matrix P whose element with row l and column m is $P(l, m)$. Further, let $Q_t(i)$ be the probability of visiting the node indexed i after t-steps of the random walk and let $Q_t = (Q_t(1), Q_t(2), ...)^T$ be the vector of probabilities. After t time steps $Q_t = (P^T)^t Q_0$. If λ_i are the eigenvalues of P and ϕ_i are the corresponding eigenvectors of unit length, then $P = \sum_{i=1}^{|V|} \lambda_i \phi_i \phi_i^T$. As a result, after t applications of the Markov transition probability matrix $P^t = \sum_{i=1}^{|V|} \lambda_i^t \phi_i \phi_i^T$. If the row and columns of the matrix

P sum to unity, then $\lambda_1 = 1$. Furthermore, from spectral graph theory [19] provided that the graph G is not a bipartite graph, then the smallest eigenvalue $\lambda_{|V|} > -1$. As a result, when the Markov chain approaches its steady state, i.e. $t \to \infty$, then all but the first term in the above series become negligible. Hence, $\lim_{t \to \infty} P^t = {}_1 \, _1^T$. This establishes that the leading eigenvector of the transition probability matrix is the steady state of the Markov chain. For a more complete proof of this result see the book by Varga [21] or the review of Lovasz [20]. As a result, if we visit the nodes of the graph in the order defined by the magnitudes of the co-efficients of the leading eigenvector of the transition probability matrix, then the path is the steady state Markov chain. In this paper we aim to perform surface height recovery by co-joining pixel sites pixel sites along the path specified by the magnitude order of the components of the leading eigenvector.

Suppose that the leading eigenvector for the transition probability matrix is denoted by ${}^* = (\phi^*(1), ..., \phi^*(|V|))^T$. Our aim is to use the sequence of nodes defined by the rank order of the magnitudes of the components of the leading eigenvector to define an integration path through the set of pixel sites. The pixel path defined by the rank order of the co-efficients of the leading eigenvector is given by the list of sorted node-indices $\Gamma = (j_1, j_2, j_3, ..., j_{|V|})$ where $\phi^*(j_1) > \phi^*(j_2) > \phi^*(j_3) > ... > \phi^*(j_{|V|})$. The subscript n of the pixel with node-index $j_n \in V$ is hence the rank-order of the eigenvector component $\phi^*(j_n)$.

5   Extracting Patches

In practice the surface under study may have a patch structure. The patches may be identified by finding the blocks of the transition probability matrix induced under a permutation of the nodes. We commence by constructing the thresholded transition probability matrix A whose elements are defined as follows

$$A(i,j) = \begin{matrix} 0 & \text{if } P(i,j) << 1 \\ P(i,j) & \text{otherwise} \end{matrix} \tag{8}$$

Suppose that there are m distinct surface patches, each associated with an adjacency matrix $B^{(i)}$. If C represents a noise matrix, then the relationship between the observed transition matrix A and the underlying block-structured transition matrix is $A = B + C$ where $B = \mathcal{P} B_D \mathcal{P}^T$, $\mathcal{P}$ is a permutation matrix and $B_D = diag(B^{(1)}, B^{(2)}, .., B^{(i)}...)$ is a block diagonal matrix in which $B^{(i)}$ is the subblock corresponding to the patch indexed i. To recover the matrix B_D, we turn to the eigenvector expansion of the matrix A and write

$$A = \boldsymbol{b}_* \boldsymbol{b}_*^T + \sum_{i=2}^{|V|} \lambda_i \boldsymbol{b}_i \boldsymbol{b}_i^T \tag{9}$$

where the leading eigenvalue is unity i.e. $\lambda_1 = 1$, $\boldsymbol{b}_*$ is the leading eigenvector and the eigenvectors are normalised to be of unit length, i.e. $|\boldsymbol{b}_i| = 1$. To identify the patches, we use the following iterative procedure. We initialise the algorithm by letting $A^{(1)} = A$. Further suppose that $\boldsymbol{b}_*^{(1)}$ is the leading eigenvector of $A^{(1)}$. The matrix $B^{(1)} = \boldsymbol{b}_*^{(1)} \boldsymbol{b}_*^{(1)T}$ represents the first block of A. The nodes with non-zero entries belong to the patch. These nodes may be identified and removed from further consideration. To do this we compute the residual transition matrix $A^{(2)} = A^{(1)} - B^{(1)}$ in which the elements of the first patch are nulled. The leading eigenvector $b_*^{(2)}$ of the residual transition matrix $A^{(2)}$ is used to compute the second block $B^{(2)} = b_*^{(2)} b_*^{(2)T}$. The process is repeated iteratively to identify all of the principal blocks of A. At iteration n, $b_*^{(n)}$ is the leading eigenvector of the residual transition probability matrix $A^{(n)}$, and the nth block is $B^{(n)} = b_*^{(n)} b_*^{(n)T}$. The index set of the patch indexed n is the set of nodes for which the components of the leading eigenvector $b_*^{(n)}$ are non-zero. Hence, the index-set for the ith patch is $S_i = \{k | b_*^{(i)}(k) \neq 0\}$. It is important to stress that the patches are non-overlapping, i.e. the inner product of the block eigenvectors for different patches is zero $b_*^{(k)} . b_*^{(l)} = 0$, where $k \neq l$.

6 Height Recovery

Our surface height recovery algorithm proceeds along the sequence of pixel sites defined by the order of the co-efficients of the leading eigenvector associated with the separate patches. For the kth patch, the path is $\Gamma_k = (j_k^1, j_k^2, j_k^3, ...)$ where the order of the co-efficients of the leading eigenvector for this patch is such that $\phi_k^*(j_k^1) > \phi_k^*(j_k^2) > \phi_k^*(j_k^3) > ....$ As we move from pixel-site to pixel-site defined by this path we increment the surface height-function. In this section, we describe the trigonometry of the height incrementation process.

At step n of the algorithm, we make a transition from the pixel with path-index j_{n-1} to the pixel with path-index j_n. The distance between the pixel-centres associated with this transition is

$$d_n = \overline{(x_{j_n}^2 - x_{j_{n-1}})^2 + (y_{j_n} - y_{j_{n-1}})^2} \qquad (10)$$

This distance, together with the surface normals $N_{j_n} = (N_{j_n}(x), N_{j_n}(y), N_{j_n}(z))$ and $N_{j_{n-1}} = (N_{j_{n-1}}(x), N_{j_{n-1}}(y), N_{j_{n-1}}(z))$ at the two pixel-sites may be used to compute the change in surface height associated with the transition. The height increment is given by

$$h_n = \frac{d_n}{2} \frac{N_{j_n}(x)}{N_{j_n}(y)} + \frac{N_{j_{n-1}}(x)}{N_{j_{n-1}}(y)} \qquad (11)$$

If the height-function is initialised by setting $z_{j_0} = 0$, then the centre-height for the pixel with path-index j_n is $z_{j_{n+1}} = z_{j_n} + h_n$.

Once the surface normals that belong to the individual patches have been integrated together, then we merge them together to form a global surface. Suppose that S_k is the integrated surface for the kth patch. We compute the mean height for the pixels belonging to this boundary. We merge the patches together by ensuring that abutting patches have the same mean boundary height.

The geometry of this procedure is illustrated in Figure 1b.

7 Region Quadric Fitting

Once the height values are availble for each pixel site in a patch, then we perform smoothing. We do this by fitting a local quadric to the height data for the patch sites. To do this we employ a simple least-squares fitting method.

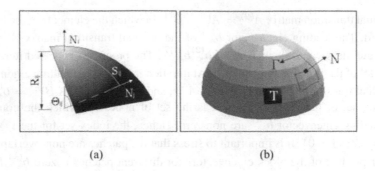

(a)   (b)

Fig. 1. Curvature and path illustration (see text).

Suppose that the pixels belonging to the patch indexed k are denoted by the set S_k. We aim to fit the quadric

$$Q_k(x,y) = a_{1,k} + a_{2,k}x + a_{3,k}y + a_{4,k}x^2 + a_{5,k}xy + a_{6,k}y^2 \qquad (12)$$

to the height data for the sites in the patch. Let $M_i = (1, x_i, y_i, x_i^2, x_i y_i, y_i^2)^T$ be a vector of co-ordinate moments and let $V_k = (a_{1,k}, ..., a_{6,k})^T$ be a vector of parameters. The least-squares parameter vector for the quadric patch satisfies the condition

$$V_k^* = \arg\min_{V_k} \sum_{i \in S_k} \left| z_i - V_k^T M_i \right|^2 \qquad (13)$$

In matrix form the solution vector is given by $V_k^* = (F_k^T F_k)^{-1} F_k^T$, where

$$F_k = \sum_{i \in S_k} z_i M_i M_i^T \qquad (14)$$

8   Surface Normal Adjustment

Turning our attention to the smoothing process, our aim is to adjust the surface normal directions so that they are consistent with the gradient of the fitted quadric and also remain on their respective irradiance cone. The opening angle of the corresponding cone will be determined by the gray-level E_i at pixel-site indexed i and the direction of the surface normal on the image plane will be determined by the gradient of the fitted quadric. As a result, we can parameterise the surface normal directions using two angles. The first of these is the angle θ_i between the surface normal and the light source direction. This is simply the opening angle of the irradiance cone, and this angle must be kept fixed in order to ensure that the recovered surface normal satisfies Lambert's law. The second is the azimuthal angle φ_i, which measures the position of the surface normal on the irradiance cone. The angles φ_i and θ_i can be defined in terms of the gradient of the local quadric patch $Q_k(x_i, y_i)$ on the image plane. Using some simple geometry, we can write

$$\varphi_i = \begin{array}{ll} 2\pi - \arccos \dfrac{\frac{\partial Q_k(x_i,y_i)}{\partial x}}{R_i} & \text{if } \frac{\partial Q_k(x_i,y_i)}{\partial y_i} < 0 \\ \arccos \dfrac{\frac{\partial Q_k(x_i,y_i)}{\partial x_i}}{R_i} & \text{otherwise} \end{array}$$

$$\theta_i = \arccos(E_i) \tag{15}$$

where R_i is the magnitude of the component of the gradient on the image plane, which is given by

$$R_i = \sqrt{\frac{\partial Q_k(x_i,y_i)}{\partial x_i}^2 + \frac{\partial Q_k(x_i,y_i)}{\partial y_i}^2}$$

Once the updated angles have been computed, then the surface normals may be updated using the equations

$$N_i(x) = \sin(\theta_i)\cos(\varphi_i)$$
$$N_i(y) = \sin(\theta_i)\sin(\varphi_i)$$
$$N_i(y) = \cos(\theta_i) \tag{16}$$

9 Algorithm Description

Having described the different steps of the surface reconstruction process, in this section we summarise how the steps are combined together in an algorithm. The sequence of processing steps is as follows:

- Step 0: The surface normals are placed in their initial positions on the irradiance cones. To do this we align them in the directions of the image gradient. The gradient is computed by first smoothing the grey-scale image by fitting local quadric patches to the raw image intensity. The smoothed image gradient is found from the derivatives of the fitted patch.
- Step 1: From the initial Gauss map (field of surface normals), we compute the sectional curvatures and hence the transition probability matrix. The blocks of the matrix are surface patches. The leading eigenvector of the transition matrix for each block is the patch integration path. Using the patch integration paths, we recover estimates of the surface height.
- Step 2: For the sites in each patch, we fit a quadric patch to the available height estimates. The fitted surface patches are used to compute an estimate of the surface gradient. At each location, the gradient estimate is used to adjust the position of the surface normals on their respective irradiance cones.
- Iteration: Steps 1 and 2 are iterated until a stable set of surface height estimates are located.

10 Experiments

We have experimented with a variety of real world images, but in this paper we concentrate mainly on images of classical statues. These objects are predominantly Lambertian, although there are local specular highlights and local albedo variations. In principle we can overcome both of these problems. In a recent paper, we have described a probabilistic method for specularity removal which uses the Torrance and Sparrow model to

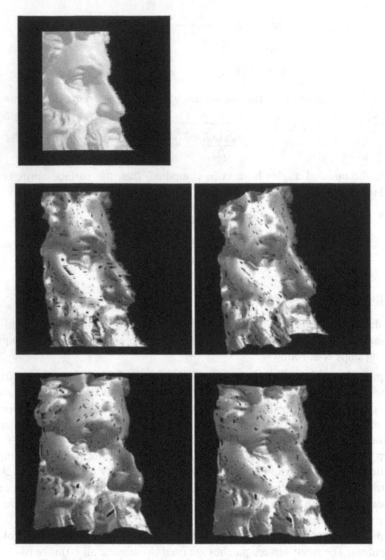

Fig. 2. Results of the shape-from-shading process on the Moses.

perform Lambertian reflectance correction for shiny objects. Local albedo changes can be accommodated using brightness normalisation or histogram equalisation.

The objects studied are a detail of Michaelangelo's Moses and a section of the "Three Graces".

In Figure 2 we show our first sequence of results. The image in the left hand of the top panel is the input to the shape-from-shading process. This is a side view of the head of the statue "Moses". The the final the field of surface normals is shown in the top right corner of Figure 2.

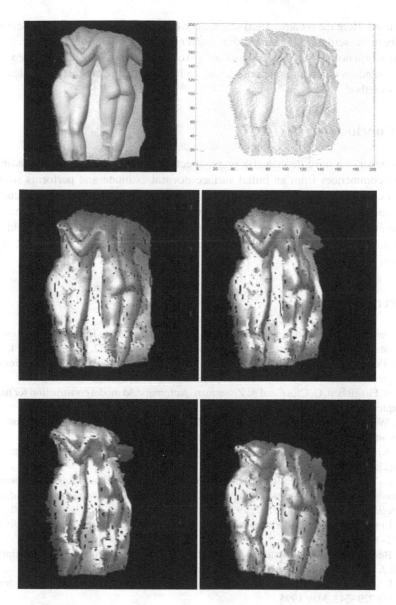

Fig. 3. Results of the shape-from-shading process on the Moses.

The two bottom rows in Figure 2 show a series of views of the reconstructed surface from different viewing directions. This figure illustrates the fine surface structure and detail recovered using our method. For instance the shape of the nose is recovered. The beard, eye-sockets and cheek bones are also well reconstructed.

In Figure 3 we show the results for a section of the relief "The Three Graces". However, only two of the subjects of the original sculpture are visible in the section of image used. Here the reconstructed surface contains most of the anatomical detail of the subjects in the sculpture. The algorithm converged after 3 iterations.

It is worth noting that the "ambiguous" pixel-sites, removed as a consequence of the Markov random chain approach used, can be interpolated using a standard least mean squares method.

11   Conclusions

In this paper, we have described a graph-spectral algorithm shape-from-shading. The method commences from an initial surface normal estimate and performs smoothing along a curvature minimising path defined by the leading eigenvector of a curvature-based transition probability matrix. By traversing this path and applying some simple trigonometry we reconstruct the surface height function. Results on real world images reveal that the method is able to deliver accurate height reconstructions for complex surfaces.

References

1. R. Fawcett, A. Zisserman, and J.M. Brady. Extracting structure from an affine view of a 3d point set with one or 2 bilateral symmetries. *IVC*, 12(9):615–622, November 1994.
2. M. Pollefeys, M. Vergauwen, F. Verbiest, K. Cornelis, and L.J. Van Gool. From image sequences to 3d models. In *Ascona01*, pages 403–410, 2001.
3. A.W. Fitzgibbon, G. Cross, and A. Zisserman. Automatic 3d model construction for turn-table sequences. In *SMILE98*, 1998.
4. K. Wong, P.R.S. Mendonca, and R. Cipolla. Reconstruction and motion estimation from apparent contours under circular motion. In *BMVC99*, pages I: 83–92, 1999.
5. B. K. P. Horn and M. J. Brooks. The variational approach to shape from shading. *CVGIP*, 33(2):174–208, 1986.
6. P. L. Worthington and E. R. Hancock. New constraints on data-closeness and needle map consistency for shape-from-shading. *IEEE Transactions on Pattern Analysis and Machine Intelligence*, 21(12):1250–1267, 1999.
7. Y. Li and R. Woodham. Orientation-based representations of 3-d shape. In *CVPR94*, pages 182–187, 1994.
8. F. Bernardini and H. Rushmeier. High-quality texture reconstruction from multiple scans. *IEEE Trans. on Visualization and Comp. Graphics*, 7(4), 2001.
9. B.J. Super and A.C. Bovik. Planar surface orientation from texture spatial-frequencies. *PR*, 28(5):729–743, May 1995.
10. J. Malik and R. Rosenholtz. Computing local surface orientation and shape from texture for curved surfaces. *IJCV*, 23(2):149–168, June 1997.
11. R.T. Frankot and R. Chellappa. Estimation of surface topography from sar imagery using shape from shading techniques. *AI*, 43(3):271–310, June 1990.
12. H. Delingette, M. Hebert, and K. Ikeuchi. Energy functions for regularization algorithms. *SPIE*, 1570:104–115, 1991.
13. R. Zhang, Ping-Sing Tsai, J. E. Cryer and M. Shah. Shape from shading: A survery. *IEEE Trans. on Pattern Analysis and Machine Intelligence*, 21(8):690–706, 1999.
14. P. Dupuis and J. Oliensis. Direct method for reconstructing shape from shading. In *CVPR92*, pages 453–458, 1992.

15. M. Bichsel and A. P. Pentland. A simple algorithm for shape from shading. In *CVPR92*, pages 459–465, 1992.
16. B. B. Kimia R. Kimmel, K. Siddiqqi and A. M. Bruckstein. Shape from shading: Level set propagation and viscosity solutions. *International Journal of Computer Vision*, (16):107–133, 1995.
17. R. Kimmel and A. M. Bruckstein. Tracking level sets by level sets: a method for solving the shape from shading problem. *Computer vision and Image Understanding*, 62(2):47–48, July 1995.
18. E. Rouy and A. Tourin. A viscosity solution approach to shape-from-shading. *Siam J. Numerical Analysis*, 29(3):867–884, 1992.
19. Fan R. K. Chung. *Spectral Graph Theory*. American Mathematical Society, 1997.
20. L. Lovász. Random walks on graphs: a survey. *Bolyai Society Mathematical Studies*, 2(2):1–46, 1993.
21. R. S. Varga. *Matrix Iterative Analysis*. Springer, second edition, 2000.
22. P. L. Worthington and E. R. Hancock. Needle map recovery using robust regularizers. *Image and Vision Computing*, 17:545–557, 1999.
23. D. Mumford and J. Shah. Optimal approximations by piecewise smooth functions and associated variational problems. *Comm. in Pure and Appl. Math.*, 42(5):577–685, 1989.
24. M. P. Do Carmo. *Differential Geometry of Curves and Surfaces*. Prentice Hall, 1976.

A Computational Algebraic Topology Model
for the Deformation of Curves

M.F. Auclair-Fortier[1], P. Poulin[1], D. Ziou[1], and M. Allili[2]

[1] DMI, Université de Sherbrooke, Sherbrooke, Canada, J1K 2R1
{auclair,poulin,ziou}@dmi.usherb.ca
[2] DCSM, Bishop's University, Lennoxville, Canada, J1M 1Z7
mallili@ubishops.ca

Abstract. A new method for the deformation of curves is presented. It is based upon a decomposition of the linear elasticity problem into basic physical laws. Unlike other methods which solve the partial differential equation arising from the physical laws by numerical techniques, we encode the basic laws using computational algebraic topology. Conservative laws use exact global values while constitutive allow to make wise assumptions using some knowledge about the problem and the domain. The deformations computed with our approach have a physical interpretation. Furthermore, our algorithm performs with either 2D or 3D problems. We finally present an application of the model in updating road databases and results validating our approach.

Keywords: Curve deformation, principle of linear momentum, computational algebraic topology, active contours, road database updating.

1 Introduction

In recent years, deformable models have been widely studied since the introduction of active contours by Kass *et al* [6]. To solve these problems, many different approaches have been proposed [5,9] in particular, physical models derived from equations of continuum mechanics. Among these models, we are concerned with those related to the deformation of curves [6,12]. They are very useful in automatic updating of road databases [2].

For a given curve S, the application of these methods often leads to a discrete stationary system of equations of the form $KS = f(S)$ where K is a matrix which encodes the regularizing constraints on S and $f(S)$ represents the data potential. Several methods have been introduced to compute the matrix K. Among them, mass-springs models [10] are physical models which use a discrete representation of the objects, modeled with point masses linked together by springs. These models offer only a rough approximation of the phenomena happening in a body and information is only available at a finite number of points [9]. Moreover, the determination of spring constants reflecting the properties of a specific material may be a fastidious work. Other models based upon the minimization of an energy functional which takes into account an internal regularizing force and an external force applied on the data are also often used. Some of them consider the deformable bodies as continuous objects by approximating their behavior with methods such as the finite element method (FEM). However, the computational requirements of the FEM make them difficult to be applied without preprocessing steps. Finite

F.J. Perales and E.R. Hancock (Eds.): AMDO 2002, LNCS 2492, pp. 56–67, 2002.

difference methods (FDM) are also used. They usually offer better efficiency than FEM but they require the computation of fourth order derivatives which make them sensitive to noise [9].

We propose to use an approach based on the principle of linear momentum. Unlike mass-springs models, our model offers a systematic method for reflecting some properties of the materials. These material properties allows to parameterize the deformation. Because this principle is a physical one, our model includes a concrete physical interpretation unlike to other techniques [9].

In problems encountered in computer vision, the continuous domain must be subdivided into many sub-domains in which there is often only one information available. These sub-domains may be either pixels-based or regions-based. The principle of linear momentum is a conservation equation which means that it is valid on a whole domain by nature. We then propose to use the global equation instead of discretize the partial differential equation (PDE) obtained by a limit process on this global equation [8,13]. Such an approach has already been used for electromagnetism [14], heat transfer [1] and mechanical engineering problems [4]. It has the advantage to minimize the approximation steps involved in the discretization process of the continuous problem. Under the same assumptions, its results and convergence rates are better than those obtained with classical numerical methods such as FDM or FEM [4].

To encode these physical global values over pixels of different dimensions, we use a computational algebraic topology-based image model. This model has been proposed by Ziou and Allili [16] and used by Auclair-Fortier et al. [1] for the resolution of the diffusion. It introduces the image support as a decomposition in terms of points, edges, surfaces, volumes, etc. Images of any dimensions can then be handled.

Our approach has several important advantages. 1) Since the linear elasticity problem is well-known in continuum mechanics, our modeling can be performed wisely in order to provide a physical interpretation of the whole deformation process and of its intermediate steps, allowing for an easier determination of the parameters used in the process. 2) The curves are modeled as material having their own physical properties such as elasticity and rigidity. They have the property of recovering their original shape when the forces applied on them are taken off which confirm the physical interpretation of the steps. 3) The deformed curves can either have high curvature points or be locally smooth. 4) Our approach can be applied to other physics-based problems by using a suitable decomposition [1].

In order to validate our model, we apply our algorithm to the correction of road databases. This paper is organized as follows. Sect. 2 introduce the basic laws involved in linear momentum principle. In Sect. 3 we summarize the algebraic topology-based image model. We propose in Sect. 4 a representation of the problem similar to the one introduced in [1]. Applications and experimental results are presented in Sect. 5.

2 Decomposition into Basic Laws

The goal of this section is to decompose the conservation of linear momentum into basic laws. This is a fundamental step to understand the discretization process of Sect. 4.

Given distributed body forces ρb and traction forces t^n depending on the surface normal vector n, the principle of linear momentum [3] states that the resultant force acting on a body, moving under the velocity field v is equal to the rate of change over time of the linear momentum:

$$\underbrace{\frac{d}{dt} \int_V \rho v \, dV}_{\text{lin. momentum}} = \underbrace{\int_S t^n \, dS + \int_V \rho b \, dV}_{\text{Forces acting on the body}}. \tag{1}$$

Using the Cauchy stress formula [7]:

$$t_i^n = \sum_{j=1}^{3} \sigma_{ij} n_j, \qquad i = 1, 2, 3 \tag{2}$$

where σ_{ij} is the stress component in the direction of x_j when n is parallel to x_i, and Gauss's divergence theorem, we have

$$\frac{d}{dt} \int_V \rho v \, dV = \int_V (\nabla \cdot \sigma + \rho b) \, dV, \tag{3}$$

where the divergence of a tensor is a vector which elements are the divergence of each column of the tensor. Since the element of volume is arbitrary, the integral sign can be taken off and the first basic law is obtained assuming a zero velocity field in Eq. 3:

$$\nabla \cdot \sigma = \rho b. \tag{4}$$

This is the usual PDE formulation used with continuous hypothesis.

In order to explain how the internal forces of an elastic body vary when it undergoes deformations, we must take into account a constitutive equation (or material law) which reflect the internal constitution of the materials. The next basic law, known as the generalized Hooke's law for linear elastic isotropic materials in plane strain situations [7], is given by the following equations:

$$\sigma_{ii} = \frac{E}{(1+\nu)(1-2\nu)} \left[(1-\nu)\varepsilon_{ii} + \nu(\varepsilon_{jj} + \varepsilon_{kk}) \right] \tag{5}$$

$$\sigma_{ij} = 2\,G\,\varepsilon_{ij} = \frac{E}{1+v}\varepsilon_{ij} \quad (i \neq j). \tag{6}$$

where E is the *modulus of elasticity of Young*, ν the *Poisson ratio* and $G = \frac{E}{2(1+\nu)}$ the *modulus of rigidity*.

The strains are defined by the well-known strain-displacements relation [11] which can be expressed by a tensor ε having elements

$$\varepsilon_{ij} = \frac{1}{2} \left(\frac{\partial u_i}{\partial x_j} + \frac{\partial u_j}{\partial x_i} \right), \qquad i, j = 1, 2, 3 \tag{7}$$

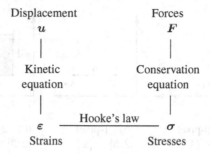

Fig. 1. Decomposition of the linear elasticity problem into basic laws.

where u_i is the displacement field of the original body in the direction of x_i. Considering another tensor

$$d = \nabla u = ((\nabla u_1)^t, (\nabla u_2)^t, (\nabla u_3)^t), \tag{8}$$

it is easy to see that is the symmetric part of d, that is $= \frac{d+d^t}{2}$.

Having this decomposition in mind, a general scheme similar to the one presented by Tonti [13] may then be introduced to summarize how the internal reaction forces of a body are related to the global displacements of that body (Fig. 1).

3   The CAT-Based Image Model

The main goal of this section is to introduce the image model used to derive the computational scheme presented in the next section. The image acquisition can be seen as a process which accumulates the total number of photons within a global area corresponding to the pixel. This can be associated then to the integration of some physical field. Moreover, as we have seen in Sect. 2, Eq. 1 is a conservation equation which makes it global by essence and then applies exactly on a whole spatial area. Conservation equations relates a global physical quantity on a domain with another global physical quantity on the boundary of this domain. This allows for an exact algebraic formulation [8]. If we consider a pixel as a n-dimensional domain, we need an image model representing this domain, the global value associated with it, the intrinsic orientation associated to the physical field, the boundary of the domain and the relation between the two global values. All these are elegantly provided by the CAT-based image model. We give here an overview of the model but a detailed version of it and some other applications in image processing may be found in [1,11,16].

An image is composed of two distinctive parts: the image support (pixels) and some field quantity associated with each pixel. This quantity may be scalar (e.g. gray level), vectorial (e.g. color, multispectral, optical flow) or tensorial (e.g. Hessian). The image support is a complex of unit cubes usually called *pixels*. A pixel $\gamma \subset \mathbb{R}^n$ is a product

$$\gamma = I_1 \times I_2 \times \ldots \times I_n$$

where I_j is either the singleton $\{k\}$ and is said to be a *degenerate* interval, or the closed interval $[k, k + 1]$ for some $k \in \mathbb{Z}$. The number $q \in \{0, 1, \ldots n\}$ of non-degenerate intervals is by definition the *dimension* of γ, which is called a *q-pixel*. Fig. 2 illustrates

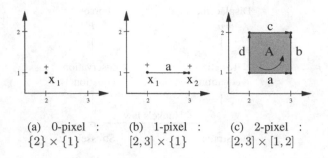

(a) 0-pixel :   (b) 1-pixel :   (c) 2-pixel :
$\{2\} \times \{1\}$ $[2,3] \times \{1\}$ $[2,3] \times [1,2]$

Fig. 2. Three examples of q-pixels in $\mathbb{R}^2$.

three elementary pixels in $\mathbb{R}^2$. For a q-pixel ($q \geq 1$), we intuitively define one of its $(q-1)$-face as $(q-1)$-pixel formed by replacing one of its non-degenerate interval $I_i = [a_i, b_i]$ by either a_i or b_i. One can define the $(q-2)$-faces, ..., down to the 0-faces of σ in the same way.

By definition, a natural orientation of the cube is assumed for each pixel. Suppose that γ denotes a particular positively oriented q-pixel. It is natural to denote the same pixel with opposite orientation by $-\gamma$. Examples of orientations are given in Fig. 2. A *cubical complex* in $\mathbb{R}^n$ is a finite collection $\mathcal{K}$ of q-pixels such that every face of any pixel of the image support is also a pixel in $\mathcal{K}$ and the intersection of any two pixels of $\mathcal{K}$ is either empty or a face of each of them. The definitions presented above allow us to consider 2-pixels (square elements), 1-pixels (line elements) and 0-pixels (point elements) simultaneously.

In order to write the image support in algebraic form, we introduce the concept of *chains*. Any set of oriented q-pixels of a cubical complex can be written in algebraic form by attributing to them the coefficient $0, 1$ or -1, if they are not in the set or if they should or should not be taken with positive orientation, resp. A formal expression for a q-chain c_q is $c_q = \sum_{\gamma_i \in \mathcal{K}} \lambda_i \gamma_i$ where $\lambda_i \in \{-1, 0, 1\}$.

Finally, given a q-pixel γ, we define its *boundary* $\partial\gamma$ as the $(q-1)$-chain corresponding to the alternating sum of its $(q-1)$-faces. The sum is taken according to the orientation of the $(q-1)$-faces with respect to the orientation of the q-pixel. For instance, in Fig. 2, the boundary of the 1-pixel a is $x_2 - x_1$ and the boundary of the 2-pixel A is $a + b - c - d$. We say that a $(q-1)$-face of γ is positively oriented relative to the orientation of γ if its orientation is compatible with the orientation of γ. Taking Fig. 2(c) a and b (resp. c and d) are positively (resp. negatively) oriented with respect to the orientation of A. By linearity, the extension of the definition of boundary to arbitrary q-chains is easy.

In order to model the discrete counterpart of field quantity over the image plane, we look for an application $\mathcal{F}$ which associates a global quantity with all q-pixels γ of a cubical complex. We denote this by $< \mathcal{F}, \gamma >$. This quantity may be any mathematical entity such as a scalar, a vector, etc. For two adjacent q-pixels γ_1 and γ_2, $\mathcal{F}$ must satisfy $< \mathcal{F}, \lambda_1\gamma_1 + \lambda_2\gamma_2 > = \lambda_1 < \mathcal{F}, \gamma_1 > +\lambda_2 < \mathcal{F}, \gamma_2 >$, which means that the sum of the quantity over each pixel is equal to the quantity over the two pixels. The resulting transformation is called a *q-cochain*.

Finally we need an operator which associates a global quantity with the $(q + 1)$-pixels according to the global quantities given on their q-faces. Given a q-cochain $\mathcal{F}$, we define an operator δ, called the *coboundary operator*, which transforms $\mathcal{F}$ into a $(q + 1)$-cochain $\delta\mathcal{F}$ such that

$$< \delta\mathcal{F}, \gamma >=< \mathcal{F}, \partial\gamma > \qquad (9)$$

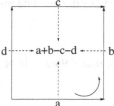

for all $(q + 1)$-chains γ. The coboundary is defined as the signed sum of the physical quantities associated with the q-faces of γ. The sum is taken according to the relative orientation of the q-faces of the $(q+1)$-pixels of γ with respect to the orientation of the pixels. Fig. 3 presents an example of the coboundary operation for a 2-pixel.

Fig. 3. Coboundary operation.

4   Encoding of the Basic Laws Using the CAT-Based Image Model

To encode the basic laws of the elasticity problem, the image support is subdivided into cubical complexes. Global quantities are applied over k-pixels via cochains according to basic laws presented in Section 2. The constitutive equations 5 and 6 are expressed as linear transformations between two cochains. Since we want to represent two kinds of global values over the image, we use two complexes. The first complex is associated with variables describing the configuration of the system (e.g. displacements) while the second complex refers to the source variables (e.g. forces) [13].

The global force (assumed to be known) over a surface is expressed as a 2-cochain $< \mathcal{F}, \gamma_F >$ for a 2-pixel γ_F of a 2-complex $\mathcal{K}^s$:

$$< \mathcal{F}, \gamma_F >= \int_{\gamma_F} \rho\boldsymbol{b}\, dS = \int_{\gamma_F} \nabla \cdot \underline{\underline{T}}\, dS.$$

Applying the divergence theorem, we have

$$< \mathcal{F}, \gamma_F >= \int_{\partial\gamma_F} \underline{\underline{T}} \cdot \boldsymbol{n}\, dP = \sum_{\gamma_{S_i} \in \partial\gamma_F} \int_{\gamma_{S_i}} \underline{\underline{T}} \cdot \boldsymbol{n}_i\, dP. \qquad (10)$$

where $\boldsymbol{n}_i$ is the normal vector to γ_{S_i}. This allows us to define a 1-cochain

$$< \mathcal{S}, \gamma_{S_i} >= \int_{\gamma_{S_i}} \underline{\underline{T}} \cdot \boldsymbol{n}_i\, dP. \qquad (11)$$

The cochain $\mathcal{F}$ is then the coboundary of $\mathcal{S}$:

$$< \mathcal{F}, \gamma_F >=< \delta\mathcal{S}, \gamma_F >=< \mathcal{S}, \partial\gamma_F >,$$

which is an exact discrete representation of Eq. 4.

We model now the global displacement gradient $\boldsymbol{d}$ as a 1-cochain $< \mathcal{D}, \gamma_D >$ for a 1-pixel γ_D over a 2-complex $\mathcal{K}^p$ with $\partial\gamma_D = \mathbf{x}_* - \mathbf{x}_\#$ (Fig. 4(a)):

$$< \mathcal{D}, \gamma_D >= \int_{\gamma_D} \boldsymbol{d} \cdot dP = \int_{\mathbf{x}_\#}^{\mathbf{x}_*} \nabla\boldsymbol{u} \cdot dP. \qquad (12)$$

Let us apply a 0-cochain $\mathcal{U}$ to $\partial \gamma_D$, we have

$$< \mathcal{U}, \partial \gamma_D > = < \mathcal{U}, \mathbf{x}_* - \mathbf{x}_\# > = < \mathcal{U}, \mathbf{x}_* > - < \mathcal{U}, \mathbf{x}_\# >$$

and use the line integral theorem on Eq. 12. Then we have

$$< \mathcal{D}, \gamma_D > = \boldsymbol{u}(\mathbf{x}_*) - \boldsymbol{u}(\mathbf{x}_\#).$$

We thus define $< \mathcal{U}, \mathbf{x} > = \boldsymbol{u}(\mathbf{x})$. The cochain $\mathcal{D}$ is then the coboundary of $\mathcal{U}$:

$$< \mathcal{D}, \gamma_D > = < \delta\mathcal{U}, \gamma_D > = < \mathcal{U}, \partial \gamma_D >$$

and it is an exact discrete representation of Eq. 8. Up to now, we only have exact discretization of the physical laws, this is an important advantage of the modelization.

We finally need to represent the Hooke's law (Eqs 5 and 6) coupled with Eq. 7 which links the local values of $\boldsymbol{d}$ and   . In cochain terms, we want to link the cochains $\mathcal{D}$ and $\mathcal{S}$. Since Eqs 5 and 6 are constitutive which are local by nature, we cannot provide a topological expression for them. We use a piecewise approximation $\boldsymbol{d}$ of $\boldsymbol{d}$ such that for each 1-face γ_D of a 2-pixel γ of $\mathcal{K}^p$ we have

$$\int_{\gamma_D} \boldsymbol{d} \cdot dP = < \mathcal{D}, \gamma_D > . \tag{13}$$

Applying the generalized Hooke's law and Eq. 7 in order to satisfy Eq. 13, we have an approximated version of   :

$$\sigma_{ii} = E \, \frac{(1 - \nu)d_{ii} + \nu \; d_{jj} + d_{kk}}{(1 + \nu)(1 - 2\nu)}$$

$$\sigma_{ij} = \frac{E}{(1 + \nu)} \, \frac{d_{ij} + d_{ji}}{2} \quad , \qquad i, j = 1, 2, 3, \quad i \neq j$$

at all points of γ.

Let us position the two cubical complexes $\mathcal{K}^p$ and $\mathcal{K}^s$ such that the 0-pixels of $\mathcal{K}^p$ correspond to the center of the image pixels and the 2-pixels of $\mathcal{K}^s$ coincide with the image pixels (Fig. 4(b)). This way of positioning $\mathcal{K}^s$ allows the use of an approximation polynomial for $\boldsymbol{d}$ of order 1 with the same accuracy as that obtained using one of order 2 [8]. For simplicity, we assume that it arises from a bilinear approximation of $\boldsymbol{u}$. Then for a 2-pixel of $\mathcal{K}^p$ (Fig. 4(a)), we have

$$\boldsymbol{d} = \left[\frac{\mathcal{D}_1}{\Delta} + \frac{\mathcal{D}_3 - \mathcal{D}_1}{\Delta^2} x_2, \frac{\mathcal{D}_4}{\Delta} + \frac{\mathcal{D}_2 - \mathcal{D}_4}{\Delta^2} x_1 \right]. \tag{14}$$

Eq. 11 is then replaced by

$$< \mathcal{S}, \gamma_{S_i} > = \int_{\gamma_{S_i}} \quad \cdot \, \boldsymbol{n}_i \, dP. \tag{15}$$

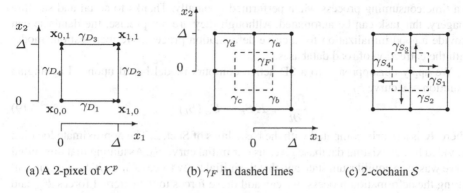

(a) A 2-pixel of $\mathcal{K}^p$ (b) γ_F in dashed lines   (c) 2-cochain $\mathcal{S}$

Fig. 4. Cochains in $\mathcal{K}^p$ and $\mathcal{K}^s$.

In order to compute $< \mathcal{S}, \gamma_{S_i} >$, we use four approximation functions ^{a}, ^{b}, ^{c} and ^{d} because each γ_F intersects four 2-pixels of $\mathcal{K}^p$ (see Fig. 4). We find the value of the cochain $\mathcal{S}$ over the four 1-faces of γ_F using Eq. 11:

$$\mathcal{S}_1 = \int_0^{\frac{\Delta}{2}} {}^a \left\langle \frac{\Delta}{2}, x_2 \right\rangle \cdot i \, dx_2 + \int_{-\frac{\Delta}{2}}^0 {}^b \left\langle \frac{\Delta}{2}, x_2 \right\rangle \cdot i \, dx_2$$

and so on for $\mathcal{S}_2, \mathcal{S}_3$ and $\mathcal{S}_4$. Using Eq. 10 we have

$$< \mathcal{F}, \gamma_F >= \mathcal{S}_1 + \mathcal{S}_2 + \mathcal{S}_3 + \mathcal{S}_4. \tag{16}$$

Eq. 16 represents the global internal forces $\rho b = (F_1, F_2)$ as a function of the displacement $u = (u, v)$. As an example, we present the values of F_1 and F_2 for the 2-pixel γ_F of Fig. 4(b) with $\Delta = 1$:

$$F_1 = C\,[(3 - 4\nu)u_{-1,1} + (2 - 8\nu)u_{0,1} + (3 - 4\nu)u_{1,1}$$
$$+(10 - 8\nu)u_{-1,0} + (-36 + 48\nu)u_{0,0} + (10 - 8\nu)u_{1,0}$$
$$+(3 - 4\nu)u_{-1,-1} + (2 - 8\nu)u_{0,-1} + (3 - 4\nu)u_{1,-1}$$
$$-2v_{-1,1} + 2v_{1,1} + 2v_{-1,-1} - 2v_{1,-1}] \tag{17}$$
$$F_2 = C\,[(3 - 4\nu)v_{-1,1} + (10 - 8\nu)v_{0,1} + (3 - 4\nu)v_{1,1}$$
$$+(2 - 8\nu)v_{-1,0} + (-36 + 48\nu)v_{0,0} + (2 - 8\nu)v_{1,0}$$
$$+(3 - 4\nu)v_{-1,-1} + (10 - 8\nu)v_{0,-1} + (3 - 4\nu)v_{1,-1}$$
$$-2u_{-1,1} + 2u_{1,1} + 2u_{-1,-1} - 2u_{1,-1}] \tag{18}$$

where $C = \frac{E}{16(1+\nu)(1-2\nu)}$. Eqs 17 and 18 set a linear relationship between a pixel and its neighbors.

5   Application and Results

Some existing road databases have been obtained by scanning road cartographic information. That means that their location are not precise and they have to be corrected. This is a time consuming process when performed manually. Thanks to aerial and satellite imagery, this task can be automated. Although they are not precise, the database can provide a good initialization for a curve deformation process. We then test our model with the correction of road databases.

We apply our approach to a 2D active contours model based upon a Lagrangian evolution of a curve S_t

$$\frac{\partial S_t}{\partial t} + K S_t = F_{ext}(S_t) \tag{19}$$

where K is a matrix computed with the basic laws of Sect. 2. The approximate location provided by the existing database gives us our initial curve S_0. Assuming that this initial curve was in an equilibrium state and that the initial body forces $F_0 = K S_0$ are constant during the deformation process, we can add these forces to the external forces F_{ext} and solve Eq. 19 with an explicit scheme

$$S_{t+\Delta t} = S_t + \Delta t(F_{ext} - K u_t) \tag{20}$$

where u_t is the displacement vector for the curve S_t.

In order to solve Eq. 20, we need global values for the body forces F_{ext} over each pixel of $\mathcal{K}^s$. In our examples, we use the line plausibility image obtained using a line detector proposed by Ziou [15]. We assume that the line plausibility is a global value valid over the whole pixel. Thus we set $F_{ext} = g'_\sigma * L$ where L is the line plausibility image and g'_σ is the Gaussian derivative at scale σ. Eqs. 17 and 18 are used to build the stiffness matrix K of Eq. 20.

For each image, we have compared the results with our physics-based method (PBM) with those obtained with a finite element method (FEM) [2]. For all results, the image force is the gradient obtained using a line detector proposed by Ziou [15] with the line detection scale set to 0.8.

The first image is a section of a RADARSAT SAR image centered on the region of Stephenville (Québec), Canada with a 25-meter resolution[1] in which the initial curves are drawn in white. Fig. 5 presents results obtained with the PBM ($E = 200$ and $\nu = 0.45$) and FEM ($\alpha = 0.03$ and $\beta = 38.8, 33.1, 43.7$ and 41.5 depending on the curve section). We zoomed the upper central parts of both images (Figs 5(c) and 5(d)) to show the major improvement on high curvature points. This is explained by the fact that unlike FEM which is energy minimization based, PBM waits until some external forces modify the initial curve, even in high-curvature points. Since the initialization is close to the shore, then the resulting curve was not greatly modified and kept its high curvature points.

Fig. 6 presents the results obtained on a portion of an orthoimage of the region of Merrit in the south of British Columbia, Canada [2] with the PBM ($E = 25$ and $\nu = 0.1$) and FEM ($\alpha = 0.03$ and $\beta = 41.8$). One can see that PBM provide results which are a little bit closer to the shore than the FEM.

All over this paper, we have insisted on the fact that the deformations obtained using our model have a physical interpretation and that the objects modeled using the PBM have their own physical properties. To illustrate this fact, Fig. 7 shows the evolution of this corrected curve when the external forces are taken off. Fig. 7(b) presents both the

---

[1] The image was provided by the Canadian Space Agency under the ADRO-2 program.

[2] © Department of Natural Resources of Canada. All rights reserved.

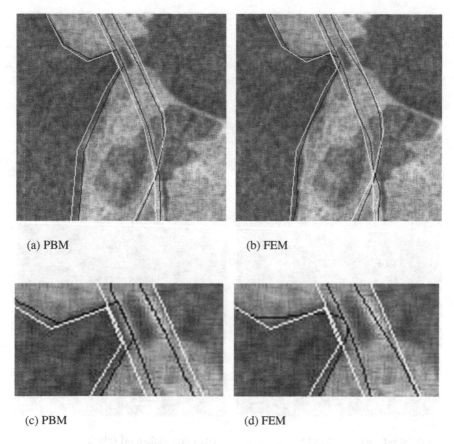

(a) PBM   (b) FEM

(c) PBM   (d) FEM

Fig. 5. Results on a SAR image.

final curve (in black) and the initial curve (in white). One can clearly notice that the curve has recovered its original shape but has also experienced a spatial shift, which is natural because this shift is not dependent on the material property of the curve.

6   Conclusion

We have presented a new model for the deformation of curves. The proposed approach starts from the principle of linear momentum. Since this equation is conservative, it can be applied directly on a whole domain. As the pixel value can be seen as a integrated value over the whole pixel area, we take directly the global conservation equation instead of the PDE usually used. This approach allows us to rely exactly some global values by algebraic equations. Two global values can not be exactly relied by algebraic equations since they depend on the material properties but the approximations can be chosen in order to give the required physical behavior.

In order to represent the elements of various dimensions involved in the process as well as all the global values, the intrinsic orientation of the physical field and the links between global values, we use an image model based on algebraic topology. This model

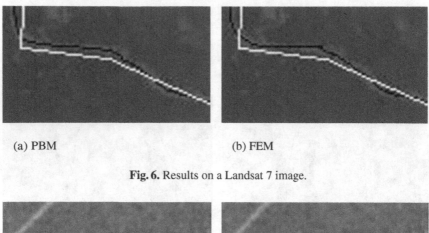

(a) PBM   (b) FEM

Fig. 6. Results on a Landsat 7 image.

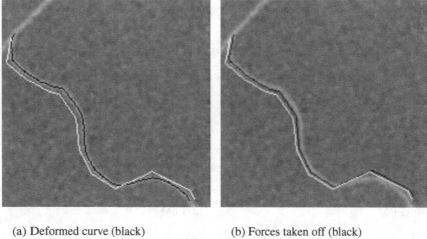

(a) Deformed curve (black)   (b) Forces taken off (black)

Fig. 7. Shape recovery of a curve when the external forces are taken off. Initial curve is in white.

uses generic elegant mathematical tools which can be applied in any dimension and to solve other problems [1,16].

Our approach presents the following differences with the other methods. 1) We use both global and local quantities. 2) It is based on the global conservation which is discrete by nature instead of using a discretization of the PDE. 3) It is based upon a decomposition into basic laws of physics. This allows us to give a physical explanation to the deformation steps. 4) The curves and surfaces have physical behaviors. 5) We make approximation only when the constitutive equation is involved, the other laws being exactly discretized. We validated our approach into a road database updating application on synthetic and real images.

References

1. M.F. Auclair-Fortier, P. Poulin, D. Ziou, and M. Allili. Physics Based Resolution of Smoothing and Optical Flow: A Computational Algebraic Topology Approach. Technical Report 269, Département de mathématiques et d'informatique, Université de Sherbrooke, 2001.

2. L. Bentabet, S. Jodouin, D. Ziou, and J. Vaillancourt. Automated Updating of Road Databases from SAR Imagery: Integration of Road Databases and SAR Imagery information. In *Proceedings of the Fourth International Conference on Information Fusion*, volume WeA1, pages 3–10, 2001.

3. A.P. Boresi. *Elasticity in Engineering Mechanics*. Prentice Hall, 1965.

4. F. Cosmi. Numerical Solution of Plane Elasticity Problems with the Cell Method. *to appear in Computer Modeling in Engineering and Sciences*, 2, 2001.

5. S.F.F. Gibson and B. Mirtich. A Survey of Deformable Modeling in Computer Graphics. Technical report, Mitsubishi Electric Research Laboratory, 1997.

6. M. Kass, A. Witkin, and D. Terzopoulos. Snakes : Active Contour Models. *The International Journal of Computer Vision*, 1(4):321–331, 1988.

7. G. T. Mase and G. E. Mase. *Continuum Mechanics for Engineers*. CRC Press, 1999.

8. C. Mattiussi. The Finite Volume, Finite Difference, and Finite Elements Methods as Numerical Methods for Physical Field Problems. *Advances in Imaging and Electron Physics*, 113:1–146, 2000.

9. J. Montagnat, H. Delingette, N. Scapel, and N. Ayache. Representation, shape, topology and evolution of deformable surfaces. Application to 3D medical imaging segmentation. Technical Report 3954, INRIA, 2000.

10. S. Platt and N. Badler. Animating Facial Expressions. *Computer Graphics*, 15(3):245–252, 1981.

11. P. Poulin, M.-F. Auclair-Fortier, D. Ziou and M. Allili. A Physics Based Model for the Deformation of Curves: A Computational Algebraic Topology Approach. Technical Report 270, Département de mathématiques et d'informatique, Université de Sherbrooke, 2001.

12. S. Sclaroff and A. Pentland. Model Matching for Correspondance and Recognition. *IEEE Transactions on Pattern Analysis and Machine Intelligence*, 17(6):545–561, 1995.

13. E. Tonti. A Direct Discrete Formulation of Field Laws: The Cell Method. *CMES-Computer Modeling in Engineering & Sciences*, 2(2):237–258, 2001.

14. E. Tonti. Finite formulation of the electromagnetic field. *Progress in Electromagnetics Research*, PIER 32 (Special Volume on Geometrical Methods for Comp. Electromagnetics):1–44, 2001.

15. D. Ziou. Finding Lines in Grey-Level Images. Technical Report 240, Département de mathématiques et d'informatique, Université de Sherbrooke, 1999.

16. D. Ziou and M. Allili. An Image Model with Roots in Computational Algebraic Topology: A Primer. Technical Report 264, Département de mathématiques et d'informatique, Université de Sherbrooke, April 2001.

P³DMA: A Physical 3D Deformable Modelling and Animation System

Miquel Mascaro Portells, Arnau Mir, and Francisco Perales

Departament de Matemàtiques i Informàtica
Unitat de Gràfics i Visió
Universitat de les Illes Balears
Crta. de Valldemossa, Km. 7,5
07071 Palma de Mallorca
http://dmi.uib.es/research/GV

Abstract. Animation and Realistic Simulation of a 3D object's elastic deformation is actually an important and challenging feature in applications where three-dimensional object interaction and behaviour is considered or explored. Also, in interactive environments we need a rapid computation of deformations. In this paper we present a prototype of a system for the animation and simulation of elastic objects in an interactive system and under real-time conditions. The approach makes use of the finite elements method (F.E.M) and Elasticity Theory. The simulation is interactively visualized in an Open Inventor environment. Using picking node selection the user can interactively apply forces to objects causing their deformation. The deformations computed with our approach have a physical interpretation based on the mathematical model defined. Furthermore, our algorithms perform with either 2D or 3D problems. Finally, a set of results are presented which demonstrate performance of the proposed system. All programs are written in C++ using POO, VRML and Open Invertor tools. Real time videos can be visualized on web site: http://dmi.uib.es/people/mascport/defweb/dd.html

Keywords: Elastic Deformation, Finite Elements Method, Elasticity Theory, Computer Animation, Physical Models, VRML.

1 Introduction and Related Work

Obviously, exible and deformable objects are inherently more di cult to model and animate in computer graphics than rigid objects. Until recent years, the computer graphic methods proposed were limited to modelling rigid objects. However, recent advances in algorithms and computer graphics hardware support the processing of exible objects. Today, there is a great need in many engineering and medical applications to be able to simulate the material and geometrical behaviour of 3D objects under real forces. In general, di erent modelling techniques are usually classi ed into three categories: geometrical, physical and hybrid:

---

* This work is partially subsidized by CICYT under grant TIC2001-0931 and by UE under grant Humodan-IST.

F.J. Perales and E.R. Hancock (Eds.): AMDO 2002, LNCS 2492, pp. 68–79, 2002.
© Springer-Verlag Berlin Heidelberg 2002

Geometrical techniques. Geometrical models do not consider the physical properties of objects. They focus on appearance and the deformation is represented by geometrical equations. This means that the user has a high degree of intervention and they are computationally faster than other approaches.

Physical techniques. In this group of techniques, the objects are modelled as a triangular or rectangular grid in 2D or voxeled volumed in 3D. Each joint or node in the grid can be a ected by forces and the global grid is governed by the interaction of physical forces on each node considered. This kind of methods are more realistic from the mathematical and physical viewpoint and the user only de nes the initial conditions and the system can simulate a real physical simulation over time. Unfortunately, they are more computationally expensive than geometrical techniques.

Hybrid techniques. Finally, we can combine physical and geometrical methods to avoid problems and improve e ciency.

In particular, the growth in hardware graphics can overcome the time-consuming restrictions of physically based methods. So in this paper we present our system called P³DMA. It is based on Finite Element Methods (F.E.M) and uses the Elasticity Theory. As we know, the solid theory used guarantees the robustness of the system and is actually widely used by other researchers [NNP02]. Thus, we are principally interested in designing a system that can run in real or near real time systems. We believe that in Virtual Reality systems the time in interaction and feedback is very critical. In this case, the e ciency of implementation is very important and results must be checked to reach this condition. In some cases, an initial o -line process can be introduced to improve e ciency.

This paper is organized in several sections. The second section includes the mathematical model proposed. The third section is dedicated to presenting the F.E.M implemented. The fourth section includes the algorithm designed to resolve the dynamical system. Finally, we conclude with some considerations about parallelization, e ciency and computational cost. The paper also includes the conclusions, future work and related bibliography.

2   Mathematical Model Proposed

Let Ω be an enclosed and connected solid in $\mathbb{R}^3$. Let us assume that the boundary of Ω, Γ, is type C^1 in parts. We divide Γ into two parts, Γ_0 and Γ_1, where Γ_1 is the part of the boundary which receives external forces and Γ_0 is the xed part of the boundary whose size we assume to be strictly positive. Note that boundary Γ does not necessarily need to be connected, which will enable us to simulate deformations of objects with holes.

The aim of this work is to study and analyse the computational cost of the evolution of Ω under the action of external forces f on the inside and external sources g on the boundary Γ_1.

The position of the object is de ned by the function $u(t, x)$. Our problem is, therefore, reduced, given the functions u_0 (initial position of the object) and u_1 (initial speed), to nding the position $u(t, x) = (u_1, \ldots, u_3)$ of these in the domain $Q_T = \Omega \times (0 \times T)$ which will verify the following evolution system in time:

$$\rho \frac{\delta^2 u_i}{\partial t^2} - \sum_{j=1}^{3} \frac{\partial}{\partial x_j} \sigma_{ij} = f_i, \ i = 1, 2, 3 \text{ en } Q_T,$$

$$u_i = 0, \ i = 1, 2, 3 \text{ en } \Gamma_0 \times (0, T),$$

$$\sum_{j=1}^{3} \sigma_{ij} n_j = g_i, \ i = 1, 2, 3 \text{ en } \Gamma_1 \times (0, T), \tag{1}$$

$$u_i(\cdot, 0) = u_{0,i}, \ i = 1, 2, 3 \text{ en } \Omega,$$

$$\frac{\partial u_i}{\partial t}(\cdot, 0) = u_{1,i}, \ i = 1, 2, 3 \text{ en } \Omega.$$

where functions σ_{ij} are the components of the tension tensor, n_j are the components of the normal vector at a point on the surface of the domain $\Gamma_1 \times (0, T)$ and ρ is the density of the object.

The resolution of the above problem is carried out by variational formulation. The solution of a discrete approximation u_h of the above formulation gives us the approximate solution to our problem.

Speci cally, we consider a subspace V_h with a nite dimension $I = I(h)$ of Hilbert s space H de ned by $H = \{ v \in (H^1(\Omega))^3, \text{ tal que } v = 0 \text{ sobre } \Gamma_0 \}$.

Our problem is reduced to nding a function u_h de ned in Q_T solution to the following di erential system:

$$\forall v_h \in V_h, \ \rho \frac{d^2}{dt^2}(u_h(t), v_h) + a(u_h(t), v_h) = L(v_h),$$

$$u_h(0) = u_{0,h}, \tag{2}$$

$$\frac{du_h}{dt}(0) = u_{1,h},$$

where $a(\cdot, \cdot)$ is the bilinear continous form de ned by $a(u, v) = \sum_{i,j=1}^{3} \int_\Omega \sigma_{i,j}(u) \times \varepsilon_{ij}(v) dx$, $(\cdot, \cdot)$ is the following scale product de ned for functions de ned in Q_T: $(u, v) = \sum_{i=1}^{3} \int_\Omega u_i(x) v_i(x) dx$ and $L(v)$ is the following continuous linear form on V_h: $L(v) = \sum_{i=1}^{3} \int_\Omega f_i v_i dx + \int_{\partial \Omega} g_i v_i d\sigma$.

Let ϕ_i be a V_h base of functions. If we write the solution to look for u_h as, $u_h(t) = \sum_{i=1}^{I} \xi_i(t) \phi_i$, the components ξ_i verify the above di erential system.

$$\rho \sum_{i=1}^{I} \xi_i''(t)(\phi_i, \phi_j) + \gamma \sum_{i=1}^{I} \xi_i'(t)(\phi_i, \phi_j) + \sum_{i=1}^{I} a(\phi_i, \phi_j)\xi_i(t) = L(\phi_j). \tag{3}$$

In the above system we have added a new term $(\gamma \sum_{i=1}^{I} \xi'(t)(\phi_i, \phi_j))$ to simulate a damping e ect of the object. The above system, written in a matrix form, is:

$$\rho M \xi'' + \gamma M \xi' + K \xi = L, \tag{4}$$

with M and K as the mass and tension matrixes respectively:

$M = ((\quad_i, \quad_j)) \ i, j = 1, \ldots, I$

$K = (a(\quad_i, \quad_j)) \ i, j = 1, \ldots, I^{\cdot}$

By dscretizing, in time, this last equation:

$$M \left(\frac{\rho}{\Delta t^2} + \frac{\gamma}{2\Delta t} \right) \xi(t + \Delta t) =$$
$$= L + \frac{\rho M}{\Delta t^2} (2\xi(t) - \xi(t - \Delta t)) + \frac{\gamma M}{2\Delta t}\xi(t - \Delta t) - K\xi(t)$$

(5)

The simulation of di erent physical phenomena such as instantaneous blows, constant forces, waves, etc. are implicit in the expression of vector L.

3 F.E.M and $K^{\varsigma} M^{\varsigma} L$. Definition

In order to choose the type of nite elements to use we will base our decision on two basic criteria:

The type of nite element to be used must correctly transmit the propagation of the tensions in the direction perpendicular to each face of the nite element. The type of nite elements to be used must possibility a real time computational process. This is why nite elements of a rectangular prism type will be chosen. This kind of nite element makes a right transmition of the propagation of the tensions in the direction perpendicular to each face of the nite element and gets a low computational cost.

Note that by means of the type of nite elements chosen it is possible to de ne uniform grids (grids which possess all the nite elements of an identical length), and non-uniform grids. This second type of grid let us make an approach of the boundary of Ω.

First of all, we will de ne the fundamental tool which will not allow us to work with the nite elements: domain with a pair of points.

Let i and j be two arbitrary nodes of the grid of nite elements of the object. Let sup $\quad_i$ be the set $\mathbb{R}^3$ where $\quad_i \neq 0$.

$\Omega_{i,j}$ is de ned as the integration domain of a pair of points (i, j) such as

$$\Omega_{i,j} = \sup \quad_i \cap \sup \quad_i .$$

3.1 Base Functions

In the three-dimensional model, there are three types of base functions:

$$^{(1)}_i = (\varphi_i, 0, 0) \ , \quad ^{(2)}_i = (0, \varphi_i, 0) \ , \quad ^{(3)}_i = (0, 0, \varphi_i) .$$

(6)

The expression of φ_i is the same in each base function: it is that function which has a value of 1 in the i-th vertex and 0 in the other vertices.

3.2　Deformations Tensor

The deformations tensor is de ned by the following expression:

$$\varepsilon_{ij}\left(\boldsymbol{v}\right) = \frac{1}{2}\left[\frac{\partial v_i}{\partial x_j} + \frac{\partial v_j}{\partial x_i}\right] , \ 1 \le i,\,j \le n\,. \tag{7}$$

3.3　The Tension Matrix K

The internal bonds of the object can be seen in tension matrix K.

The components of matrix K are: $K_{ij} = K(\varphi_i, \varphi_j)$, where φ_i and φ_j are the base functions de ned in (6) and the expression of $K(\boldsymbol{u}, \boldsymbol{v})$ is the following where $\boldsymbol{u}$ and $\boldsymbol{v}$ are any H functions:

$$K\left(\boldsymbol{u}, \boldsymbol{v}\right) = \lambda \int_{\Omega} \left(\sum_{k=1}^{n} \frac{\partial u_k}{\partial x_k}\right)\left(\sum_{k=1}^{n} \frac{\partial v_k}{\partial x_k}\right) dx_1 dx_2 dx_3$$

$$+ 2\mu \sum_{i,j=1}^{n} \int_{\Omega} \varepsilon_{ij}\left(\boldsymbol{u}\right)\varepsilon_{ij}\left(\boldsymbol{v}\right) dx_1 dx_2 dx_3\,, \quad \forall\, \boldsymbol{u}, \boldsymbol{v} \in H. \tag{8}$$

The expression of matrix K is the following:

$$K = \begin{pmatrix} K\left(\varphi_i^{(1)}, \varphi_j^{(1)}\right) & K\left(\varphi_i^{(1)}, \varphi_j^{(2)}\right) & K\left(\varphi_i^{(1)}, \varphi_j^{(3)}\right) \\ K\left(\varphi_i^{(2)}, \varphi_j^{(1)}\right) & K\left(\varphi_i^{(2)}, \varphi_j^{(2)}\right) & K\left(\varphi_i^{(2)}, \varphi_j^{(3)}\right) \\ K\left(\varphi_i^{(3)}, \varphi_j^{(1)}\right) & K\left(\varphi_i^{(3)}, \varphi_j^{(2)}\right) & K\left(\varphi_i^{(3)}, \varphi_j^{(3)}\right) \end{pmatrix}. \tag{9}$$

The space of functions we consider is that generated by the polynomes $\mathbb{R}^3$ $< 1, x_1, x_2, x_3, x_1 \cdot x_2, x_1 \cdot x_3, x_2 \cdot x_3, x_1 \cdot x_2 \cdot x_3 >$. Therefore, the function φ_i will have a linial combination of theese polynomes.

In order to nd $K_{ij} := K(\varphi_i, \varphi_j)$ for instance, we must carry out two integrals on the domain of the pair of points Ω_{ij}. Below, we write $\Omega_{ij} = \cup Q_k$, where Q_k is a square prism type nite element which forms part of Ω_{ij}.

Therefore, we can calculate K_{ij} in the following way: $K_{ij} = \sum_k K_{ij}^{(k)}$, where $K_{ij}^{(k)}$ corresponding to $K(\varphi_i, \varphi_j)$, for instance, would have the expression:

$$K_{ij}^{(k)} = (\lambda + 2\mu) \int_{Q_k} \frac{\partial \varphi_i}{\partial x_1}\frac{\partial \varphi_j}{\partial x_1} dx_1 dx_2 dx_3 + \mu \int_{Q_k} \left(\frac{\partial \varphi_i}{\partial x_2}\frac{\partial \varphi_j}{\partial x_2} + \frac{\partial \varphi_i}{\partial x_3}\frac{\partial \varphi_j}{\partial x_3}\right) dx_1 dx_2 dx_3.$$

With k xed, there will be $64 = 8 \times 8$ di erent $K_{ij}^{(k)}$ values since each square prism Q_k has a total of 8 vertices.

Let $Q_s = [0,1] \times [0,1] \times [0,1]$. The calculation of each of the integrals that appear in the expression $K_{ij}^{(k)}$ can be carried out in the following way:

$$\int_{Q_k} \frac{\partial \varphi_i}{\partial x_i}\frac{\partial \varphi_j}{\partial x_j} dx_1 dx_2 dx_3 = V_k \int_{Q_s} \frac{\partial \varphi_i'}{\partial x_i'}\frac{\partial \varphi_j'}{\partial x_j'} dx_1' dx_2' dx_3'\,,$$

where V_k is the volume of Q_k, $\dfrac{\partial \varphi_i}{\partial x_i} = \sum_j \dfrac{\partial \varphi_i'}{\partial x_j'}\dfrac{\partial x_j'}{\partial x_i} = a_i \dfrac{\partial \varphi'}{\partial x_i'}$ and the variable change of Q_k a Q_s is $x_i' = b_i + a_i x_i$, $i = 1, 2, 3$.

The calculation of $\int_{Q_s} \frac{\partial \varphi'_i}{\partial x'_i} \frac{\partial \varphi'_j}{\partial x'_j} dx'_1 \, dx'_2 \, dx'_3$ is quite simple as we are working with a standard cube.

In this way, the 64 possible values $K_{ij}^{(k)}$ can be obtained. It can be seen that there are only 8 different values.

3.4 The Mass Matrix M

The mass matrix M will be made up of nine sub-matrixes whose expression is the following:

$$M = \begin{pmatrix} \binom{(1)}{i}, \binom{(1)}{j} & 0 & 0 \\ 0 & \binom{(2)}{i}, \binom{(2)}{j} & 0 \\ 0 & 0 & \binom{(3)}{i}, \binom{(3)}{j} \end{pmatrix}, \text{ where:}$$

$\binom{(1)}{i}, \binom{(1)}{j} = \binom{(2)}{i}, \binom{(2)}{j} = \binom{(3)}{i}, \binom{(3)}{j} \neq 0$ si $\Omega_{ij} \neq \emptyset$.

In order to calculate (φ_i, φ_j) in an effective way, we will use a method of approximate integration using the vertices of the finite elements as nodes. That is, using: $\binom{(1)}{i}, \binom{(1)}{j} = \sum_{k|Q_k \subset \Omega_{ij}} \int_{Q_k} \varphi_i(x)\varphi_j(x)dx$, we approximate the integration as:

$$\int_{Q_k} \varphi_i(x)\varphi_j(x)dx \approx \sum_{l=1}^{8} A_i \varphi_i(P_l)\varphi_j(P_l), \tag{10}$$

where P_l are the vertices of the finite element Q_k and A_i are the coefficients of the approximate integration formula.

In this way, we manage to make the mass matrix M diagonal since $\varphi_i(P_l) = \delta_{il}$. Furthermore, since the numerical integration error is less than the error we make in the variational approximation of the problem which is in the order of h^3 where h is the maximum length of the sides Q_k (see appendix and [Cia80]), the use of the integration method does not increase the overall error in the approximation.

In order to find $\int_{Q_k} \varphi_i(x)\varphi_j(x)dx$, we will move onto a standard cube $Q_s = [0, 1] \times [0, 1] \times [0, 1]$ by the adequate change in variable and there we will use the expression (10). In this way coefficients A_i will not depend on the finite element Q_k chosen. In the standard cube, coefficients A_i equal: $A_i = \frac{1}{8}$.

By the way,
$$\int_{Q_k} \varphi_i(x)\varphi_j(x)dx = \frac{\delta_{ij}V_k}{8}.$$

3.5 The External Force Vector L

The external force vector L will be of the type:

$L = \left(L_i^{(1)}, L_i^{(2)}, L_i^{(3)} \right)^T$, where $L_i^{(k)}$, $k = 1, 2, 3$, are dimension vectors N with N as the number of nodes of the grid of finite elements which does not belong to Γ_0, that is, non fixed nodes.

The expressions of the vectors $L(\quad_i)$, $L(\quad'_i)$ and $L(\quad''_i)$ are the following:

$$L\quad_i^{(k)} = \int_{\mathrm{sup}\,\varphi_i} f_k(\boldsymbol{x})\varphi_i(\boldsymbol{x})d\boldsymbol{x} + \int_{\partial\Omega\cap\mathrm{sup}\,\varphi_i} g_k(\boldsymbol{x})\varphi_i(\boldsymbol{x})d\sigma,$$

where $k = 1, 2, 3$.

In all the experiments carried out, we have assumed that $f = 0$. Therefore, the rst addends in the above expressions will be null.

If the external forces $\boldsymbol{g}$ applied on the boundary are constant, the above expressions are reduced to: $L\quad_i^{(k)} = g_k \int_{\partial\Omega\cap\mathrm{sup}\,\varphi_i} \varphi_i(\boldsymbol{x})d\sigma$.

Our problem is, therefore, reduced to nding $\int_{\partial\Omega\cap\mathrm{sup}\,\varphi_i} \varphi_i(\boldsymbol{x})d\sigma$.

We will assume that the boundary of Ω is approximated by square prism type nite elements. Therefore, we have the case in which the integration domain $\partial\Omega \cap \mathrm{sup}\,\varphi_i$ will be: $\partial\Omega \cap \mathrm{sup}\,\varphi_i = \cup \Pi_{ik}$, where Π_{ik} are at rectangles situated on a plane $x =$constant.

We have, therefore, the case in which the value of the above integral can be calculated as: $\int_{\partial\Omega\cap\mathrm{sup}\,\varphi_i} \varphi_i(\boldsymbol{x})d\sigma = \sum_k \int_{\Pi_{ik}} \varphi_i(\boldsymbol{x})d\sigma$

The above integral $\int_{\Pi_{ik}} \varphi_i(\boldsymbol{x})d\sigma$ can be reduced by the variable change adapted to a double integral on the standard square $[0, 1] \times [0, 1]$.

4   Dynamic Solution System, Parallelization and Computational Cost

The matrix of the system (5) is diagonal, so the i-th component of the value $\xi(t + \Delta t)$ can be obtained as:

$$\xi(t + \Delta t)(i) = \frac{L(i) + \xi_1(i) + \xi_2(i) - \xi_3(i)}{M_1(i, i)} \,,\, i \in \{0, \dots, 3N\} \,,$$

where

$$M_1 := M\left(\frac{\rho}{\Delta t^2} + \frac{\gamma}{2\Delta t}\right), \quad \xi_1 := \frac{\rho M}{\Delta t^2}(2\xi(t) - \xi(t - \Delta t)),$$
$$\xi_2 := \frac{\gamma M}{2\Delta t}\xi(t - \Delta t), \quad \xi_3 := K\xi(t).$$

4.1   Parallel Computation of the Tension Matrix K

Using the fact that component ij of matrix K can be calculated as $K_{ij} = \sum_{Q_k \subset \Omega_{ij}} K_{ij}^{(k)}$, we can parallelize the computation of K_{ij} by assigning the calculation of $K_{ij}^{(k)}$ to each CPU.

4.2   Parallel Computation of the Solution of the Problem

If the external forces are variable during the deformation process the calculation of vector L will be depending of the time parameter.

If these forces are constant or constant in parts, we can calculate the value of the L vector in a parallel process. We assign to each CPU the compute of $\partial\Omega\cap\sup\varphi_i\,\varphi_i(x)d\sigma$.

In the gure 1 the calculation process of the deformation is outlined, where the system, from the conditions of the material to be deformed and the application of the external forces in time, is capable of launching a totally parallelizable calculation process.

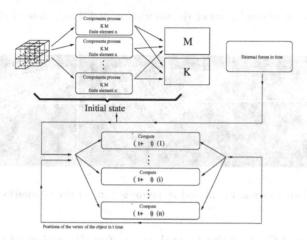

Fig. 1. Outline of the parallel calculation process of the dynamic solution system of deformations.

4.3   Computational Cost of the Calculation of the Matrixes K and M

The computational cost of the tension and mass matrixes will be a function of the number of simultaneous processes that the system can bear, and a function of the quantity of nite elements of the object to be deformed.

Let ne the number of the nite elements of the object. Let np the number of simultaneous processes the computerized system can bear. Let Q_l an arbitrary nite element.

Let C_{MK_l} the computational cost associated to calculate $\sum_{i,j}(K_{ij}^{(l)}) + \frac{\delta_{ij}V_l}{8}$ and the additions to reach the nal values of the matrixes M and K associated to each independent process. Then we can de ne:

$$C_{MK} = \max_{1<=l<=ne} C_{MK_l}.$$

Finaly, we obtain the computational cost to calculate the matrixes M,K:

$$Cost_{MK} <= \frac{C_{MK}*ne}{np} \,--> \frac{O(ne)}{np}.$$

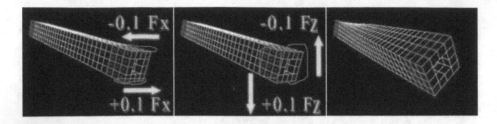

Fig. 2. Initial forces conditions of the simulation and 2 sec. time of the deformation process.

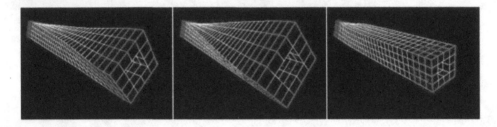

Fig. 3. Left to right 13, 24 and 26 seconds time of the simulation process.

Computational Cost of the Calculation of an Iteration of the Solution.
The computational cost of the solution of one iteration step in the dynamic system is linear $O(n)$ where n is the number of nodes in the grid of nite elements such that the matrix of the system is diagonal.

5   An Elastic Simulation Example

In gures 2, 3, 4 we can see the simulation process of a 60 seconds elastic deformation. We apply some forces in a kind of a latex square tube of dimensions $0.028 \times 0.028 \times 0.224$ meters. We apply some Fx newton forces in the upper and lower marks during the rst 24 seconds (left, gure 2). Between 12-24 seconds we apply some Fz newton forces in right and left marks (middle, gure 2). In two seconds time of the simulation process we can observe a little tube expansion and rotation (right, gure 2).

At 13 seconds time we can note the efect of the Fx forces result, a greather expansion and anti-clock wise rotation of the latex tube (left, gure 3). At 24 seconds time we can see the nal state of the object after the Fx znd Fz forces action (middle, gure 3). At 26 seconds the action forces have been stoped an the object is returning to its initial state (right, gure 3).

At 27 seconds time the elastic energy of the tube has made a clock-wise rotation (left, gure 4). Here to the nal state of the simulation process the object makes an armonic rotation balance to reach its initial state (middle-right, gure 4).

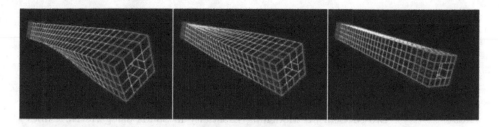

Fig. 4. Left to right 27, 30 and 60 seconds time of the simulation process.

6   Conclusions and Future Work

In this work we have presented a 3D deformation model based on the Theory of Elasticity. This model uses a rectangular parallepiped grid of nite elements that let us make a pre-computation values of the matrixes M & K. That cause possibility a real time simulation of the deformation process. The main contributions can be summed up in the following points:

The calculation of deformations is totally parallelizable. We assign the computation process for the nite elements grid matrix values to several CPU s. Values acording to one voxel of the nite elements grid are assigned to one CPU. The nal values for the tension and mass matrixes are the additions of the partial results computed for each parallel process. The solution of the dynamic system can be parallelizated too cause the system is diagonal.

The chosen nite elements correctly transmit the tensions in a direction perpendicular to the boundary of the same. Therefore, the deformations presented are quite realistic. Whatever quadrangular parallelepiped voxel can be used in this deformation model to makes the nite elements grid of the object.

The computational cost has been reduced so that the deformations can be represented in real time. Experiments have been realized using an ATHLON 900 CPU with 512 MB of RAM memory. The model supports real time process in an objetc with 12000 voxels.

A study of the computational cost of the algorithm has been carried out. We reach a lineal computational cost deppending on the number of voxels of the object and the quantity of simultaneous processes that the system can bear

In the context of future work, we would like to highlight the following:

A study of the deformations of two-dimensional varieties such as the study of clothes deformations or the deformation of the human skin.

A study of deformations when internal forces are not null, $f \neq 0$.

A study of deformations when the external force g depends on the speed of the object. Integrating inertial forces to the model and collision checking techniques.

References

AnsOLK00.   Anshelevich, E., Owens, S., Lamiraux, F., Kavraki, L. E. Deformable Volumesin Path Planning Applications. ICRA 2000, Department of Computer Science, Rice University, Houston, 2000.

Aon90.   Aono, M. A. Wrinkle Propagation Model for Cloth. Proc. CG. Int'l, Springer-Verlag, 95-115, 1990.

Bro94.   Bro-Nielsen. M. Modelling Elasticity in Solids using Active Cubes - Application to Simulated Operations. Institute of Mathematical Modelling Technical University of Dennmark. 1994.

Cia80.   Ciarlet, P.G.. The Finite Element Method for Elliptic Problems. Université Pierre et Marie Curie, París. North-Holland Publishing Company, Amsterdam-New York, Oxford. 1980.

CohC91.   Cohen, L. D., Cohen, I. Finite Element Methods for Active Contour Models and Ballons for 2D and 3D Images. CEREMADE, France. Cahiers de Mathématiques de la Decisión, MD n° 9124 November 1991.

DebDBC99.   Debunne, G., Desbrun, M., Barr, A., Cani, M. P. Interactive multiresolution animation of deformable models. Computer Animation and Simulation '99. Eurographics Workshop, Milan, 1999.

Dec96.   Decaudin, P. Geometric Deformation by Merging a 3D-Object with a Simple Shape. INRIA. Graphics Interface'96 proceedings, Toronto. 1996.

ErdDJC01.   Erdan, G., Duaquing, X., Jingbin, W., Chen, C. Dynamic Cloth Motion Simulation Using a Novel Fast Collision Detection. Computer Science and Engineering Department, ZheJiang Univ. Conference Paper, 2001.

FalPT97.   Faloutsos, P. and M. van de Panne. And Demetri Terzopoulos. IEEE Transaction on Visualization and Computer Graphics, vol 3, n. 3, 1997.

FanRR94.   Fang, S. and Raghavan, R. and Richtsmeier, T. Volume Morphing Methods for Landmark Based 3D Image Deformation. National University of Singapore, - School of Medicine, Baltimore, 1994.

Far97.   Farin, G. Curves and surfaces for computer-aided geometric design: a practical guide. San Diego, California. London: Academic Press, ISBN: 0122490541, 1997

FenK98.   Fenster, D., Kender, J.R. Sectored Snakes: Evaluating Learned-Energy Segmentations. Department of Computer Science, Columbia University, New York, NY 1027 USA, 1998.

GibM97.   Gibson, S.F.F. and Mirtch, B. A Survey of Deformable Modelling in Computer Graphics. Technical Report, Mitsubishi Electrical Research, 1997.

HagF98.   Hagenlocke, M., Fujimura, K. CFFD: a tool for designing flexible shapes. The Visual Computer (1998) 14:271-287, Springer-Verlag 1998.

HinG96.   Hing, N. Ng and Grimsdale, R. L. Computer Graphics Techniques for Modelling Cloth. IEEE Computer Graphics and Applications, 28-41, 1996.

KavLH98.   Kavraki, L.E., Lamiraux, F., Holleman, C. Towards Planning for
             Ellastic Objects. Department of Computer Science, Rice University
             (Huston). Workshop of Algorithmic Foundations of Robotics, pages
             313-325, 1998.

MasMP00.   Mascaró, M., Mir, A., Perales, F. Elastic Deformations Using Finite
             Element Methods in Computer Graphic Applications. AMDO 2000,
             pp. 38-47, 2000. Springer-Verlag Berlin Heidelberg 2000.

McIT97.   McInerney, T., Terzopoulos, D. Dept. of Computer Science, University
             of Toronto, Canada. Published in the Proc. CVRMed'97, Grenoble,
             France, march, 1997.

McQW00.   McDonnell, K.T., Quin, H., Wlodarczyk, R.A. . Dept. of Computer
             Science, University of New York at Stony Brook.

Met97.   Metaxas, D. N. Physics-Based Deformable Models. University of Pen-
             sylvania, USA. KluwerAcademic Publishers, 1997.

MonDSY00.   Montagnat, J., Delingette, H., Scapel, N., Ayache, N. Representation,
             shape, topology and evolution of deformable surfaces. Application to
             3D medical image segmentation. INRIA, 2000.

NNP02.   I. Nikitin, L. Nikitina, P. Frolov. Real Time simulation of elastic ob-
             jetcs in Vitual Environments usign finite element method and precom-
             puted Green's functions. Eight EG Workshop on VE, 2002, 47-52, S.
             Muller, W. Sturzlinger (editors), 2002.

NurRR01.   Nürnberger, A., Radetzky, A., Kruse R. Using recurrent neuro-fuzzy
             techniques for the identification and simulation of dynamic systems.
             Neurocomputing 36, 123-147, Elsevier Science B. V., 2001.

RavT92.   Raviart, P. A., Thomas, J. M. Introduction à l'analyse numérique des
             equations aux dérivées partielles. Ed. Masson, 3ª edición, 1992.

Rud90.   Rudomin, I.J. Simulating Cloth using a Mixed Geometry-Phisycal
             Method. Doctoral Dissertation, Dept. of Computer and Information
             Science, Univ. Of Pennsylvania, 1990.

ShiHCJ01.   Shi-Min, H., Hui, Z., Chiew-Lang, T., Jia-Guang, S. Direct manipu-
             lation of FFD: efficient explicit solutions and decomposible multiple
             point constraints. The Visual Computer (2001) 17:370-379. Springer-
             Verlag 2001.

TerQ94.   Terzopoulos, D. , Qin, H. Dynamic NURBS with geometric constraints
             for interactive sculpting. ACM Transactions on Graphics, 13(3):103-
             136, 1994.

ThalCCVW98. Thalmann, N. M., Carion, S., Courchesne, M., Volino, P., Wu, Y.
             Virtual Clothes, Hair and Skin for Beutiful Top Models. MIRAlab,
             University of Geneva, 1998.

ZabS99.   Zabaras, N. Srikanth, A. An Object-Oriented Programming Approach
             to the Lagrangian FEM Analysis of Large Inelastic Deformations and
             Metal-Forming Processes. International Journal for Numerical Meth-
             ods in Engineering. Int. J. Numer. Meth. Engng. 45, 399-445 (1999).

A Novel Approach to Generate Multiple Shape Models for Tracking Applications

Daniel Ponsa and F. Xavier Roca

Centre de Visió per Computador, Universitat Autònoma de Barcelona
08193 Bellaterra (Barcelona), Spain
daniel@cvc.uab.es

Abstract. Many proposals to generate shape models for tracking applications are based on a linear shape model, and a constraint that delimits the parameter values which generate feasible shapes. In this paper we introduce a novel approach to generate such models automatically. Given a training set, we determine the linear shape model as classical approaches, and model its associated constraint using a Gaussian Mixture Model, which is fully parameterized by a presented algorithm. Then, from this model we generate a collection of linear shape models of lower dimensionality, each one constrained by a single Gaussian model. This set of models represents better the training set, reducing the computational cost of tracking applications. To compare our proposal with the usual one, a comparison measure is defined, based on the Bayesian Information Criterion. Both modeling strategies are analyzed in a pedestrian tracking application, where our proposal claims to be more appropriate.

1 Introduction

Active Contours (AC)[3] are a common technique used in many computer vision applications, specially in the ones that require tracking the shape of targets along an image sequence (human-machine interfaces, medical diagnosis, etcetera). Basically, AC represent totally or partially the pro le of an object by means of a parametric curve, who is readjusted in every frame in order to recover the changes in the outline of tracked objects. Usual approaches to solve this task rely on estimation methods as the Kalman Filter [12] and the Condensation Algorithm [11]. This two methods estimate in every frame the probability density function (pdf) of the shape parameters of the tracked target. The principal difference between them is that while the Kalman lter assumes a Gaussian pdf, the Condensation algorithm makes none assumption about it. It approximates the real shape pdf by means of a population of samples. The performance of both methods rely strongly on how well the shape of the target and its dynamics are modeled. Linear models (required for the Kalman Filter, and commonly used in many Condensation implementations) are usual insu cient to achieve good tracking performances in real applications. So more complex models are usually considered, and the usual tracking frameworks are adapted to deal with them.

F.J. Perales and E.R. Hancock (Eds.): AMDO 2002, LNCS 2492, pp. 80–91, 2002.
© Springer-Verlag Berlin Heidelberg 2002

This paper proposes a multiple model approach to describe the shape variability in a training set. This models are generated unsupervisedly from training data, de ning a collection of shape spaces of small dimensionality. A measure of comparison between shape models is also presented, in order to evaluate quantitatively the improvements contributed by our proposal.

The layout of the paper is as follows: Section 2 reviews previous works in shape modeling, concentrating in the proposals based on de ne a constrained linear shape model. Then, Section 3 describes a novel unsupervised algorithm to generate this models from training sets. Section 4 presents a new proposal to shape modeling, based on convert the previously described models into a set of gaussian-constrained linear shape models. Section 5 concentrates in the de nition of a comparison criteria to evaluate our proposal against others. Finally, Section 6 provides results concerning pedestrian modeling. The paper concludes with a discussion of the di erent proposals, and with a brief description of our current work-in-progress in this area.

2   Contour Models

The objective of a good shape model is maintaining compactly the possible appearances of an object s shape, excluding at the same time all unfeasible shapes. Several proposals have been done to generate models automatically from training sets. The pioneer work of Cootes et al. [6] compacts the variations of a polygonal contour in what they called a Point Distribution Model. Given several examples of valid shapes of the object, they construct a training set by normalizing and aligning them respect a given reference frame. The objective of this normalization is exclude the global variations the shape may su er (translations, changes of scale, ...), while preserving the di erent feasible shapes of the object. A short review of several alignment methods can be found in [5]. Once the training set is aligned, a principal component analysis (PCA) is done to construct an statistical linear shape model. By arranging the eigenvectors with biggest eigenvalues in a matrix W, and being $\hat{Q}$ the mean shape in the aligned training set, the training shapes $\mathbf{Q} = \{Q_1, \ldots, Q_n\}$ can be approximately synthesized using the expression

$$Q_k = WX_k + \hat{Q}, \ k \in \{1, \ldots, M\} \ , \tag{1}$$

where $\mathbf{X} = \{X_1, \ldots, X_n\}$ are shape vectors in space W with a dimensionality signi cantly inferior to the elements in $\mathbf{Q}$. They correspond to the projection of $\mathbf{Q}$ to the shape space W, done with the expression

$$X_k = W'(Q_k - \hat{Q}), \ k \in \{1, \ldots, M\} \ . \tag{2}$$

The reduced dimensionality of the generated shape space W contributes e ciency in the shape management, as well as lters the noise present in the training set (which is mainly concentrated in the rejected eigenvectors). Moreover, as an inferior dimensionality suppose having less degrees of freedom, the set of representable shapes is more constrained. In [2], Baumberg extended this method to work with parameterizations of shapes based on B-spline curves.

An important drawback of this linear shape space is that in practical problems its representability is far bigger than an ideal generalization of $\mathbf{Q}$. That is, exist con gurations of X able to synthesize invalid shapes of the object. To solve this, di erent authors have proposed to constrain the values of X, so only *valid* linear combinations of the eigenvectors in W should be added to $\bar{Q}$. This is commonly done by delimiting the (usually) non-linear Subspace of Valid Shapes (SVS) in W (which correspond to the region occupied by $\mathbf{X}$), using a combination of small linear subregions. Heap and Hogg [9] propose to do that using the k-means algorithm, which delimits the SVS by means of a combination of hiperellipsoids. Similarly, Cootes and Taylor [4] specify the SVS using a Gaussian Mixture Model, tted to it using the *EM* algorithm (see Figure 1). Both proposals use the SVS in tracking application, forcing the shape estimations to be inside the de ned SVS. When an estimation is outside this region, their value is replaced with the value in the SVS nearer to it.

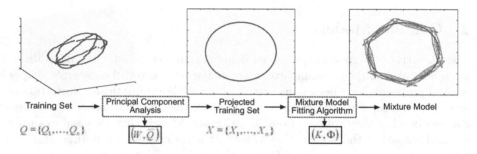

Fig. 1. Process involved in the construction of a Linear Shape Model constrained with a Gaussian Mixture Model. *Solid square boxes* mark the parameters estimated

In tracking applications, shape models are enclosed with dynamic models that describe the expected shape variations along time. The classical approach to model this variations is by means of an stochastic autoregressive process. Another possibility is using the SVS constraint of a shape model to represent its dynamics from a discrete point of view. Each patch de ning the SVS can be interpreted as a discrete state for the shape of an object. So being the training set a temporal sequence of shape changes, each training sample can be associated to the patch of SVS where it projects. Next, the *labeled* training sequence can be used to construct a State Transition Matrix (STM), which maintain the state transition probabilities re ecting typical shape changes (a Markov Chain). Figure 2 show an schematic of this process.

So from this review it is clear that linear shape models, to be useful in real tracking applications, need to be properly constrained (i.e. have a precise SVS model). Furthermore, advantage can be took from the SVS model to describe the temporal behavior of shape changes. So it is very important having a good model of the SVS to obtain reliably tracking performances. In the next section, we detail a novel approach to determine it unsupervisedly.

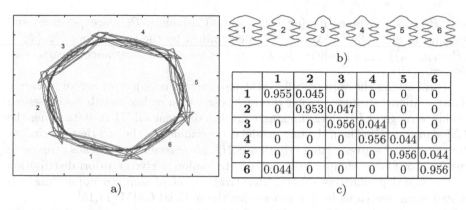

	1	2	3	4	5	6
1	0.955	0.045	0	0	0	0
2	0	0.953	0.047	0	0	0
3	0	0	0.956	0.044	0	0
4	0	0	0	0.956	0.044	0
5	0	0	0	0	0.956	0.044
6	0.044	0	0	0	0	0.956

a)   c)

Fig. 2. Dynamic learning process of a Markov Chain model, for a synthetic training set. a) A GMM models the SVS. b) Labeled figures display the mean shape of each SVS patch. c) The STM computed from a training sequence, using the procedure described in [10]. It can be seen that the shapes in the training sequence progress along the SVS in clockwise order

3   Unsupervised Learning of the SVS

The delimitation of the SVS in **X** is usually posed as the problem of approximate the distribution of **X**. In general, this can not be accurately described by classical parametric distributions. Semi-parametric approaches as the Gaussian Mixture Models (GMM) achieve more accurate descriptions, while the number of parameters that need to be estimated is still reduced. Previous approaches have used the k-means and the EM algorithm to t GMM to **X** [9,4]. However, this iterative methods depend strongly on the number of Gaussian component K assumed, and also in its initial placement in the W-space. In the papers reviewed, the value K is set manually by inspection on the training set, but how they are initially placed is not reported. However, it is common to do this at random.

In the next section we present a novel algorithm to establish all the parameters of a GMM automatically, given a data set **X**. Our algorithm determines iteratively a near-to-optimal amount of components K, initializing them in a data-driven manner.

3.1   Fully Gaussian Mixture Models Parameterization

GMMs approximate data distributions by means of a linear combination of Gaussian components. They can be expressed as,

$$p(x) = \sum_{i=1}^{K} p(x|i)P(i) ,\tag{3}$$

where K indicates the amount of mixture components (the order of the model), $p(x|i)$ the probability density function of the i-th component of the mixture, and $P(i)$ its weight or mixing coe cient. The values $P(i)$ are positive, and sum up to unity. So GMM are fully determined by the parameters $\{K, \{\Phi_i = (P(i), \mu_i, \Sigma_i)\}_{i=1...K}\}$, where (μ_i, Σ_i) are the mean and covariance of each component $p(x|i)$.

Establishing the value of all GMM parameters is object of active research. The traditional strategy to solve this task is based on realize an exhaustive search within a range of K values, making converge di erent GMM to data using the EM algorithm [7]. Then, the best model is determined as the one that maximizes (or minimizes) a given tting criterion [8,16]. More recent approaches propose to use Markov Chain Monte Carlo methods to explore a given a priori distribution of the GMM parameters re ning iteratively a set of samples populating this distribution, searching in this process for the optimal GMM [14,15].

Our proposal to deal with this problem achieves results comparables to the ones obtained by exhaustive search proposals, but requiring less computational time. It is based on introducing the notion of GMM inside the procedure of Divisive Hierarchical Clustering Algorithms.

Given a data set $\mathbf{X} = (X_1, \cdots, X_n)$, a rst GMM is stated considering a single component, being its parameters $K = 1, \Phi = \Phi_1 = \{(P(1) = 1, \mu_1 = \mu_X, \Sigma_1 = \Sigma_X)\}$. If this representation describes precisely the real data distribution, there is no need to explain it using more components. Otherwise, more components should be considered. So rst we need to de ne a criterion to measure the *fitness* of the GMM with respect to data. Our proposal is requiring that the components of a GMM represent normally distributed data clusters. In the initial GMM considered (i.e. a single Gaussian), this means to apply a *Test of Multivariate Normality* to $\mathbf{X}$. To do this we apply the method described in [18]. If the test fails, the Gaussian is split in two, and the EM algorithm is applied to make converge the new de ned GMM. Figure 3 show an example of this process.

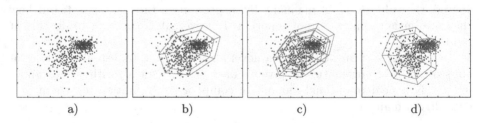

Fig. 3. Basic process of the unsupervised method to parameterize GMM. a) Data set b) Initial GMM. c) The test of Multivariate Normality fails. The component is split. d) Final GMM obtained by applying the *EM* algorithm

When the GMM has more than one component, First $\mathbf{X}$ is subdivided into clusters by assigning each X_i to the component k which provides the maximum conditional probability $p(X_i|k)P(k)$. Then, the normality of each cluster is checked in decreasing order of its $P(i)$, so analyzing rst the components that support more strongly $\mathbf{X}$. When a cluster fails the test, its corresponding component is split in two, the EM applied to the resultant new GMM, and the overall process repeated again. We add in this process an stop condition for situations where $\mathbf{X}$ cannot be accuratelly represented by GMM. With this we want to avoid splitting components that represent *underpopulated* clusters, which appear in such situations. Figure 4 summarizes the proposed procedure. A detailed description of this method can be found in [13], where its performance is also evaluated.

---

0 set $K \leftarrow 1,\ \varPhi \leftarrow \{\varPhi_1\} \leftarrow \{(1, \mu_X, \Sigma_X)\}$
1 Sort components in $\varPhi$ in decreasing order of $P(i)$
2 set $i \leftarrow 1,\ Split \leftarrow$ FALSE
3 **while** $i \leq K$ and $Split =$ FALSE
    if NumElements$(\varPhi_i) > Threshold$ and NormalityTest$(\varPhi_i)$ =FALSE
    $Split \leftarrow$ TRUE
    else $i \leftarrow i + 1$
4 **if** $Split =$ TRUE
    $(\varPhi_a, \varPhi_b) \leftarrow$ SplitComponent$(\varPhi_i)$
    set $K \leftarrow K + 1$.
    set $\varPhi \leftarrow \varPhi \backslash \{\varPhi_i\}$.
    set $\varPhi \leftarrow \varPhi \cup \{\varPhi_a\} \cup \{\varPhi_b\}$
    $\varPhi \leftarrow$ EM$(\varPhi)$
    goto 1.

Fig. 4. Our proposed Adaptive Gaussian Mixture Model Fitting Algorithm

4   Generation of Multiple Shape Models

At this point it has been described the necessity for constrained linear models, and a novel method to model this constraint from a training sequence. In this section, we propose a new method to model shapes, constructed form a SVS constraint model.

As explained before, the GMM constraining the SVS can be used to determine discrete states of a shape model. Each one of this states groups elements whose shape variability can be delimited by a Gaussian distribution. This fact suggest us to replace the linear model constrained by a GMM with a set of linear models, each one constrained by a single Gaussian. First we assign each projected training sample X_i to the component k that maximizes its likelihood. This allow us to de ne K subsets Q^i in the training sequence $\mathbf{Q}$, where

$$Q^i = \cup \{Q_j\}\ \forall X_j \mid i = \arg \max_{k=1}^{K} p(X_j, k) P(k)\ . \tag{4}$$

Now we have the training set in groups similar in shape. We propose to de ne an speci c linear shape model for each of them, constraining its respective SVS with a single Gaussian. Figure 5 summarizes this procedure.

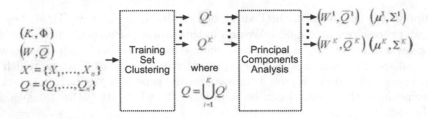

Fig. 5. Construction of multiple models, from a linear shape model constrained with a mixture of models

As each $Q^i \subset Q$ and its elements present in some extent similarity, it seems logical to expect that the each W^i requires a dimensionality less or equal than W. We determine the dimensionality of W^i by the minimal dimensionality d^i for which its mean squared reconstruction error is smaller or equal to the obtained using W. That is,

$$\min_{} d^i \mid \sum_{Q_j \in Q^i} Q_j - (W^i X_j^i + \overline{Q}^i)^2 \le \sum_{Q_j \in Q^i} Q_j - (W X_j + \overline{Q})^2 , \quad (5)$$

where X_j^i is the projection of Q_j onto the W^i space. We found that the most important bene t of proceed in that way, more than the gain of accuracy (that is set at a feasible minimum), is the reduction in dimensionality of shape spaces. This fact reduces the computational load of tracking algorithms, which favors to obtain more robust performances (allow a better temporal sampling of sequences, considering more so sticated image measurement, etc). Also, having a lower dimensionality supposes implicitly a gain in the constraining of the SVS, as the degrees of freedom of the shape parameterizations are reduced. Moreover, the Gaussian constraint of each model can be elegantly applied in a tracking algorithm by assuming a constrained Brownian motion for the dynamics of shape parameters (see [3] for a description).

Despite this arguments favoring the practical application of the model, remains to ascertain if the new proposal represents indeed an improvement in shape modeling. This subject is object of study in the next section.

5   Comparison between Shape Models

To compare our proposal with the linear shape model constrained with a GMM, we use the Bayesian Information Criterion (BIC) [17]. This criterion (known as Minimum Description Length(MDL) in the Information Theory eld) simultaneously judges both the complexity and the correctness of a given model. So it discourages models than using a bigger number of parameters outperform just slightly the accuracy of representation of simple models. This criterion is de ned by

$$BIC = \ln p(I|\Theta) - \frac{1}{2} M \ln N , \quad (6)$$

where $I = \{I_1, \ldots, I_N\}$ is the data set of N elements to be modeled, Θ the parameters of the model, and M the amount of parameters. As the models to be compared maintain separately a shape model and a constraint model (i.e, the SVS model), we have de ned its overall BIC value as

$$BIC(\text{Model}) = BIC(\text{Linear Shape Model}) + BIC(\text{SVS Model}) . \quad (7)$$

5.1 BIC of a GMM-Constrained Linear Shape Model

Given a training set of shapes $\mathbf{Q} = \{Q_1, \ldots, Q_N\}$ of dimension d_o, and a linear shape space $(W, \bar{\Phi})$ of dimension d_i, we de ne the terms involved in equation (6) as,

$$\ln\ p(\mathbf{Q}|W, \bar{\Phi}) = \sum_{i=1}^{N} -\frac{1}{2}(Q_i - (WX_i + \bar{\Phi}))^2 , \quad (8)$$

$$M = d_o(d_i + 1) , \quad (9)$$

where (8) corresponds to the mean squared reconstruction error of the shape model, given the training set. X_i is computed with equation (2).

To validate the constraint model, we evaluate how well the projected training set $\mathbf{X} = \{X_i, \ldots, X_M\}$ is represented by the GMM. So if the number of components in the GMM is K, the terms in the BIC expression are,

$$\ln\ p(\mathbf{X}|\Phi) = \sum_{i=1}^{N} \ln p(X_i|\Phi) = \sum_{i=1}^{N} \ln \sum_{j=1}^{K} p(X_i|\mu_j, \Sigma_j)P(j) , \quad (10)$$

$$M = K\ \frac{d_i(d_i + 1)}{2} + d_i + 1 , \quad (11)$$

considering Gaussians of full covariance in the GMM.

5.2 BIC of a Collection of G-Constrained Linear Shape Models

For our proposal, we compute the terms of the BIC expression as,

$$\ln\ p(\mathbf{Q}|W^1, \ldots, W^K, \bar{\Phi}^1, \ldots, \bar{\Phi}^K) = \sum_{k=1}^{K} \sum_{Q_i \in Q^k} -\frac{1}{2}(Q_i - (W^k X_i^k + \bar{\Phi}^k))^2, (12)$$

$$M = Kd_o + \sum_{k=1}^{K} d_i^k d_o . \quad (13)$$

where d_i^k is the dimension of shape space k, and X_i^k the projection of Q_i in the shape space $(W^k, \bar{\Phi}^k)$. For the SVS model, the BIC terms reduce to

$$\ln\ p(\mathbf{X}|\mu^1, \ldots, \mu^K, \Sigma^1, \ldots, \Sigma^K) = \sum_{k=1}^{k} \sum_{X_i \in Q^k} \ln p(X_i|\mu^k, \Sigma^k) , \quad (14)$$

$$M = \sum_{k=1}^{K} \frac{d_i^k(d_i^k + 3)}{2} . \quad (15)$$

From the presented expression, still both proposals can not be compared, as the computations involved depend on the modeled data set. Next section evaluates both methods in a concrete tracking problem.

6   Experiments

The performance of the method proposed in this papers has been analyzed in a pedestrian tracking application. Given a training sequence of a pedestrian walking sideways, a training set has been generated by delimiting its outline in the di erent frames. This sequence presents discontinuous shape changes due to the legs movement, which will results in a non-linear SVS. From the PCA of the training sequence, an initial linear shape model $(W, \bar{q})$ of dimension 7 is determined. Figure 6 shows the projection of the training set on the W-space, and the GMM obtained with the method described in Section 3, which models the SVS.

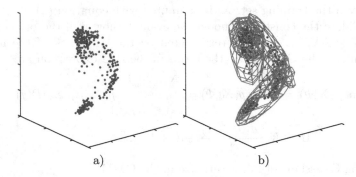

a)   b)

Fig. 6. a) Training data projected into the 3 first dimensions of a 7-dimensional learned shape space. b) The 8 component GMM estimated to constrain the SVS

From the GMM, the collection of linear shape models is constructed. Figure 7 display graphically the dimensionality selected for each shape model. It is also shown the mean shape of each model generated. Clearly, our method have recognized unsupervisedly a reduced number of silhouette states which synthesize a typical pedestrian walking cycle.

Figure 8 shows a qualitative comparison between our multi-model approach and the usual constrained single model. The lines perpendicular to the silhouettes show the shape variability captured in the di erent models. Our proposal seems to be more speci c in localizing the zones of change of the silhouettes.

Table 1 shows the result of applying the described BIC to the di erent models. It can be stated that despite the multi-model approach represents more accurately the training set (i.e., has a minor reconstruction error), a single model is preferable. The gain of using 8 di erent models for this task does not justi es the amount of parameters needed. However, the restriction that complements the

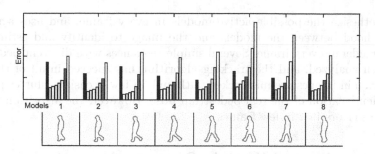

Fig. 7. *Up*: Mean squared reconstruction error for the new shape models considered. Each group of bars show in black color the reconstruction error of the initial 7-dimensional shape model applied to Q^i. The rest of the bars show the error of the model constructed from Q^i, considering dimensionalities from 7 (the *white bar* closer to the *black one*) till 1. The *gray bar* marks the dimensionality selected. *Down*: Mean shape of the models generated

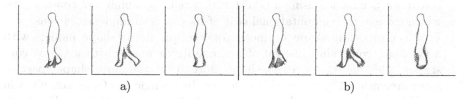

Fig. 8. a) Our proposal. b) The usual approach. The variability in b) is the one associated to the component in the GMM used to generate the models displayed in a)

Table 1. a) Usual approach. b) Our proposal

	BIC(Shape)			BIC(SVS)			Global
	$\ln p(\mathbf{Q}, \Theta_{Shape})$	$-\frac{1}{2}M\ln N$	Sum	$\ln p(\mathbf{X}, \Theta_{SVS})$	$-\frac{1}{2}M\ln N$	Sum	BIC
a)	-1096.4	-1522.7	-2619.1	-9040.2	-856.5	-9896.7	-12516
b)	-441.1	-6090.8	-6531.9	-5020.7	-223.0	-5243.7	-11776

shape model can be better modeled if a collection of simple models is considered, as show the bigger BIC(SVS) value. Taking into account both aspects of shape models, our proposal is more appropriate for modeling the studied training set, as has bigger global BIC value.

To apply our models in a real tracking application, we have augmented them to include Euclidean transformations. So for a given model k, shapes are synthesised by

$$Q_k = E_{T,s,\rho}(W^i X_k + \bar{Q}^i) , \qquad (16)$$

where $E_{T,s,\rho}$ performs a translation T, and scaling s and a rotation ρ to the shape corresponding to X_k. This model has been used in a simple multiple model tracking algorithm based on the generalized pseudo-Bayesian estimator of rst order (see [1] for a description). Basically the algorithm uses the information in a STM to hypothesize the possible active models in every frame, and uses a measure of likelihood between the models and the image to identify and estimate the active model in every frame. Several simple sequences with di erent pedestrians has been analyzed, and the tracking algorithm has succeed in all of them. No pedestrian in images are mistracked, although in few occasions clutter provokes a misidenti cation of the real pedestrian pose. However, the algorithm recovers form this errors just in few frames.

7   Discussion and Work-in-Progress

This paper has three main contributions:

> Presents a novel method to determine the SVS of linear shape models. The method makes easier the construction of constrained linear shape models, as it provides an unsupervised data-driven algorithm to generate them. The constraint is modeled using a GMM with a reduced number of components, which reduces the computational cost of its practical implementations.
>
> Proposes modeling shape by means of multiple linear shape models with a Gaussian constraint, instead of a single linear model with a GMM constraint. This models represent shape more accurately, in a shape space of lower dimensionality. Their SVS is de ned by a single one Gaussian, what in tracking applications can be easily controlled using a constrained Brownian motion to model shape changes.
>
> Suggests an objective criterion to compare between di erent shape models, based on the use of the Bayesian Information Criterion.

Our current work focuses on using the models described in complex tracking scenarios. We are evaluating di erent published tracking frameworks that manage multiple shape models, in terms of its cost and performance. We are also working in complementing shape models with appearance models, in order to obtain better descriptions of objects.

Acknowledgments

This work has been partially supported by TIC2000-0382, Spain.

References

1. Y. Bar-Shalom, X. R. Li, and T. Kirubarajan. *Estimation with Applications to Tracking and Navigation*. John Wiley & Sons, 2001.
2. A.M. Baumberg. *Learning Deformable Models for Tracking Human Motion*. PhD thesis, The University of Leeds. School of Computer Studies, 1995.
3. A. Blake and A. Isard. *Active Contours*. Springer, 1998.
4. T. Cootes and C. Taylor. A mixture model for representing shape variation. *Image Vision Computing*, 1999.

5. T.F. Cootes and C.J. Taylor. Statistical models of appearance for computer vision. Technical report, Wolfson Image Analysis Unit. Imaging Science and Biomedical Engineering, University of Manchester, 2000.

6. T.F. Cootes, C.J. Taylor, D. Cooper, and J.Graham. Active shape models- their training and application. *Computer Vision and Image Understanding*, 1995.

7. N. M. Dempster, A.P. Laird and D.B. Rubin. Maximum likelihood from incomplete data via the EM algorithm. *J. R. Statist. Soc. B*, 39:185–197, 1977.

8. C. Fraley and A. Raftery. How many clusters? which clustering method? answers via model-based cluster analysis. *Computer Journal*, 41:578–588, 1998.

9. A. Heap and D. Hogg. Improving specificity in pdms using a hierarchical approach. In *In Proc. British Machine Vision Conference, volume 1*, pages 80–89, 1997.

10. T. Heap and D. Hogg. Wormholes in shape space: Tracking through discontinuous changes in shape. In *Sixth International Conference on Computer Vision*, pages 344–349, 1998.

11. M. Isard and A. Blake. Condensation – conditional density propagation for visual tracking. *International Journal of Computer Vision*, 1998.

12. R. Kalman. A new approach to linear filtering and prediction problems. *Transactions of the ASME*, 1960.

13. D. Ponsa and X. Roca. Unsupervised parameterisation of gaussian mixture models. Lecture Notes in Artificial Intelligence, to appear, 2002.

14. S. Richardson and P.J. Green. On Bayesian analysis of mixtures with an unknown number of components. *Journal of the Royal Statistical Society (Series B)*, 59(4):731–758, 1997.

15. S. Roberts, C. Holmes, and D. Denison. Minimum entropy data partitioning using Reversible Jump Markov Chain Monte Carlo. *IEEE Transactions on Pattern Analysis and Machine Intelligence*, 23(8):909–915, August 2001.

16. S.J. Roberts, D. Husmeier, I. Rezek, and W. Penny. Bayesian Approaches To Gaussian Mixture Modelling. *IEEE Transaction on Pattern Analysis and Machine Intelligence*, 20(11):1133–1142, 1998.

17. Gideon Schwarz. Estimating the dimension of a model. *Annals of Statistics*, 6(2):461–464, March 1978.

18. Stephen P. Smith and Anil K. Jain. A test to determine the multivariate normality of a data set. *IEEE Transactions on Pattern Analysis and Machine Intelligence*, 10(5):757–761, September 1988.

Real-Time Human Motion Analysis Based on Analysis of Silhouette Contour and Color Blob

Ryuya Hoshino[1], Daisaku Arita[1],
Satoshi Yonemoto[2], and Rin-ichiro Taniguchi[1]

[1] Department of Intelligent Systems, Kyushu University
HTTP://LIMU.IS.KYUSHU-U.AC.JP
[2] Department of Intelligent Systems, Kyushu Sangyo University

Abstract. This paper presents real-time human motion analysis for human-machine interface. In general, man-machine 'smart' interface requires real-time human motion capturing systems without special devices or markers. Although vision-based human motion capturing systems do not use such special devices and markers, they are essentially unstable and can only acquire partial information because of self-occlusion. When we analyze full-body motion, the problem becomes severer. Therefore, we have to introduce a robust pose estimation strategy to deal with relatively poor results of image analysis. To solve this problem, we have developed a method to estimate full-body human postures, where an initial estimation is acquired by real-time inverse kinematics and, based on the estimation, more accurate estimation is searched for referring to the processed image. The key points are that our system combines silhouette contour analysis and color blob analysis for feature extraction to achieve robust feature extraction and that our system can estimate full-body human postures from limited perceptual cues such as positions of a head, hands and feet, which can be stably acquired by feature extraction process. In this paper, we outline a real-time and on-line human motion analysis system.

1 Introduction

Man-machine seamless 3-D interaction is an important tool for various interactive systems such as virtual reality systems, video game consoles, etc. To realize such interaction, the system has to estimate motion parameters of human bodies in real-time. Up to the present, as a method for human motion sensing, many motion capture devices with special markers or magnetic sensor attachments have been employed, which often impose physical restrictions on the object, and which are not comfortable for their users. On the other hand, recently, fully image-feature-based motion capturing systems, which do not impose such restrictions have been developed as computer vision applications [1]. Although the vision-based approach still has problems to be solved, it is a very smart approach that can achieve seamless human-machine interaction.

F.J. Perales and E.R. Hancock (Eds.): AMDO 2002, LNCS 2492, pp. 92–103, 2002.

To analyze human motion, image features such as blobs (coherent region) [1][2][3] or silhouette contours [4][5] are usually employed. Blob-based, or skin-color-based, image analysis is not very robust, because it is often dependent on target individuals such as their wearing clothes (long sleeve shirts or short sleeve shirts etc). On the other hand, a silhouette-based approach has a problem that important features such as hands do not always appear in a body silhouette. Therefore, in this paper, we combine both approaches. However, even with a combined approach, features which can be detected robustly are limited and view dependent, and, thus, we have to develop a mechanism to estimate human full-body posture from the limited number of cues. In addition, to deal with the view dependency and the self-occlusion problem when a human makes various poses, we have employed an approach of multi-view image analysis and have developed a view selection mechanism.

In this paper, we present multi-view-based real-time human motion analysis system and its application to real-time human-machine interface. The key point of our system is that it can estimate human postures from limited perceptual cues such as positions of a head, hands and feet, which are stably detected by image analysis. In the viewpoint of practical applications, real-time feature is quite important, and, therefore, to realize a real-time system with multiple cameras, which produce enormous amount of information, we use a PC-cluster, a set of PCs connected via high-speed network, and acquire quite high performance of image processing.

2 System Overview

2.1 Outline of the Algorithm

The basic algorithm ow of our real-time motion capturing is as follows:

1. Perception (Detection of cues)
   Silhouette detection, skin color blob detection, and 2-D feature extraction
   Calculation of 3-D positions of features using multi-view fusion
2. Human Motion Synthesis
   Generation of human gure full-body motion and rendering in the virtual space and calculation of the interaction.

In order to analyze various human postures, we arrange multiple cameras so as to capture horizontal views and vertical views of a human body. As we mentioned, to make the system real-time and on-line, we have implemented the system on the PC cluster. Figure 1 shows the con guration of processing modules on the PC cluster, which is a parallel-pipeline structure. Each rectangle in the gure indicates one PC. At rst, each view image is processed, or applied to 2D image processing, in a pipelined combination of ICM and HPM (or TPM). This means that the degree of parallelism at this stage is equal to the number of views, or the number of cameras. Then the processed results of all views are integrated and processed at 3DPM (3D image processing) and reconstructed at

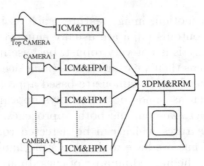

Fig. 1. Image processing modules on PC cluster

RRM (real-time rendering) sequentially. Therefore, when we use N views, or N cameras, we need $N + 1$ PCs.

Details of the processing modules are as follows:

a) Perception Module:

Image Capturing Module (ICM)

These modules work as image-capturing modules. Each ICM_v ($v = 1, \cdots, N$; N is the number of cameras) captures images with 320×240 pixel (YUV:422 pixel format) and sends them to TPM and HPMs.

Horizontal view Processing Module (HPM)

These modules work as 2-D image processing modules for horizontal-view-cameras. The image processing algorithm contains silhouette detection, skin-color blob detection and 2D feature extraction). Each HPM receives the image data from ICM, and sends 2-D extracted image feature data (positions of detected cues) to 3DPM.

Top view Processing Module (TPM)

This module works as 2-D image processing modules for a vertical-view-camera (or top-view-camera). Since usually the rotation of body around the body axis is not easy to estimate accurately, we have introduced the top view. The role of this module is almost the same as that of HPM, except that image processed here is captured from top view.

3-D Processing Module (3DPM)

This module works as a 3-D vision processing module. It receives and integrates the 2-D image feature data from HPM_v ($v = 1, \cdots, N - 1$) and TPM, and estimates 3-D model parameters (3-D positions of cues). The estimated parameters are sent to the RRM.

b) Human Motion Synthesis:

Real-time Rendering Module (RRM)

This module works as a real-time renderer of the virtual space. It receives the 3-D cue positions from 3DPM and estimates 3-D pose and motion of the human body based on the received data.

3   2D Image Analysis

3.1   Analysis for Horizontal-View-Camera

Feature points to detect in horizontal-view-camera images are a head top, right/left hands (ngertips), right/left foot points. Knees and elbows, which are very important features to estimate human postures, are not easy to detect from the images, since they do not appear as distinctive image features. Therefore, to estimate knee and elbow positions, we have introduced multi-view approach and 3D pose estimation based on inverse kinematics and search by reverse projection. Details will be presented in section 5.

The feature points, or a head top, hands (ngertips), foot points, usually appear as relatively sharp convex points on a silhouette contour of a human body image. Therefore, the convex points are good cues for the feature points, and silhouette contour analysis seems to be a good approach to detect them. However, hands are sometimes occluded by other parts of human body, especially by torso, and, in such cases, skin-color blob analysis is an alternative approach for feature point detection. Therefore, to make the feature point detection robust, we combine both approaches, i.e., silhouette-based approach and color-blob-based approach. For a head top and foot points, it is enough for the system to detect convex points from a silhouette contour, and we will omit its details. For hands, the following combined procedure is applied, which is designed to handle both cases when a target person wears a long sleeve shirt and when he/she wears a short sleeve shirt:

1. In HIS color space, skin-color pixels are detected. Then, they are clustered into blobs based on the distance from the blobs detected in the previous frame.
2. Major axis of a hand blob is calculated.
3. Crossing points of the major axis and the contour of the blob are calculated. A crossing point nearest to the previously detected position becomes a hand position.
4. If a hand blob makes a circular shape, or if its major axis can not be calculated, its centroid becomes a hand position.

Here, we have assumed that in successive image frames shapes of a human body region do not change very largely, and the system generally searches for the feature points in the neighborhood of its corresponding feature point detected in the previous frame. At the initial frame, we assume a standard initial posture, which is a standing posture with arms and legs open.

We show some results of 2D feature point detection (Figure 2), where a silhouette contour and skin-color blobs of a human body are presented. Circles in this gure indicate left hand positions, which shows that the system can correctly detect a left hand in either case of wearing a long sleeve shirt or of wearing a short sleeve shirt. It is satisfactory result for single view image analysis of human motion.

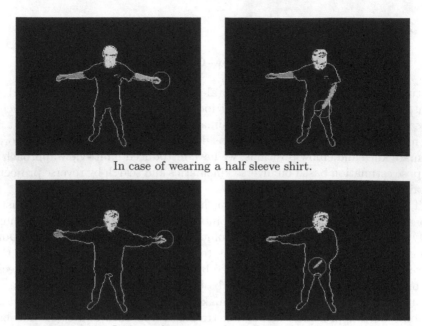

In case of wearing a half sleeve shirt.

In case of wearing a long sleeve shirt.

Fig. 2. Results of Feature Point Detection

3.2 Analysis for Vertical-View-Camera

In TPM, the 2D positions of right and left ngertips, those of both shoulders, and the rotation angle of torso around the body axis are estimated. The ngertip positions are estimated by a method similar to one described in section 3.1. For estimation of the rotation around the body axis, the orientation of the major axis of the silhouette region is a good cue, and it is calculated from the second order moment and moment of inertia.

However, the angle of the major axis of a silhouette region in the top view is often severely a ected by con gurations of both arms, and, as a result, it is sometimes di erent from the torso angle. To diminish the in uence of the arm con gurations, we erase arm parts from the silhouette region by applying a morphology operation, opening, and extract the torso part. The structuring element in this case is very simple, $\{(0,0),(1,0),(-1,0),(0,1),(0,-1)\}$, and we iterate the opening operation seven times. The number of iteration is decided according to preliminary experiments[1].

As for the 2D positions of both shoulders, referring to a pre-de ned value of the shoulder width, we simply estimate them from the position of the centroid of the silhouette region and the rotation angle of torso. Figure 3 shows examples of the image analysis results in TPM. Gray regions are extracted torso parts, and a line in each region indicates the rotation angle of torso. Bright dots in the

---

[1] The number of iteration should be further considered. Probably, it is better to change the iteration number depending on input images

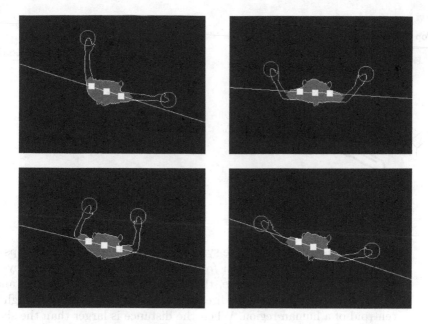

Fig. 3. Image analysis on TPM

region are the centroid and estimated 2D positions of the shoulders. It shows our image analysis works correctly.

4   3D Feature Analysis

In principle, when at least two views of an object point are available, we can calculate its 3D position based on the binocular stereo mechanism. However, only two views are not enough to analyze various body postures because of the self-occlusion. Therefore, in our system, we use multiple, or redundant, views including a top view. In 3DPM, the system dynamically selects good views for stereo calculation referring to the result of TPM (described in section 3.2). Outline of the algorithm is as follows:

1. Referring to the body rotation acquired in TPM, the system selects two cameras (*front cameras*) facing to the front of the body and one camera (*side camera*) viewing the side of the body. The selection is done referring to inner products of a vector of the body direction and vectors from the centroid of the silhouette region in the top view to cameras (Figure 4). Two cameras giving two maximum inner products are selected as *front cameras* and a camera giving inner product nearest to zero is selected as *side camera*.
2. Two cameras for stereo calculation are selected among two *front cameras*, *side camera* and *top camera*.
   For positions of a head, a torso and both feet ends, two *front cameras* are selected. The torso position here is calculated from the position of the centroid of the human region.

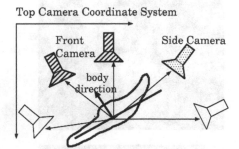

Fig. 4. View Selection

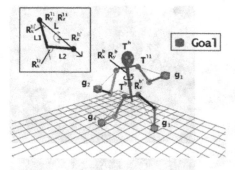

Fig. 5. Our Human Figure Model Geometry

For positions of ngertips, the system checks whether the ngertips appear on silhouette contours in *front camera* views. This is done by calculating, in a top view image, the distance between a ngertip and a line which is parallel to body direction and which is passing through the centroid of a human region. When the distance is larger than the shoulder width, which means that arms are widely open, two *front cameras* are selected. Otherwise, it is judged that a ngertip does not appear on the silhouette contour in *front camera* views, and *top camera* and *side camera* are selected for stereo calculation.

5   3D Pose Estimation

5.1   Basic Concept

Since information acquired in the perception process is just 3-D positions of a torso, a head, hands and feet of a human body, we have to estimate the body posture from these cues, the number of which is less than the degree of freedom of the body. Actually, we have to estimate 3D positions of elbows and knees. In our system, based on a very simple human body model (see Fig.5), we have adopted two analysis approaches: real-time inverse kinematics (IK) and search by reverse projection (SRP). The former is a general and elegant (and fast!) approach but it can only calculate a sub-optimal solution. On the other hand, the latter is rather brute force and searches for the solution referring to original silhouette regions, not to the 3D feature points. The system, at rst, estimates the elbow and knee positions using inverse kinematics, and after once the estimation is acquired the system searches for optimal solution referring to the estimated result. In analyzing an image sequence, those positions in a frame are usually searched by the latter approach based on the results in the previous frame. An important point is that when something wrong happens, or the elbow and knee positions can not be detected, because of noise and other reasons, the inverse kinematics is invoked as an error recovery process. Because of page limitation, we omit the inverse kinematics part, and, for detail, please refer to [8].

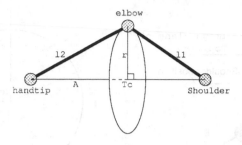

Fig. 6. Positional relation among shoulder, elbow and hand

For torso posture, the axis of the torso is estimated as an axis connecting the centroids of a head part and a torso part. The pan angle around the torso axis can be estimated by moment analysis of the silhouette region in the top view (it cf. section 3.2).

5.2 Search by Reverse Projection

Basic idea of estimation of elbow and knee positions based on *search by reverse projection* is not very di cult. After we estimate the positions of a ngertip and a shoulder for one arm, if we know the lengths of its upper arm and forearm, the position of its elbow is restricted on a circle in 3D space shown in Figure 6, and we only have to search for the elbow position on the circle. When we select a point on the circle and map it onto an image plane of each view, the point should be included in every silhouette region. In other words, points which satisfy the above condition might coincide with the elbow position with high probability.

Suppose that

the position of the shoulder point is (x_1, y_1, z_1),
$A = (A_x, A_y, A_z)$ is a vector from the shoulder point to the ngertip,
the length of the upper arm is l_1 and that of the forearm is l_2,

the radius r and the center T_c of the circle are represented as follows:

$$r = \frac{4|A|^2(l_1^2 + l_2^2) + 4l_1^2 l_2^2 - (l_1^2 + l_2^2 + |A|^2)^2}{2|A|} \tag{1}$$

$$T_c = (x_1 + A_x t, \; y_1 + A_y t, \; z_1 + A_z t) \tag{2}$$

$$\text{where } t = \frac{l_1^2 - r^2}{|A|^2}.$$

Actual procedure of elbow position estimation is as follows:

1. **Estimation of 3D position of shoulder**
   A z coordinate of the shoulder point can be calculated by adding the height of torso (D in Figure 7), which is a pre-de ned value, to the position of the

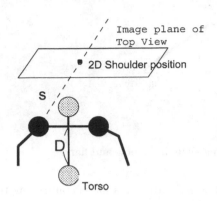

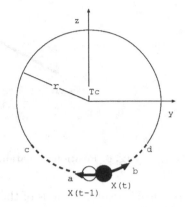

Fig. 7. Shoulder position in the world coordinates

Fig. 8. Estimation of elbow position

torso (*cf.* section 4). As for its x and y coordinates, rst, a line of sight passing through the shoulder point in the image plane is calculated (dotted line s in Figure 7) based on camera calibration parameters and the 2D position of a shoulder in a top view. Then x, y coordinates of the shoulder position is calculated from its z coordinate and the line of sight.

2. **Setup of local coordinates for elbow position estimation**
   A local coordinate system whose origin is T_c, whose x axis is A, whose z axis coincides with an axis which is the projection of the z axis of the world coordinate system onto a plane including the search circle. Then, the search circle becomes to lie on the y-z plane of the de ned local coordinate system, and, therefore, the calculation of elbow position search can be simpli ed. The reverse transformation from this local coordinate system into the world coordinate system is very simple as well.

3. **Estimation of elbow position**
   Figure 8 shows the process of elbow position search in the t-th frame. At rst, the possible range of the elbow position is established as a neighborhood of the elbow position estimated in the (t-1)-th frame (or by IK) (*cd* in Figure 8). Then, the possible range is reversely projected onto all the image planes, and the possible range which is inside of all of the silhouette regions becomes the nal possible range of the elbow position (*ab* in Figure 8). Generally, the nal possible range does not become a single point, and, therefore, the center of the possible range is decided as the estimated elbow position.

Fig.9 shows di erence of a result by IK and one by SRP, which shows that SRP gives more accurate posture estimation.

6   Implementation and Experiments

In this experiment, we have used 6 IEEE1394-based color cameras (Sony DFW-V500) with f:4mm lenses. Five of them are horizontal-view-cameras and arranged

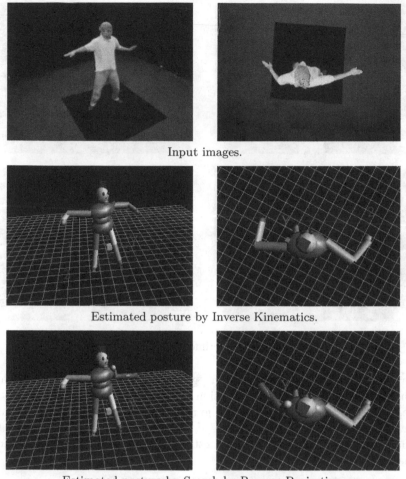

Input images.

Estimated posture by Inverse Kinematics.

Estimated posture by Search by Reverse Projection.

Fig. 9. Comparison between IK and SRP

circularly at intervals of about 30 degrees, and the rest is a vertical-view-camera. These cameras are geometrically calibrated in advance. The images are captured with the size of 320×240 pixels, and the frame rate is 15 fps[2]. The number of PC s in the system is seven, each of which has dual PentiumIII s(700MHz) running Linux.

The goal of our method is that, referring to multiple, or redundant, view images, the system can analyze human postures in such situations that a hand overlaps with a torso part, which cannot be analyzed by usual silhouette analysis. Fig.10 shows several snap shots of a real-time online experiment. Displays at the

---

[2] When an external trigger is given to our cameras, the maximum frame rate becomes 15fps, not 30fps. However, the potential performance of the system can be 30fps, normal video rate.

Fig. 10. Online Experiment of Motion Capture

lower right show re-generated human gures analyzed by our motion capture method. Detailed quantitative evaluation of its estimation accuracy has not been done, but from re-generated human gures we see our method achieves almost correct human posture estimation.

In this method the system can not estimate very complex postures, since the human model is very simple:

Twist of the neck can not be detected. However, it can be detected after we introduce face detection to the system.

Postures in which hands or feet can not be detected are almost impossible to estimate.

In spite of these problems, we can apply this system to various interactive applications.

7   Conclusion

In this paper, we have shown a real-time human motion capturing without special marker-sensors and its application to real-time human-machine interaction. For real-time motion analysis, we have adopted silhouette-based multi-view fusion to realize full-body motion analysis. The key point is that we have established a framework of estimation of full-body motion from a limited number of perceptual cues, which can be stably extracted from input images. Since the system implemented on PC-cluster works in real-time and online, it can be applied to various *real-virtual* applications. We will improve each image analysis algorithm to make more robust human motion analysis possible, which leads our real-time human motion analysis more applicable. In future work, we will investigate more practical applications of human-machine interface based on real-time human motion analysis.

Acknowledgments

This work has been partly supported by Intelligent Media Technology for Supporting Natural Communication between People project (13GS0003, Grant-in-Aid for Creative Scienti c Research, the Japan Society for the Promotion of Science).

References

1. C.Wren, A.Azarbayejani, T.Darrell, A.Pentland, "Pfinder: Real-Time Tracking of the Human Body", *IEEE Transactions on Pattern Analysis and Machine Intelligence*, Vol.19, No.7, pp.780-785, 1997.
2. C.Bregler, "Learning and Recognizing Human Dynamics in Video Sequences", *in Computer Vision and Pattern Recognition*, pp.568–574, 1997.
3. M.Etoh, Y.Shirai, "Segmentation and 2D Motion Estimation by Region Fragments", *International Conference on Computer Vision*, pp.192–199, 1993.
4. M.K.Leung, Y-H.Yang, "First Sight: A Human Body Outline Labeling System", *IEEE Transactions on Pattern Analysis and Machine Intelligence*, Vol.17, No.4, pp.359-377, 1995.
5. K.Takahashi, T.Sakaguchi, J.Ohya, "Remarks on a Real-Time 3D Human Body Posture Estimation Method using Trinocular Images," *International Conference on Pattern Recognition*, Vol.4, pp.693–697, 2000.
6. Y.Okamoto and R.Cipolla and H.Kazama and Y.Kuno, "Human Interface System Using Qualitative Visual Motion Interpretation", *Transactions of Institute of Electronics, Information and Communication Engineers*, Vol.J76-D-II, No.8, pp.1813–1821, 1993 (in Japanese).
7. J.Zhao and N.Badler: Inverse Kinematics Positioning Using Nonlinear Programming for Highly Articulated Figures, *Transactions on Computer Graphics*, Vol.13, No.4, pp.313–336, 1994.
8. S.Yonemoto, D.Arita and R.Taniguchi: "Real-Time Visually Guided Human Figure Control Using IK-based Motion Synthesis", Proc. 5th Workshop on the Application of Computer Vision, pp.194-200, 2000.

Human Body Model Acquisition and Motion Capture Using Voxel Data

Ivana Mikić[2], Mohan Trivedi[1], Edward Hunter[2], and Pamela Cosman[1]

[1]Department of Electrical and Computer Engineering
9500 Gilman Drive, La Jolla, California 92093-0407
phone: 858 822-0002, fax: 858 822-5336
trivedi@ece.ucsd.edu, pcosman@code.ucsd.edu
[2]Q3DM, Inc.
{imikic,ehunter}@q3dm.com

Abstract. In this paper we present a system for human body model acquisition and tracking of its parameters from voxel data. 3D voxel reconstruction of the body in each frame is computed from silhouettes extracted from multiple cameras. The system performs automatic model acquisition using a template based initialization procedure and a Bayesian network for refinement of body part size estimates. The twist-based human body model leads to a simple formulation of the extended Kalman filter that performs the tracking and with joint angle limits guarantees physically valid posture estimates. Evaluation of the approach was performed on several sequences with different types of motion captured with six cameras.

1   Introduction

Motion capture is of interest in many applications such as advanced user interfaces, entertainment, surveillance systems, or motion analysis for sports and medical purposes. In the past few years, the problem of markerless, unconstrained motion capture has received much attention from computer vision researchers [1, 2, 3, 4]. Many systems require manual initialization of the model and then perform the tracking. The systems that use multiple camera images as inputs, most often analyze the data in the image plane, comparing it with the appropriate features of the model projection [5, 6]. Promising results have been reported in using the depth data obtained from stereo [7, 8] for pose estimation. However, only recently the first attempts at using voxel data obtained from multiple cameras to estimate body pose have been reported [9]. This system used a very simple initialization and tracking procedure that did not guarantee a valid articulated body model.

In [10] we have introduced the framework for articulated body model acquisition and tracking from voxel data: video from multiple cameras is segmented and a voxel reconstruction of the person's body is computed from the 2D silhouettes; in the first frame, an automatic model initialization is performed – the head is found first by template matching and the other body parts by a sequential template growing procedure. An extended Kalman filter is then used for tracking. In this system, a body pose

F.J. Perales and E.R. Hancock (Eds.): AMDO 2002, LNCS 2492, pp. 104–118, 2002.

where all four limbs were visible as separate was expected in the first frame for successful initialization. The orientation of each body part was modeled independently and therefore the physically invalid joint rotations were possible. Also, the voxel labeling approach used to compute the measurements for the tracker was based on Mahalanobis distance and worked well only for small frame-to-frame displacements.

We have, therefore, designed a new system with a greatly improved performance (Fig. 1). During model initialization, we have introduced a model refinement phase where a Bayesian network that incorporates the knowledge of human body proportions improves the estimates of body part sizes. A twist-based human body model is now used, which leads to a simple extended Kalman filter formulation and guarantees physically valid posture estimates. We have also designed a voxel labeling approach that takes advantage of the unique qualities of voxel data and of the Kalman filter predictions to obtain quality measurements for tracking. Section 2 contains the description of the twist-based human body model and the formulation of the extended Kalman filter. In Section 3 the voxel labeling and tracking are presented. The model acquisition algorithm is described in Section 4. Experimental evaluation is presented in Section 5. Concluding remarks follow in Section 6.

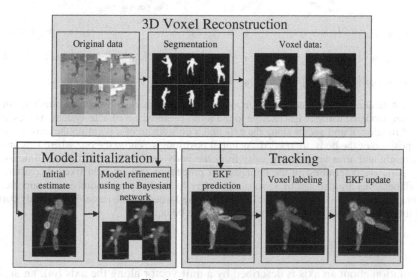

Fig. 1. System components.

2   Human Body Model and the Kalman Filter Formulation

The articulated body model we use is shown in Fig. 2. Sizes of body parts are denoted as $2 l_i^{(j)}$, where i is the body part index, and j is the dimension order – smallest dimension is 0 and largest is 2. For all parts except torso, the two smaller dimensions are set to be equal to the average of the two dimensions estimated during initialization. The positions of joints are fixed relative to the body part dimensions in the torso coordinate system (for example, the hip is at $\begin{bmatrix} 0 & d_H{}_0^{(1)} & {}_0^{(2)} \end{bmatrix}^T$ - see Fig. 2). Sixteen axes of rotation are modeled in different joints. Two in the neck, three in each shoulder, two in each hip and one in each elbow and knee. The range of allowed values is set for each angle. For example, the rotation in the knee can go from 0 to 180 degrees - the knee cannot bend forward. The rotations about these axes (relative to the torso) are modeled using twists [11, 12].

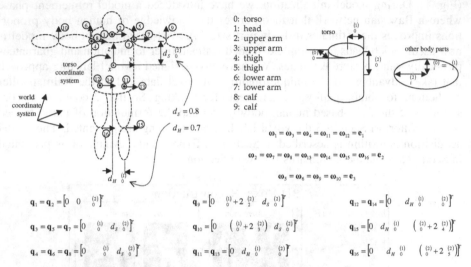

Fig. 2. Articulated body model. Sixteen axes of rotation (marked by circled numbers) in body joints are modeled using twists relative to the torso-centered coordinate system. To describe an axis of rotation, a unit vector along the axis and a coordinate of a point on the axis in the "initial" position of the body are needed. As initial position, we chose the one where legs and arms are straight and arms are pointing away from the body as shown in the figure. Dimensions of body parts are determined in the initialization procedure and are held fixed thereafter. Body part dimensions are denoted by λ; subscript refers to the body part number and superscript to dimension order – 0 is for the smallest and 2 for the largest of the three. For all body parts except the torso, the two smaller dimensions are set to be equal.

Rotation about an axis is described by a unit vector along the axis (ω), an arbitrary point on the axis ($\mathbf{q}$) and the angle of rotation (θ_i). A twist associated with an axis of rotation is defined as:

$$\xi = \begin{matrix} \omega \\ v \end{matrix} \quad , \text{where } \mathbf{v} = \omega \cdot \mathbf{q} \tag{1}$$

An exponential map, $e^{\hat{\xi}}$ maps the homogeneous coordinates of a point from its initial values to the coordinates after the rotation is applied [12]:

$$\mathbf{p}(\ ) = e^{\hat{\xi}}\,\mathbf{p}(0) = \mathbf{T}\mathbf{p}(0) \tag{2}$$

where

$$\mathbf{p}(\ ) = \begin{bmatrix}\mathbf{x}^T(\ ) & 1\end{bmatrix}^T = \begin{bmatrix}x(\ ) & y(\ ) & z(\ ) & 1\end{bmatrix}^T, \quad e^{\hat{\omega}} = \mathbf{I} + \hat{\omega}\sin\ + \hat{\omega}^2(1\ \cos\ )$$

$$\mathbf{T} = e^{\hat{\xi}} = \begin{array}{cc} e^{\hat{\omega}} & \left(\mathbf{I}\ e^{\hat{\omega}}\right)\!\left(\omega\cdot\mathbf{v}\right) + \omega\omega^T\mathbf{v} \\ 0 & 1 \end{array} = \begin{bmatrix}\mathbf{R} & \mathbf{t} \\ 0 & 1\end{bmatrix}, \quad \hat{\omega} = \begin{bmatrix} 0 & _2 & _1 \\ _2 & 0 & _0 \\ _1 & _0 & 0 \end{bmatrix} \qquad (3)$$

Even though the axes of rotation change as the body moves, in the twists formulation the descriptions of the axes stay fixed and are determined in the initial body configuration. We chose the configuration with extended arms and legs and arms pointing to the side of the body (as shown in Fig. 2). In this configuration, all angles θ_i are zero. The figure also gives values for the vectors ω_i and $\mathbf{q}_i$ for each axis.

Knowing the dimensions of body parts and using the body model shown in Fig. 2, the configuration of the body is completely captured with angles of rotation about each of the axes (θ_1 - θ_{16}) and the centroid and orientation of the torso. Orientation (rotation matrix) of the torso is parameterized with a quaternion, which is equivalent to the unit vector ω_0 and the angle θ_0. Therefore, the position and orientation of the torso are captured using seven parameters – three coordinates for centroid location and four for the orientation. The configuration of the described model is fully captured by 23 parameters, which we include into the Kalman filter state, $\mathbf{x}_k$. For the measurements of the Kalman filter (contained in the vector $\mathbf{z}_k$) we chose 23 points on the human body: centroids and endpoints of each of the ten body parts, neck, shoulders, elbows, hips, knees, feet and hands (Fig. 3).

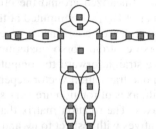

Fig. 3. 23 points on the human body, chosen to form a set of measurements for the Kalman filter.

To design the Kalman filter, the relationship between the measurement and the state needs to be described. For a point $\mathbf{p}$, we define the "set of significant rotations" that contains the rotations that affect the position of the point – if $\mathbf{p}$ is the fingertip, there would be four: three in the shoulder and one in the elbow. Set of angles θ_p contains the angles associated with the set of significant rotations. The position of a point $\mathbf{p}_t(\theta_p)$ with respect to the torso is given by the product of exponential maps that correspond to the set of significant rotations and of the position of the point in the initial configuration $\mathbf{p}_t(0)$ [12]:

$$\mathbf{p}_t(\theta_p) = \mathbf{T}_{i1}\mathbf{T}_{i2}...\mathbf{T}_{in}\mathbf{p}_t(0), \text{ where } \theta_p = \{\ _{i1},\ _{i2},...,\ _{in}\} \qquad (4)$$

We denote with $\mathbf{T}_0$ the mapping that corresponds to the torso position and orientation:

$$T_0 = \begin{array}{cc} R_0 & t_0 \\ 0 & 1 \end{array} = \begin{array}{cc} e^{\hat{\omega}_0 \circ} & t_0 \\ 0 & 1 \end{array} \tag{5}$$

where $R_0 = e^{\hat{\omega}_0 \circ}$ and t_0 is the torso centroid. The homogeneous coordinates of a point with respect to the world coordinate system can now be expressed as:

$$p_0(\theta_p, \omega_0, t_0) = T_0 p_t(\theta_p) \tag{6}$$

It follows that Cartesian coordinate of this point in the world coordinate system is:

$$x_0(\theta_p) = R_0(R_{i1}(R_{i2}(..(R_{in}x_t(0) + t_{in}) + ...) + t_{i2}) + t_{i1}) + t_0 \tag{7}$$

For any of the chosen 23 measurement points, its location relative to the torso centroid in the initial configuration $x_t(0)$ is a very simple function of the body part dimensions and the joint locations (which are also defined relative to the body part dimensions). For example, left foot is at $\begin{bmatrix} 0 & d_H & \binom{1}{0} & \left(\begin{smallmatrix}(2)\\0\end{smallmatrix} + 2\begin{smallmatrix}(2)\\4\end{smallmatrix} + 2\begin{smallmatrix}(2)\\8\end{smallmatrix}\right)\end{bmatrix}^T$.

In the Kalman filter equations [13]:

$$x_{k+1} = Fx_k + u_k \tag{8}$$
$$z_k = H(x_k) + w_k$$

the relationship between the measurements and the state is nonlinear, except for the torso centroid. It is, therefore, linearized around the predicted state in the extended Kalman filter, i.e. the Jacobian of $H(x_k)$ is computed at the predicted state. This Jacobian consists of partial derivatives of coordinates of each of the 23 measurement points with respect to the torso centroid, torso quaternion and the 16 angles of rotation. All these derivatives are straightforward to compute from the Equation 7, since only one rotation matrix and one translation vector depend on any given angle θ_i. Rotation matrices associated with axes of rotation are very simple since all axes coincide with one of the coordinate axes. The rotation matrix that describes the torso orientation is arbitrary, but its derivatives with respect to ω_0 and θ_0 are also easy to compute.

To ensure that the model configuration represents a valid posture of the human body, the angles in different joints need to be limited. We impose these constraints on the updated Kalman filter state that contains the estimate of these angles by setting the value of the angle to the interval limit if that limit has been exceeded.

3   Voxel Labeling and Tracking

The algorithm for model acquisition, which estimates body part sizes and their locations in the beginning of the sequence, will be presented in the next section. For now, we will assume that the dimensions of all body parts and their approximate locations in the beginning of the sequence are known. For every new frame, the tracker updates model position and configuration to reflect the motion of the tracked person. The labeling of the voxel data is necessary for obtaining the measurements used for tracking. From the labeled voxels, it is easy to compute the locations of the 23 points shown in Fig. 3, since those points are either centroids or endpoints of different body parts.

Initially, we labeled the voxels based on the Mahalanobis distance from the predicted positions of body parts. However, in many cases, this led to loss of track. This was due to the fact that labeling based purely on distance cannot produce a good result when the prediction is not very close to the true positions of body parts. We have, therefore, designed an algorithm that takes advantage of the unique qualities of voxel data to perform reliable labeling even for very large frame-to-frame displacements.

Due to its unique shape and size, the head is easiest to find and is located first (Fig. 4). We create a spherical crust template whose inner and outer diameters correspond to the smallest and largest head dimensions. For the head center we choose the location of the template center that maximizes the number of surface voxels that are inside the crust. Then, the voxels that are inside the sphere of the larger diameter, centered at the chosen head center are labeled as belonging to the head, and the true center is recomputed from those voxels. The location of the neck is found as an average over head voxels with at least one neighbor a non-head body voxel. The prediction of the head center location is available and we therefore search for it only in the neighborhood of the prediction. This speeds up the search and also decreases the likelihood of error.

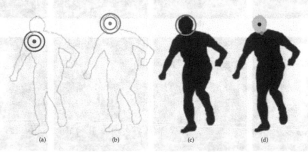

Fig. 4. Head location procedure illustrated in a 2D cross-section. (a) search for the location of the center of a spherical crust template that contains the maximum number of surface voxels (b) the best location is found (c) voxels that are inside the sphere of a larger diameter are labeled as belonging to the head (d) head voxels (green), the head center (black) and the neck (red).

Next, the torso voxels are labeled. The template of the size of the torso (with circular cross-section whose radius is the larger of the two torso base dimansions) is then placed with its base at the neck and with its axis going through the centroid of non-head voxels. The voxels inside this template are then used to recompute a new centroid, and the template is rotated so that its axis passes through it (torso is anchored to the neck at the center of its base at all times). This procedure is repeated until the template stops moving, which is accomplished when the template is entirely inside the torso or is well centered over it. Even with an initial centroid that is completely outside the body, this procedure converges, since in the area close to the neck, the template always contains some torso voxels that help steer the template in the right direction (see Fig. 5). The voxels inside the template are labeled as belonging to the torso.

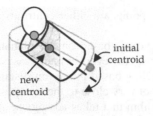

Fig. 5. Fitting the torso. Initial torso template is placed so that its base is at the neck and its main axis passes through the centroid of non-head voxels. Voxels that are inside the template are used to calculate new centroid and the template is rotated to align the main axis with the new centroid. The process is repeated until the template stops moving which happens when it is entirely inside the torso or is well centered over it.

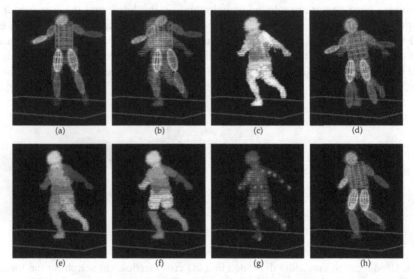

Fig. 6. Voxel labeling and tracking. (a) tracking result in the previous frame (b) model prediction in the new frame; (c) head and torso located; (d) limbs moved to preserve the predicted hip and joint angles for the new torso position and orientation; (e) four limbs are labeled by minimizing the Mahalanobis distance from to the limb positions shown in (d); (f) upper arms and thighs are labeled by fitting them inside the limbs, anchored at the shoulder/hip joints. The remaining limb voxels are labeled as lower arms and thighs; (g) the measurement points are easily computed from the labeled voxels (h) tracker adjusts the body model to fit the data in the new frame.

Then, the predictions for the four limbs are modified to maintain the predicted hip and shoulder angles with the new torso position. The remaining voxels are then assigned to the four limbs based on Mahalanobis distance from these modified limb positions. To locate upper arms and thighs inside the appropriate limb voxel blobs, the same fitting procedure used for torso is repeated, with templates anchored at the shoulders/hips. When the voxels belonging to upper arms and thighs are labeled, the remaining voxels in each of the limbs are labeled as lower arms or calves. Using modified predictions of the limb locations enables the system to handle large frame to frame displacements. Once all the voxels are labeled, the 23 measurement points are easily computed as centroids or endpoints of appropriate blobs. The extended Kalman described in the previous section is then used to adjust the model to the measurements in the new frame and to produce the prediction for the next frame. Fig. 6 illustrates the voxel labeling and tracking.

4   Model Acquisition

The human body model is chosen a priori and is the same for all humans. However, the actual sizes of body parts vary from person to person. Obviously, for each captured sequence, the initial locations of different body parts will vary also. Model acquisition, therefore, involves both locating the body parts and estimating their true sizes from the data in the beginning of a sequence. It is performed in two stages. First, the rough estimates of body part locations and sizes in the first frame are generated using a template fitting and growing algorithm. In the second stage, this estimate is refined over several subsequent frames using a Bayesian network that takes into account both the measured body dimensions and the known proportions of the human body. During this refinement process, the Bayesian network is inserted into the tracking loop, using the body part size measurements produced by the voxel labeling to modify the model, which is then adjusted to best fit the data using the extended Kalman filter. When the body part sizes stop changing, the Bayesian network is "turned off" and the regular tracking continues.

4.1   Initial Estimation of Body Part Locations and Sizes

This procedure is similar to the voxel labeling described in Section 6.2. However, the prediction from the previous frame does not exist (this is the first frame) and the sizes of body parts are not known. Therefore, several modifications and additional steps are needed.

The algorithm illustrated in Fig. 4 is still used to locate the head, however, the inner and outer diameters of the spherical crust template are now set to the smallest and largest head diameters we expect to see. Also, the whole volume has to be searched. The errors are more likely than during voxel labeling for tracking, but are still quite rare: in our experiments on 600 frames, this version located the head correctly in 95% of the frames.

To locate the torso, the same fitting procedure described for voxel labeling is used (Fig. 5), but with the template of an average sized torso. Then, the torso template is shrunk to a small, predetermined size in its new location and grown in all dimensions until further growth starts including empty voxels. At every step of the growing, the torso is reoriented as shown in Fig. 5 to ensure that it is well centered during growth. In the direction of the legs, the growing will stop at the place where legs part. The voxels inside this new template are labeled as belonging to the torso (Fig. 7).

Next, the four regions belonging to the limbs are found as the four largest connected regions of remaining voxels. The hip and shoulder joints are located as the centroids for voxels at the border of the torso and each of the limbs. Then, the same fitting and growing procedure described for the torso is repeated for thighs and upper arms. The lower arms and calves are found by locating connected components closest to the identified upper arms and thighs. Fig. 8. shows the described initial body part localization on real voxel data.

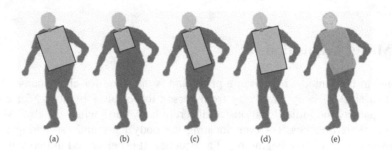

(a)   (b)   (c)   (d)   (e)

Fig. 7. Torso locating procedure illustrated in a 2D cross-section. (a) Initial torso template is fitted to the data; (b) It is then replaced by a small template of predetermined size which is anchored at the same neck point and oriented the same way; (c) the template is then grown and reoriented at every step of growing to ensure the growth does not go in the wrong direction; (d) the growing is stopped when it starts including empty voxels; (e) voxels inside the final template are labeled as belonging to the torso.

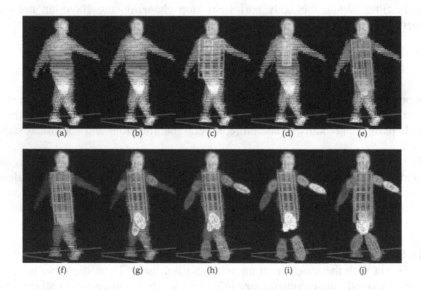

Fig. 8. Initial body part localization. (a) 3D voxel reconstruction; (b) head located; (c) initial torso template anchored at the neck centered over the non-head voxels; (d) start of the torso growing; (e) final result of torso growing with torso voxels labeled; (f) four limbs labeled as four largest remaining connected components; (g) upper arms and thighs are grown anchored at the shoulders/hips with the same procedure used for torso; (h) lower arms and calves are fitted to the remaining voxels; (i) all voxels are labeled; (j) current model adjusted to the data using the EKF to ensure a kinematically valid posture estimate.

4.2 Model Refinement

The estimates of body part sizes and locations in the first frame produced by the algorithm described in the previous section performs robustly, but the sizes of the torso and the limbs are often very inaccurate and depend on the body pose in the first frame. For example, if the person is standing with legs straight and close together, the initial torso will be very long and include much of the legs. The estimates of the thigh and calf sizes will be very small. Obviously, an additional mechanism for estimating true body part sizes is needed.

In addition to the initial estimate of the body part sizes and of the person's height, a general knowledge of human body proportions is available. To take that important knowledge into account when reasoning about body part sizes, we are using Bayesian networks (BNs). A BN is inserted into the tracking loop (Fig. 9), modifying the estimates of body part lengths at each new frame. The EKF tracker adjusts the new model position and configuration to the data, the voxel labeling procedure provides the measurements in the following frame, which are then used by the BN to update the estimates of body part lengths. This procedure is repeated until the body part lengths stop changing.

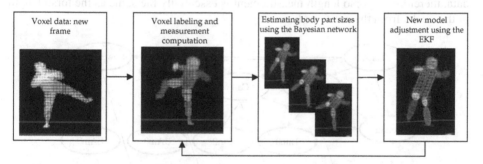

| Voxel data: new frame | Voxel labeling and measurement computation | Estimating body part sizes using the Bayesian network | New model adjustment using the EKF |

Fig. 9. Body part size estimation.

The domain knowledge that is useful for designing the Bayesian network is: the human body is symmetric, i.e., the corresponding body parts on the left and the right sides are of the same dimensions; the lengths of the head, the torso, the thigh and the calf add up to person's height; the proportions of the human body are known.

The measurements that can be made from the data are the sizes of all body parts and the person's height. The height of the person, the dimensions of the head and the two width dimensions for all other body parts are measured quite accurately. The lengths of different body parts are the ones that are inaccurately measured. This is due to the fact that the measured lengths depend on the borders between body parts, which are hard to locate accurately. For example, if the leg is extended, it is very hard to determine where the thigh ends and the calf begins, but the two width dimensions can be very accurately determined from the data.

Taking into account what is known about the human body and what can be measured from the data, we can conclude that there is no need to refine our estimates of the head dimensions or the width dimensions of other body parts since they can be accurately estimated from the data, and our knowledge of body proportions would not be of much help in these cases anyway. However, for body part lengths, the refinement is necessary and the available prior knowledge is very useful. Therefore, we have built a Bayesian network shown in Fig. 10 that estimates the lengths of body parts and that takes into account what is known and what can be measured.

Each node represents a continuous random variable. Leaf nodes Thm, Cm, UAm and LAm are the measurements of the lengths of the thigh, calf, upper and lower arm in the current frame. Leaf node Height is the measurement of the person's height (minus head length) computed in the first frame. If the person's height is significantly smaller than the sum of measured lengths of appropriate body parts, we take that sum as the true height – in case the person is not standing up. Leaf nodes Thm0, Cm0, UAm0 and LAm0 are used to increase the influence of past measurements and speed up the convergence. Each of these nodes is updated with the mean of the marginal distribution of its parent from the previous frame. Other nodes (Torso, Thigh, Calf, UpperArm and LowerArm) are random variables that represent true body part lengths. Due to the body symmetry, we include only one node for each of the lengths of the limb body parts and update the corresponding measurement node with the average of the measurements from the left and right sides. The measurement of the torso length is not used because the voxel labeling procedure just fits the known torso to the data, therefore the torso length measurement is essentially the same as the torso length in the model from the previous frame.

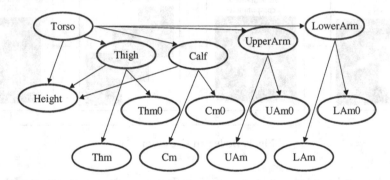

Fig. 10. The Bayesian network for estimating body part lengths. Each node represents a length. The leaf nodes are measurements (Thm represents the new thigh measurement, Thm0 reflects the past measurements etc.). Nodes Torso, Thigh, Calf, UpperArm and LowerArm are random variables that represent true body part lengths.

All variables are Gaussian and the distribution of a node Y with continuous parents **Z** is of the form:

$$p(Y/\mathbf{Z} = \mathbf{z}) = \mathcal{N}\left(\alpha + \boldsymbol{\beta}^T \mathbf{z}, \sigma^2\right) \tag{9}$$

Therefore, for each node with n parents, a set of n weights $\boldsymbol{\beta} = \begin{bmatrix} \beta_1 & \cdots & \beta_n \end{bmatrix}^T$, a standard deviation σ and possibly a constant α are the parameters that need to be chosen. These parameters have clear physical interpretation (body proportions) and are quite easy to select.

5   Experimental Evaluation

We have evaluated the described system on several sequences with different types of motion such as walking, running, jumping, sitting and dancing, captured with six cameras. Data was captured at frame rates between 5 and 10 frames/second. Each camera was captured at resolution of 640×480 pixels. We illustrate the tracking results on two sequences - dance and walking.

First, we show the results of the model acquisition. Fig. 11 shows the original camera views and the corresponding acquired models for five people. The models successfully capture the main features of these very different human bodies. All five models were acquired using the same algorithm and the same Bayesian network with fixed parameters. The convergence is achieved in three to four frames.

Fig. 12 and 13 show the tracking results for the dance and walking sequences. Fig. 14 shows some joint angles as functions of time for the walking sequence. The sequence contained fourteen steps, seven by each leg – which are easily correlated with the joint angle plots.

Tracking results look very good. However, the resolution of the model that was chosen limits the types of motions that can be accurately tracked. For example, we do not model the rotation in the waist, i.e. the shoulders and hips are expected to lie in the same plane. This will result in tracking errors when waist rotation is present in the analyzed motion. However, including additional axes of rotation or additional body parts to the model is very simple, following the framework described in this paper.

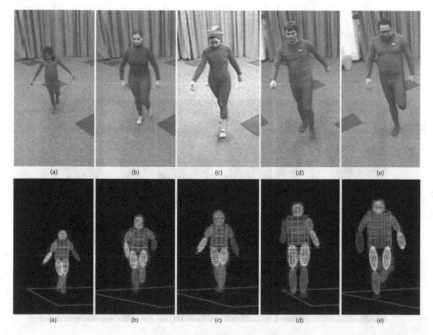

Fig. 11. Original views and estimated models of the five people (a) Aditi (height: 1295.4mm); (b) Natalie (height: 1619.25mm); (c) Ivana (height: 1651mm); (d) Andrew (height: 1816.1mm); (e) Brett (height: 1879mm).

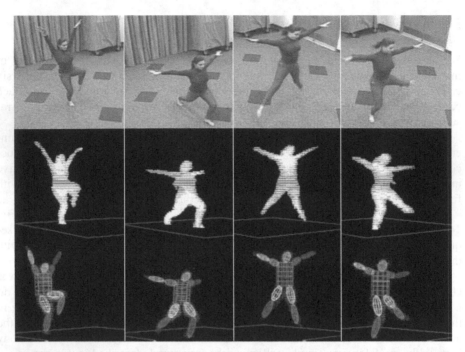

Fig. 12. Tracking results for the dance sequence and one of the six original camera views.

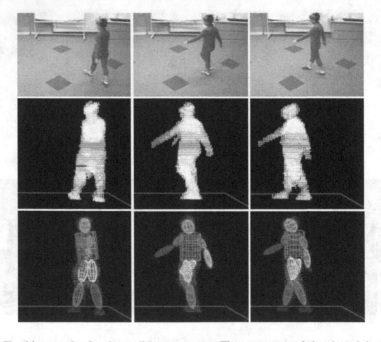

Fig. 13. Tracking results for the walking sequence. First row: one of the six original camera views. Second row: 3D voxel reconstruction viewed from a similar viewpoint. Third row: tracking results.

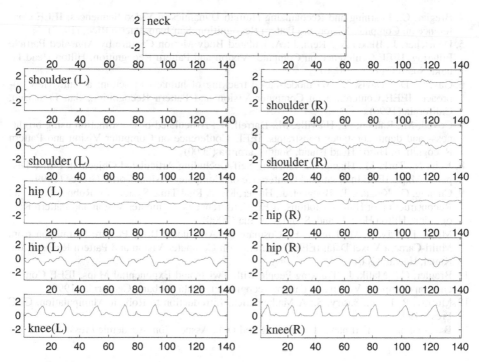

Fig. 14. Joint angles as the functions of the frame number for the walking sequence.

6   Concluding Remarks

We have demonstrated that the body posture estimation from voxel data is robust and convenient. Since the voxel data is in the world coordinate system, algorithms that take advantage of the knowledge of average dimensions and shape of some parts of the human body are easily implemented. This leads to effective model acquisition and voxel labeling algorithms. The use of the Bayesian network to impose known human body proportions during model acquisition phase gives excellent results. The twist-based human body model leads to a simple extended Kalman filter formulation and with imposed angle limits guarantees physically valid posture estimates. The framework is easily expandable for more detailed body models, which are sometimes needed.

References

1. Gavrila, D.: Visual Analysis of Human Movement: A Survey. Computer Vision and Image Understanding, vol. 73, no. 1 (1999) 82-98
2. Kakadiaris, I., Metaxas, D.: Model-Based Estimation of 3D Human Motion with Occlusion Based on Active Multi-Viewpoint Selection. IEEE Conference on Computer Vision and Pattern Recognition, San Francisco, California (1996)
3. Delamarre, Q., Faugeras, O.: 3D Articulated Models and Multi-View Tracking with Physical Forces. Computer Vision and Image Understanding, Vol. 81, No. 3 (2001) 328-357

4. Bregler, C.: Learning and Recognizing Human Dynamics in Video Sequences. IEEE Conference on Computer Vision and Pattern Recognition, San Juan, Puerto Rico, (1997)
5. Deutscher, J., Blake, A., Reid, I.: Articulated Body Motion Capture by Annealed Particle Filtering. IEEE Conference on Computer Vision and Pattern Recognition, Hilton Head Island, South Carolina (2000)
6. Gavrila, D., Davis, L.: 3D model-based tracking of humans in action: a multi-view approach. IEEE Conference on Computer Vision and Pattern Recognition, San Francisco, California (1996)
7. Covell, M., Rahimi, A., Harville, M., Darrell, T.: Articulated-pose estimation using brightness- and depth-constancy constraints. IEEE Conference on Computer Vision and Pattern Recognition, Hilton Head Island, South Carolina (2000)
8. Jojić, N., Turk, M., Huang, T.: Tracking Self-Occluding Articulated Objects in Dense Disparity Maps. IEEE International Conference on Computer Vision, Corfu, Greece (1999)
9. Cheung, G., Kanade, T., Bouguet, J., Holler, M.: A Real Time System for Robust 3D Voxel Reconstruction of Human Motions. IEEE Conference on Computer Vision and Pattern Recognition, Hilton Head Island, South Carolina (2000)
10. Mikić, I., Trivedi, M., Hunter, E., Cosman, P.: Articulated Body Posture Estimation from Multi-Camera Voxel Data. IEEE Conference on Computer Vision and Pattern Recognition, Kauai, Hawaii (2001)
11. Bregler, C., Malik, J.: Tracking People with Twists and Exponential Maps. IEEE Conference on Computer Vision and Pattern Recognition, Santa Barbara, California (1998)
12. Murray, R. Li, Z., Sastry, S.: A Mathematical Introduction to Robotic Manipulation, CRC Press (1993)
13. Bar-Shalom, Y., Fortmann, T.: Tracking and Data Association. Academic Press (1987)

3D Body Reconstruction for Immersive Interaction

Isaac Cohen and Mun Wai Lee

Institute for Robotics and Intelligent Systems
University of Southern California
Los Angeles, CA 90089-0273
{icohen,munlee}@iris.usc.edu

Abstract. In this paper we present an approach for capturing 3D body motion and inferring human body posture from detected silhouettes. We show that the integration of two or more silhouettes allows us to perform a 3D body reconstruction while each silhouette can be used for identifying human body postures. The 3D reconstruction is based on the representation of body parts using Generalized Cylinders providing an estimation of the 3D shape of the human body. The 3D shape description is refined by fitting an articulated body model using a particle filter technique. Identifying human body posture from the 2D silhouettes can reduce the complexity of the particle filtering by reducing the search space. We present an appearance-based learning method that uses a shape descriptor of the $2D$ silhouette for classifying and identifying human posture. The proposed method does not require an articulated body model fitted onto the reconstructed 3D geometry of the human body: It complements the articulated body model since we can define a mapping between the observed shape and the learned descriptions for inferring the articulated body model.

Keywords: 3D body reconstruction, articulated body model, particle filter, posture recognition, support vector machines

1 Introduction

Human body motion tracking and analysis has received a significant amount of attention in the computer vision research community in the past decade. This has been motivated by the ambitious goal of achieving a vision-based perceptual user interface in which the state and the action of the user(s) are automatically inferred from a set video cameras. The objective is to extend the current mouse-keyboard interaction techniques in order to allow the user to behave naturally in the immersed environment, as the system perceives and responds appropriately to user actions. Understanding human action in an environment is a challenging task as it involves different granularity in its analysis and description according to the targeted application. For example, describing a human activity in term of its trajectory constitutes a first level of representation, which may be satisfactory for surveillance applications but remains quite insufficient for understanding human gesture in an interactive environment. Indeed, in such situations richer descriptions are required in order to understand the human activity. Deriving a compact description or signature of the perceived 2D silhouette or of the reconstructed body model is challenging task since the object is an articulated object.

F.J. Perales and E.R. Hancock (Eds.): AMDO 2002, LNCS 2492, pp. 119–130, 2002.

Expensive and cumbersome motion capture systems such as body suits, optical (marker-based) or magnetic tracking systems, and data gloves provide a partial solution. These systems while reasonably accurate and in some cases fast, are restrictive enough that they cannot be used as part of the widely and easily accessible immersive environments we envision: very often a recalibration for specific gestures is required.

Various methods have been proposed for the estimation and analysis of full-body structure (see [10] and references therein). The objective is the development of real-time interactive systems with more sophisticated 2D and 3D tracking and representations [14,20]. Understanding the human motion from a single visual stream is challenging since only the 2D projection of these motions is captured. Recently several researchers focused on the inference of 3D body model from a monocular 2D camera using a human body model [18,7]. The main drawback of these techniques is that roughly one third of the degrees of freedom of the human model are nearly unobservable due to motion ambiguities and self-occlusion. Multiple views are therefore required to disambiguate or identify the human motion.

In this paper we present our approach for capturing 3D body motion and inferring human body posture from detected silhouettes. We show that body silhouettes allow to identify the human body posture and furthermore the integration of two or more silhouettes allows us to perform a 3D body reconstruction. Several approaches have been proposed for estimating human postures in 3D, these approaches rely on three to an array of cameras to capture the human motion [8,15]. Our approach is based on an incremental integration of 2D silhouettes captured by two or more cameras and the representation of the human body shape using generalized cylinders (GC). This GC-based reconstruction is then augmented by fitting an articulated body model. The articulated model selected in this paper consists of 10 joints and 14 segments leading to a 32 degrees of freedom model. The articulated body model is fitted and tracked in time using a particle filter method. We have defined a likelihood function based on similarity between the extracted body medial axes and the articulated body model. This allows us to avoid the need of estimating the widths of body segments that vary among people. The skeleton structure, on the other hand, does not have a significant variance among people (except for a global scaling factor), and can be used for fitting the model to the extracted data without any additional information.

Identifying the human posture from the set of degrees of freedom (dof) of the reconstructed articulated body model requires the mapping of the large space defined by the dof onto the corresponding canonical description of human postures. We present an appearance-based learning formalism that uses a shape descriptor of the $2D$ silhouette for classifying and identifying human posture. The proposed method does not require an articulated body model fitted onto the reconstructed 3D geometry of the human body. It complements the articulated body model since we can define a mapping between the observed shape and the learned descriptions for inferring the state of the dof of the articulated body model. Our approach is based on a shape descriptor of the 2D silhouettes and a learning algorithm based on Support Vector Machine (SVM) in order to account for variability in human posture.

2   3D Articulated Body Model

2.1   3D Shape from Silhouettes

The integration of the silhouettes of the object captured from the different view points allows us to reconstruct the 3D object shape. The 2D body silhouettes detected using a background learning method, define a set of rays from the camera center to the object in the scene. For each camera, this set of rays defines a generalized cone within which the object lies. Integrating the multiple views by intersecting the corresponding generalized cones defines a volume in the scene where the object lies. This volume provides an approximation of the true 3D shape that depends on the complexity of the shape of the object and on the number of views. Several algorithms have been proposed for the construction of volumetric models from a set of silhouettes. These techniques are based on the discretization of the visible volume by voxels which back-projection corresponds to the observed silhouettes cones. These techniques rely on various implementations of the intersection of the generalized cones. These volume intersection techniques are time consuming and require a large number of views (i.e. cameras). The construction of the 3D human body shape is based on the use of two or more apparent contours and *a priori* geometric model of the body shape. Shape from silhouettes techniques methods focus on inferring a surface description of the object from its occluding contours. They also require a large number of views in order to infer a good shape representation. The *a priori* shape model based on the description of body parts using Generalized Cylinder (GC) allows us to derive a 3D reconstruction from two or more silhouettes.

The human body silhouettes are extracted from multiples calibrated cameras. The estimation of the epipolar geometry between any two views is performed beforehand using a set of feature points. Image pair from these two views are rectified using a planar homography transformation so that the epipolar lines are aligned to image scan lines using the method described in [9]. This rectification reduces the numerical complexity of the registration of apparent contours along the epipolar lines. Cross sections of the extracted silhouettes in the two images are matched along the rectified scan lines. This is repeated for every image pairs to obtain multiple sets of matched cross sections.

Each pair of matched cross sections defines a quadrilateral in the 3D space. A GC is formed by fitting a circle within this quadrilateral. After fitting, the center of the circle defines a median axis of the GC. If more than two cameras are used, a reconstructed circle can be validated by projecting the circle to other views and check if it falls within the silhouette. This validation process eliminates false matches of the silhouettes cross sections.

2.2   Initialization of the Articulated Body Model

A human articulated body model is used for tracking. This model consists of 10 joint and 14 segments, representing the head, torso and limbs. Body constraints such as the limits of the joint angles are expressed in the model. The model consists of 32 degrees of freedom that include the global translation, rotation and scale, and local joint rotations. Fitting and tracking are performed using particle filter, which is described in the next section. The tracking however requires good initialization. This section describes the initialization process during which the model is fitted to the set of median points using a 3-level hierarchical approach.

1. *Extract the main axis of the body:* The main axis can be extracted using applying principle component analysis (PCA) on the median points and choosing the first principle axis. However, outstretched arms can affect the principal axes. Therefore, we perform the PCA in two stages. The PCA is performed on all the median points, and the first principle axis is extracted. We then remove half of the median points that are furthest away from the first principle axis. Using the remaining half set of median points, we performed PCA again, and extract the first principle axis as the main axis of the body. In this way, the extracted main axis is less sensitive to an outstretched arm or other outliers.

2. *Extract the position of neck and torso:* Using the body's main axis extracted in Level 1, the height of the person can be determined. We can also coarsely estimate the positions of the neck and the torso. We use these estimates to define search regions in which we locate the neck and torso more accurately using heuristics rules. For the neck, we find the position along the main axis where the width of the silhouette is the narrowest. For the torso, we find a maximal-sized rectangle box that is enclosed by the middle section of the silhouette.

3. *Extract the limbs:* The limbs are extracted from the median points using a PCA approach on the points that are not close to the main body axis. In addition, we use geometric constraints that characterize the human body such as the length ratio of the limbs. This is especially useful in extracting the positions of elbows and knees.

In Figure 1.a we show three views of a gesturing person captured by the system and the corresponding silhouettes extracted using background subtraction. After matching of the silhouettes cross sections, the 3D body reconstruction using GCs is performed as shown in Figure 1.b. Due to the effect of shadows, some parts of the ground are reconstructed around the legs of the person, but these can be easily removed using the knowledge of the ground plane. The obtained GC-based 3D body reconstruction displayed in Figure 1.c is used for initializing the articulated body model. The errors of the initialization can be seen at the intermediate nodes such as shoulders and elbows. This is expected because the locations of these joints are not precisely extracted during this initialization. Nonetheless, this coarse fitting provides a sufficiently good initialization of the articulated model. In the subsequent tracking process, the particle filter will provide a better fitting.

2.3 Articulated Model Fitting and Tracking

The tracking method is based on particle filtering, also known as the Condensation algorithm [12]. This method, which uses the Bayesian framework, is a robust online filtering technique for tracking in the presence of clutters.

In particle filtering, the posterior density is represented by a set of N particles denoted by $\{\theta_{t-1}^i\}_{i=1..N}$, with weights $\{q_{t-1}^i\}_{i=1..N}$. There are 3 basic steps: selection, prediction and updating.

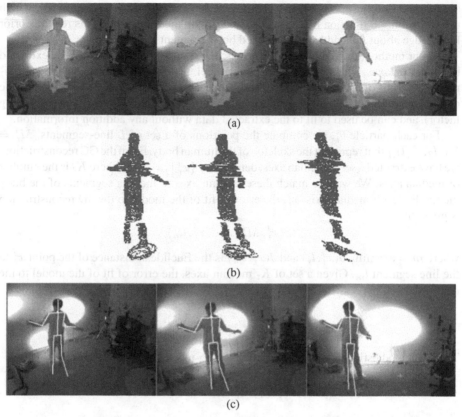

Fig. 1. 3D body reconstruction from three views using a GC-based shape description. (a) displays the views of a gesturing person with the corresponding silhouettes. (b) shows three view points of the reconstructed 3D model. (c) shows the derived initialization of the 3D articulated body model back-projected onto 2D views.

1. *Selection.* Resample with replacement the N particles $\{\theta^i_{t-1}\}_{i=1..N}$, from the set $\{\theta^i_{t-1}\}_{i=1..N}$. The probability of selecting a particle θ^i_{t-1} is proportional to its normalized weight q^i_{t-1}.

2. *Prediction.* The samples are updated according to a stochastic diffusion model,

$$\theta^i_t = \theta^i_{t-1} + w$$

where w is a vector of standard normal random variables.

3. *Updating.* Given an observation z_t, the weights are updated by the likelihood estimates,

$$q^i_t \propto p(z_t|\theta^i_t)$$

The weights are normalized so that $\sum_{i=1}^{N} q^i_t = 1$.

Particle filtering has previously been used for human body tracking in [6], which uses a likelihood function based on edge and region measurements. This requires prior knowledge about the widths of articulated body segments.

In our method, the likelihood function is based on similarity between the extracted body median axes, with the articulated body model. In this way, we avoid the need to estimate the widths of body segments that vary among people. The skeleton structure, on the other hand, does not have significant variance among people (except for a global scaling factor), and can be used to fit to the extracted data without any addition information.

For each particle θ_t^i, we compute the positions of a set of L line-segments, $M_t^i = \{l_1, l_2, ..., l_L\}$ that represent the skeleton of the human body. From the GC reconstruction, we have extracted a set of median axes, denoted by $\{x_t^j\}_{j=1...K_t}$, where K_t is the number of median axes. We want to match these median axes to the line segments of the body model. For each median axis, x_t^j, the error of fit of the model to the 3D reconstruction is given by:

$$\mathcal{E}(x_t^j, M_t^i) = d(x_t^j, l_m)$$

where $m = \arg\min \ d(x_t^j, l_i)$ and $d(x_t^j, l_m)$ is the Euclidean distance of the point x_t^j to the line segment l_m. Given a set of K_t median axes, the error of fit of the model to the data is defined by:

$$\delta_t^i = \frac{1}{K_t} \sum_{j=1}^{K_t} \mathcal{E}(x_t^j, M_t^i).$$

The likelihood estimate is computed using a zero-mean Gaussian function,

$$p(z_t|\theta_t^i) = p\left(\{x_t^j\}_{j=1,...,K_t}|M_t^i\right) = \mathcal{N}(\delta_t^i, 0, \sigma).$$

where σ^2 is the noise variance. This likelihood estimate is used to update the weight q_t^i of the particle θ_t^i.

We have used this particle-based tracking method for fitting and tracking an articulated body model from multi-view video sequences. The video sequences were captured in our laboratory using three synchronized cameras. The particle filter is initialized using the hierarchical fitting method described in Section 2.2. A total of 400 particles were used for tracking. The 2D projection of the fitted articulated body model is shown in Figure 2, along with the corresponding 3D body model rendered at arbitrary views.

3   Human Posture Recognition

Identifying the human posture from the set of degrees of freedom (*dof*) of the reconstructed articulated body model requires the mapping of the large space defined by the *dof* onto the corresponding canonical description of human postures. We present in this paper a global description or signature of human shape allowing to identify the posture of the observed human from 2D silhouettes. This signature has to account for variability in characterizing a posture or a gesture. Indeed, several people will perform similar gestures differently and therefore identifying a gesture from the 2D/3D shape descriptions will require a learning step. We present an appearance-based learning formalism

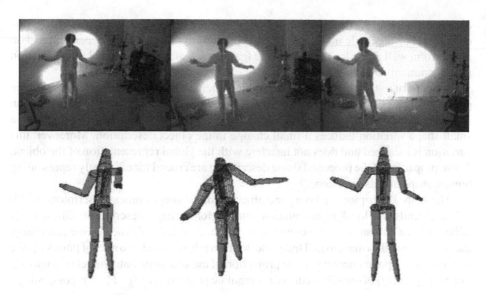

Fig. 2. Articulated body model fitting and tracking derived from the GC-based 3D reconstruction. The first row illustrates the back-projection of the articulated model onto the acquired 2D images. The reconstructed 3D model obtained using 400 particles is rendered from different view points.

that uses a shape descriptor of the $2D$ silhouette for classifying and identifying human posture. The proposed method does not require an articulated body model fitted onto the reconstructed 3D geometry of the human body. In fact, it complements the articulated body model since we can define a mapping between the observed shape and the learned descriptions for inferring the articulated body model. In the following section we will present the shape descriptor considered and the learning algorithm based on Support Vector Machine (SVM).

3.1 Human Body Shape Description

Shape descriptors have been well studied in various fields as they are used for determining the similarity between two shapes. The derived descriptors can be classified in terms of the shapes they characterize *i.e.* 2D contours, 3D surfaces, 3D volumes... to name a few; bending energy functions [23], spin images [13], harmonic shape images [24], shape context descriptors [2]. These descriptors were mainly used for shape matching and therefore focused on characterizing the local properties of the shape. Global models, assume a description of the objects into a set of features or parts segment. Common description rely on parametric models [3,19,22], deformable regions [1,4,5], shock graphs [17]... Shape similarity is then measured by comparing location of features and their spatial distributions. The performances of these approaches depend on the difficult task of segmenting the shape into its corresponding parts. These techniques perform well in the case of shapes of fixed configurations and are not suitable for modeling variability in the observed shapes such as a gesturing person. Finally, a third description approach is based on modeling the geometric distribution of the shape properties such as histograms of angles [11], algebraic moments [16]... These descriptions are view dependent and do not perform well as the localization of the features is lost in the statistical representation used (commonly a histogram).

We present a statistical shape description model that preserves the localization of the geometric features considered. This global representation allows a robust description of shape that accommodates variation of the shape. Indeed, as one would expect a small shape variation induces a small change in the object description. Moreover, this variation is localized and does not interfere with the global representation of the object. These properties of the proposed shape description are crucial for efficiently representing human shape and its variations.

The shape descriptor used is a generalization of the shape context descriptors (SCD) [2], it extends the local representation into a global shape description. Given a 2D silhouette of a human shape we compute a reference circle $\mathcal{C}_\mathcal{R}$ defined by the centroid of the silhouette and its main axis. This circle is uniformly sampled into a set of points P_i. We then consider a polar encoding of the projection of the silhouette onto the set of points P_i. For every point Q_j of the silhouette we accumulate (r, q) where $Q_j - P_i = r(\cos q, \sin q)$.

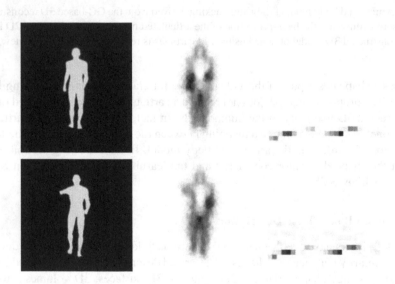

Fig. 3. Examples of global shape descriptors of a walking person (first row), and walking and pointing (second row). The middle column depicts the encoding process while the right column displays the shape signature in polar coordinates.

The polar maps derived for each point P_i are then summed and constitute the signature of the shape. In Figure 3 we show an example of such representation where the signature function, in polar coordinates was centered on the centroid and rendered in Cartesian coordinates. Note that this only a visualization of the representation map. The real signature is in the polar coordinate system.

3.2 Human Posture Inference

Deriving the human posture from the shape descriptor of its silhouettes in 2D or from the reconstructed shape in 3D is a challenging task since it requires taking into account posture variability across people. A method commonly used relies on the articulated body model in order to infer the human posture. The recovery of an articulated body model still requires the interpretation of the 30plus-degree of freedom in order to infer the human posture. This interpretation has to take into account posture variability and errors in the estimation of the articulated model in order to perform an efficient analysis of the 30plus-D parameter space.

In this paper we combine model-based and appearance-based description of human activity for the inference of the person posture. We reduce the complexity of the search in the large parameter space of articulated body model by integrating the appearance-based shape descriptor introduced in the previous section.

We use a Support Vector Machine formalism [21] to learn and classify the set of heterogeneous information provided by the appearance-based descriptors and the degrees of freedom of the articulated body model. The main advantage of using a SVM is its ability to compress the information contained in the training set, since only support vectors are required for the classification.

The main issues in using a machine learning approach are the selection of the features used as training data set and the choice of the data set for training the model. While an articulated body model provides a natural set of features to consider for training purposes, it is time consuming and it is difficult to acquire the 30plus degrees of freedom of the selected model. Conversely, appearance-based shapes are very easy to collect but a correct representation of the shape has to be selected in order to be significant for learning.

The problem we are addressing here is the definition of a decision function that from a set of observations $x \in \mathcal{X} = \{x_i, i = 0..N\}$ and the corresponding labels $y \in \mathcal{Y} = \{y_i, i = 0..N\}$ will make accurate classification of unseen values of x. A very successful approach for solving this supervised learning problem is the support vector machine (SVM) [21]. In this work we are interested in a classification of the observed human postures, therefore the set of available labels is limited to $\mathcal{Y} = \{-1, 1\}$. The decision function is defined by the SVM is:

$$f(x) = sgn \left(\sum_{i=0}^{l-1} \alpha_i^0 y_i K(x_i, x) + b \right),$$

where the coefficients α_i^0 are obtained by maximizing the functional:

$$W(\alpha) = \sum_{i=0}^{l-1} \alpha_i - \frac{1}{2} \sum_{i,j=0}^{l-1} \alpha_i \alpha_j y_i y_j K(x_i, x_j)$$

under the constraints:

$$\sum_{i=0}^{l-1} \alpha_i y_i = 0 \quad \text{and} \quad \alpha_i \geq 0.$$

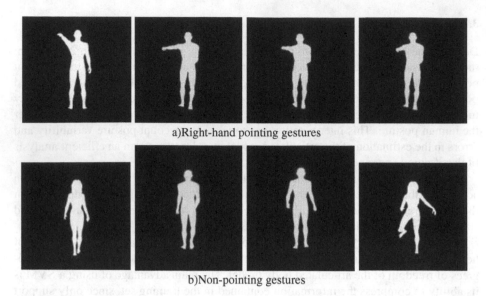

a)Right-hand pointing gestures

b)Non-pointing gestures

Fig. 4. a) and b) Examples of silhouettes used for training the SVM for recognizing right-hand pointing gesture.

The coefficients α_i^0 define a maximal margin hyper-plan in the high dimensional feature space where the data are mapped through the non linear function Φ such that $\Phi(x_i) \cdot \Phi(x_j) = K(x_i, x_j)$. Various kernels K are commonly used (linear, exponential, polynomial...) we will use a linear kernel K using therefore a linear mapping between the feature space and the representation space.

3.3   Training the Support Vector Machine and Classification

The SVM is trained using vectors containing both the 2D shape descriptors defined in the previous section complemented by the degrees of freedom of the articulated body model. The set of instances used for learning are obtained from natural observation as well as computer graphics simulation of human gestures. In the Figure 4 we show some 2D examples used for training the model to identify a right hand pointing from a front view camera. This training dataset was successfully used to classify the right hand pointing gestures captured by a front-view camera and illustrated in Figure 5. This simple example illustrates the use of a global shape description and a SVM for human posture recognition.

4   Conclusion

We have presented in this paper a method for 3D body reconstruction from multiple silhouettes. The integration of silhouettes using a GC-based description of human parts allows us to derive a good description of the human body in 3D. An articulated body

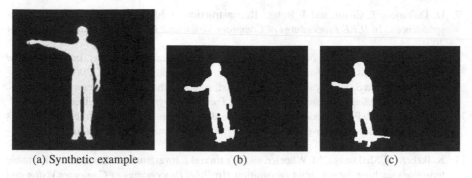

(a) Synthetic example   (b)   (c)

Fig. 5. Examples of right-hand pointing silhouettes identified by the SVM. The SVM classified synthetic examples (generated by Poser) as well as real pointing silhouettes acquired by our system as shown in (b) and (c).

model is fitted to the reconstructed 3D data using a particle filter. The likelihood function used for the particle filtering relies on the similarity between the extracted body median axes and the articulated body model.

The large numerical complexity of the particle filtering prevents us from considering a real-time implementation. However the appearance-based body posture recognition from the 2D silhouettes provides a solution to be considered in the future for reducing the search space of the particle filter technique. Indeed the shape description used along with the SVM learning algorithm allows us to account for variability in body posture while providing a good classification rate.

Acknowledgment

This research was supported by a grant from the Institute for Creative Technologies (ict.usc.edu).

References

1. R. Basri, L. Costa, D. Geiger, and D. Jacobs. Determining the similarity of deformable shapes. *Vision Research*, (38):2365–2385, 1998.
2. S. Belongie, J. Malik, and J. Puzicha. Matching shapes. In *IEEE Proceedings of the International Conference on Computer Vision*, Vancouver, Canada, July 2001.
3. T. Binford. Visual perception by computer. In *IEEE Conference on Systems Science and Cybernetics*, 1971.
4. I. Cohen, N. Ayache, and P. Sulger. Tracking points on deformable objects using curvature information. In *Proceedings of the Second European Conference on Computer Vision*, Santa Margherita Ligure, Italy, May 1992.
5. I. Cohen and I. Herlin. Curves matching using geodesic paths. In *IEEE Proceedings of Computer Vision and Pattern Recognition*, Santa Barbara, June 1998.
6. J. Deutscher, A. Blake, and I. Reid. Articulated body motion capture by annealed particle filtering. In *IEEE Proceedings of Computer Vision and Pattern Recognition*, Hilton-Head, 2000.

7. D. DiFranco, T. Cham, and J. Rehg. Reconstruction of 3d figure motion from 2d correspondences. In *IEEE Proceedings of Computer Vision and Pattern Recognition*, December 2001.

8. S. Iwasawa et al. Human body postures from trinocular camera images. In *International Conference on Automatic Face and Gesture Recognition*, pages 326–331, 2000.

9. J. Gluckman and S. K. Nayar. Rectifying transformations that minimize resampling effects. In *IEEE Proceedings of Computer Vision and Pattern Recognition*, Kauai, December 2001.

10. A. Hilton and P. Fua. Modeling people toward vision-based understanding of a person's shape, appearance, and movement. *Computer Vision and Image Understanding*, 81(3):227–230, 2001.

11. K. Ikeuchi, T. Shakunaga, M. Wheeler, and T. Yamazaki. Invariant histograms and deformable template matching for sar target recognition. In *IEEE Proceedings of Computer Vision and Pattern Recognition*, 1996.

12. M. Isard and A. Blake. Visual tracking by stochastic propagation of conditional density. In *Proceedings of the European Conference on Computer Vision*, pages 343–356, 1996.

13. A. E. Johnson and M. Hebert. Using spin-images for efficient multiple model recognition in cluttered 3-D scenes. *IEEE Transactions on Pattern Analysis and Machine Intelligence*, 21(5):433–449, 1999.

14. I.A. Kakadiaris and D.Metaxas. Three-dimensional human body model acquisition from multiple views. *International Journal of Computer Vision*, 30(3):227–230, 1998.

15. T. Kanade, H. Saito, and S. Vedula. The 3D room: Digitizing time-varying 3D events by synchronized multiple video streams. Technical report, CMU-RI, 1998.

16. R. J. Prokop and A. P. Reeves. A survey of moment-based techniques for unoccluded object representation and recognition. *CVGIP: Graphics Models and Image Processsing*, 54(5):438–460, 1992.

17. K. Siddiqi, A. Shokoufandeh, S. J. Dickinson, and S. W. Zucker. Shock graphs and shape matching. *Computer Vision*, pages 222–229, 1998.

18. C. Sminchisescu and B. Triggs. Covariance scaled sampling for monocular 3d body tracking. In *IEEE Proceedings of Computer Vision and Pattern Recognition*, December 2001.

19. F. Solina and R. Bajcsy. Recovery of parametric models from range images: The case for superquadrics with global deformations. *IEEE Transactions on Pattern Analysis and Machine Intelligence*, 1990.

20. M. Turk and G. Robertson. Perceptual user interfaces. *Communications of the ACM*, March 2000.

21. V.N. Vapnik. *Statistical Learning Theory*. Wiley, New York, 1998.

22. K. Wu and M. Levine. Recovering parametrics geons from multiview range data. In *IEEE Proceedings of Computer Vision and Pattern Recognition*, pages 159–166, June 1994.

23. I. Young, J.Walker, and J. Bowie. An analysis technique for biological shape. *Computer Graphics and Image Processing*, (25):357–370, 1974.

24. D. Zhang and M. Hebert. Harmonic maps and their applications in surface matching. In *IEEE Proceedings of Computer Vision and Pattern Recognition*, 1999.

Wide-Range Tracking of Hands in Real-Time

Yoshio Iwai[1], Tomohiro Mashita[1], and Masahiko Yachida[1]

Graduate School of Engineering Science, Osaka University
1-3, Machikaneyama, Toyonaka, Osaka 560-8531, Japan
iwai@sys.es.osaka-u.ac.jp

Abstract. We propose a method for wide-range tracking of hands in real-time by a vision sensor. By using random sampling and importance sampling, our method can track hands and estimate hand positions in real-time. We use an omnidirectional vision sensor in order to cover the wide range of hand operations. The camera is mounted on the head, which enables the system to be tolerant of the occlusion problem.

1   Introduction

A human being can generate a new idea from others' suggestions by communicating with them. Everyone has had the experience of solving a problem which cannot be addressed alone but only by communicating with others. It is a fact that communication with others is an effective way to generate a new idea or activate creativity. In such a case, what means and information we use for communication with others is important. What place we exchange communications in is also important.

General means of communication are facial expression, gesture, and speaking. These are performed face to face. Only text and voice are used for communication when people are apart from each other. If a system is developed which can send and receive realistic facial expressions and gestures, we will be able to communicate with each other more effectively. The important components in such a system are a natural interface and a real-time process. The pointing gesture is one of the natural interfaces for man-machine interaction. We therefore propose a method for hand tracking in real time and conduct experiments to evaluate its performance.

Many methods for human posture and gesture estimation have been proposed. These methods are divided into two classes: one uses a monocular camera and the other uses multiple cameras.

A method using a monocular camera[1] has the advantage that the system is simple, but has the disadvantage that the occlusion problem occurs frequently. Absolute depth information cannot be estimated, so some posture estimation methods require known parameters such as link length, initial position, and so on. There is another posture estimation method which uses constraints and evaluation functions without known parameters, but this method takes much time for computation.

A method using multiple cameras[2,3] is tolerant of the occlusion problem because it has a wide field of view and absolute depth information is estimated by feature matching. A 3D position can also be estimated. However, a system using multiple cameras is more complex and takes much time for feature matching.

F.J. Perales and E.R. Hancock (Eds.): AMDO 2002, LNCS 2492, pp. 131–141, 2002.

Our proposed method avoids occlusion problems by using a head-mounted camera and by capturing images from the top. A 3D hand position is estimated from the hand regions by giving the lengths of arms in advance. The detecting and tracking of hands is quickly performed by random sampling and importance sampling. The pointing gesture is also recognized in real time. We use a camera with an omnidirectional sensor (HyperOmni Vision)[4] in order to cover the wide range of hand operations.

1.1 Related Work

Many tracking methods using vision sensors have been proposed. Especially, the color model is important in the case of tracking skin regions such as face, hand, and body. The distribution of skin color has been studied by Yang et al.[5]. They concluded that human skin colors cluster in a small region in a color space, that human skin colors differ more in intensity than in color, and that under a certain lighting condition, a skin color distribution can be characterized by a multivariate normal distribution in the normalized color space. Therefore, many methods for visual tracking using a target's color have been proposed[6,7,8,9]. For more robust tracking, a target's shape is also used with performing edge detection[6,10].

Feiguth et al. proposed a fast visual tracking method which reaches up to 30 Hz[11]. Raja et al. use a mixture of Gaussian distributions for skin, clothes, and background models, but the parameters of the mixture Gaussians are fixed[8]. Such a method which fixes color models can be used only if the light condition is stable. Wren et al. use a Kalman filter in order to update the parameters of the color model[2]. Oliver et al. also use a Kalman filter in order to update the parameters of the color model and target position[9]. A Kalman filter is a good estimator if a system noise is Gaussian, but such an assumption is easily broken. Sigal et al. use a histogram for a color model which is a non-parametric representation of distribution[7]. Their tracking method consists of two steps: target motion estimation and target color histogram reconstruction.

MCMC (Monte Carlo Markov Chain)[12] is also used for visual tracking[13]. MCMC has the advantage that an object moving randomly can be tracked because MCMC keeps the distribution of a moving object. By using factor sampling or importance sampling, tracking can be processed quickly. The method in this paper also uses importance sampling and also has the above advantage.

The proposed method uses an omnidirectional image sensor which covers the wide range of hand operations. A spatially independent color model is inadequate for the color expression of hands which move around, therefore we propose a spatially dependent color model for objects that move widely. A spatially dependent color model can express the skin color changes of widely moving objects like hands because the color distribution changes in response to the spatial parameters of the tracked objects.

We explain a pointing operation model in section 2, an algorithm for tracking hands in section 3 and the system which implements the proposed algorithm in section 4. We conduct experiments to evaluate our proposed method in section 5, and conclude in section 6.

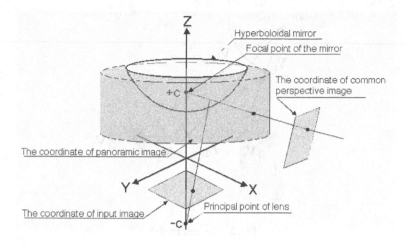

Fig. 1. HyperOmni Vision

2 Models

2.1 Camera Model

We use an omnidirectional image sensor for observation of pointing gestures in our system. This sensor covers the wide range of hand operations and has the same optical characteristics of a common camera, so we can easily estimate the object position. We briefly explain the sensor below.

The sensor consists of a camera fixed upward and a hyperboloidal mirror fixed downward. A hyperboloidal plane of the mirror is expressed by equation 1. A hyperboloidal plane has two focal points: $(0, 0, +c)$ and $(0, 0, -c)$. The hyperboloidal mirror is fixed at the upper focal point, $(0, 0, +c)$, and a focal point of the camera is fixed at the lower focal point, $(0, 0, -c)$, as shown in figure 1. The image plane, xy, is parallel to the XY-plane, and the image plane is fixed at $(0, 0, f - c)$. f is a focal length of the camera.

$$\frac{X^2 + Y^2}{a^2} - \frac{Z^2}{b^2} = -1, \tag{1}$$

$$c = \overline{a^2 + b^2},$$

$$Y/X = y/x, \tag{2}$$

$$Z = \overline{X^2 + Y^2} \tan\alpha + c, \tag{3}$$

$$\alpha = \tan^{-1}\frac{(b^2 + c^2)\sin\beta - 2bc}{(b^2 - c^2)\cos\beta}, \tag{4}$$

$$\beta = \tan^{-1}\frac{f}{x^2 + y^2}, \tag{5}$$

where a, b are parameters of a hyperboloidal plane, α is a depression angle, and β is an angle between the optical axis and projected point (x, y).

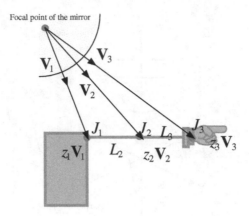

Fig. 2. The arm model

2.2   Arm Model

The human arm model is shown in figure 2. $z_i \mathbf{V_i} \equiv (X_i, Y_i, Z_i)$ expresses the 3D position of each joint, J_i. V_i is the unit vector from the focal point of the mirror to the joint. z_i is the depth of the joint. L_i is the length of the arm.

We can estimate the unit vector, V_i, by target tracking, and also estimate the depth, z_i. We describe depth estimation in the next section.

2.3   Depth Estimation

We can estimate the depth of each joint and then calculate the 3D position of the joint from equation 2 and equation 3 by giving the lengths of arms, L_i, and the vectors to the joints, V_i.

The following constraint is established when the arm length, L_i, is given:

$$\|z_i \mathbf{V}_i - z_{i-1} \mathbf{V}_{i-1}\| = L_i, \tag{6}$$

where $\mathbf{V}_i$ is a view line from the focal point of the mirror to joint i. The above equation can be explicitly solved as follows:

$$z_i = (\mathbf{V_i}, \mathbf{V_{i-1}})z_{i-1} \pm \overline{[(\mathbf{V_i}, \mathbf{V_{i-1}})^2 - 1]z_{i-1}^2 + L_i^2}. \tag{7}$$

All the positions of links are determined relative to z_1 from the above equation. The solution of equation 7 is real when the following condition is satisfied:

$$(\mathbf{V_i}, \mathbf{V_{i-1}})^2 - 1 \ z_i^2 + L_i^2 \geq 0. \tag{8}$$

$(\mathbf{V_i}, \mathbf{V_{i-1}})^2 \leq 1$ and let $-\alpha^2 \equiv (\mathbf{V_i}, \mathbf{V_{i-1}})^2 - 1, \alpha > 0$, then we obtain

$$0 < z_i \leq L_i/\alpha. \tag{9}$$

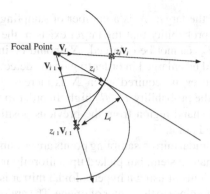

Fig. 3. Solution adjustment in case of imaginary number

When the solution is an imaginary number, we calculate the solution again by using the following equation:

$$z_i = \overline{L_i^2 - z_{i-1}^2}.$$ (10)

The geometrical explanation is shown in figure 3.

3 Tracking

The proposed method uses a centroid of colored region for depth estimation in order to determine the vector V_i. The region of interest (ROI) should be small in order to track the region in real time, but the region should be large enough in order to detect it robustly. The size of the ROI is the cost-time trade-off. While many studies for tracking have been done, it is accepted that random sampling reduces computation time more than processing a whole image. We therefore use random sampling and importance sampling for tracking regions, and also use the color information of the sampling points for object detection.

3.1 Sampling Points

For random sampling, sampling points are uniformly selected in an input image. The color information of the sampling point is compared with the object color model. Random sampling is used for detection and estimation of hand regions when hand regions have not yet been detected.

For importance sampling, sampling points are uniformly selected in the ROI of an input image. Importance sampling is used for estimation of a centroid of the hand region more accurately. The probability that a sampling point is on the tracked object can be defined as follows:

$$P = 1 - \left(\frac{R - T_a}{R}\right)^N P_r(R) \quad (0 < T_a < R),$$ (11)

where T_a is the area of the target, N is a number of sampling points, R is the area of ROI, and $P_r(R)$ is the probability that the target exists in the ROI. In the case where the area of the target, T_a, cannot be enlarged, N should be increased or R should be reduced or $P_r(R)$ should be enlarged in order to gain the detection probability P. Much computation time, however, is required when N is increased. R should therefore be reduced while keeping the probability $P_r(R)$ high. In order to reduce the area of R, we predict a position of the hand region from the previous position, and then we sample data around the predicted point.

As we use a hyperboloidal mirror, sampling points are not simply picked up uniformly in the xy-image coordinate system, but picked up uniformly in the $r\theta$-polar coordinate system. One of the problems of using a hyperboloidal mirror is that the object becomes small when the object gets close to the center of image. The area of the object is dependent on not only the distance between the camera and the object, but also the depression angle. XY-uniform random sampling on such a sensor causes an estimation bias which drifts an estimate outward. We addressed this problem by performing random sampling uniformly in the $r\theta$-polar coordinate system. Sampling points therefore become sparse in proportion to r.

3.2   Color Model with State

There are many methods for visual tracking using an object color model or using an object contour model. Most color models are static, C_μ, C_Σ, or even supports temporal change of color, $C_\mu(t), C_\Sigma(t)$. This is inadequate for modeling changes of object color captured by the omnidirectional sensor because the light condition differs at each location owing to the wide field of view. Figure 4 shows the intensity distribution in the room used for experiments.

The object color model should be changed as the state of the object changes. So we use a color model with state, $C_\mu(s), C_\Sigma(s)$. In this paper, we use the quantized position value as the state. The hand operations are quantized by M clusters.

3.3   Position Estimation of Targets

A target is tracked by comparing the color models, $C_\mu(s), C_\Sigma(s)$, with the color of a sampled point, $C(\mathbf{x}_i)$, determined by random and importance sampling. The dissimilarity, $D(\mathbf{x}_i)$, is defined by the following equation:

$$D(\mathbf{x}_i) \equiv \min_{s=0}^{M} \ (C(\mathbf{x}_i) - C_\mu(s))^T C_\Sigma^{-1}(s)(C(\mathbf{x}_i) - C_\mu(s)) \ . \tag{12}$$

Sampling point, $\mathbf{x}_i$, is a target if the dissimilarity is less than a certain threshold value, K. The area S and the centroid G of the target are estimated by the following equation:

$$d(\mathbf{x}_i) = \begin{array}{ll} 1 & D(\mathbf{x}_i) < K \\ 0 & \text{otherwise} \end{array} , \tag{13}$$

$$S = \sum_{i=0}^{N} d(\mathbf{x}_i), \tag{14}$$

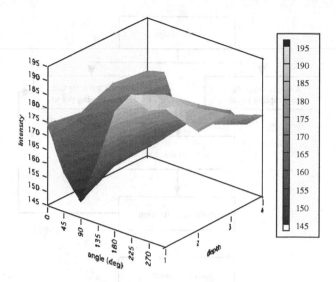

Fig. 4. Intensity distribution in the room used for experiments

$$G = \frac{\sum_{i=0}^{N} d(\mathbf{x}_i)\mathbf{x}_i}{S}, \tag{15}$$

where N is the sum of sampling points. In the case of $S = 0$, the target cannot be found and importance sampling is stopped. The positions of tracked centroids are used for depth estimation of the arm.

4   Implementation

The outline of our system is shown in figure 5. The sum of random sampling points and importance sampling points is fixed at constant N, so the computation is performed at a constant rate. The importance sampling points are picked up around the region centering a centroid of a tracking target.

5   Experimental Results

We conduct experiments on real images by using an SGI workstation (Onyx2, MIPS R12K, 400 MHz) with an omnidirectional sensor (TOM-02-0013, Suekage). The size of an image is 720×243 pixels. The lengths of all arms, L_i, are given in advance, and the root depth, z_1, is also given.

Figure 9 shows the marker tracking using importance and random sampling. Figure 10 shows the results of tracking. The processing time is shown in figure 7. The processing time of sampling and color evaluation at $N = 1000$ is about 150 ms per frame. The processing time of image capturing and posture estimation is 20 ms per frame. Of course, the processing time increases in proportion to the number of sampling points. Figure 8

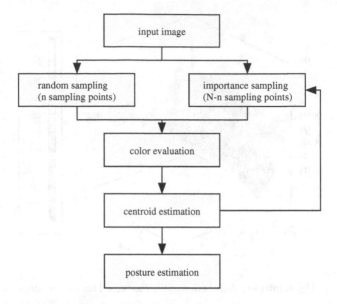

Fig. 5. Tracking and estimation system

Fig. 6. Experimental environment

shows variances of estimation of a hand position. The hand position is stably estimated by increasing sampling points because the variances decrease in proportion to the number of sampling points.

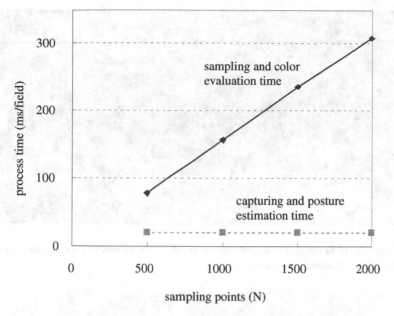

Fig. 7. processing time

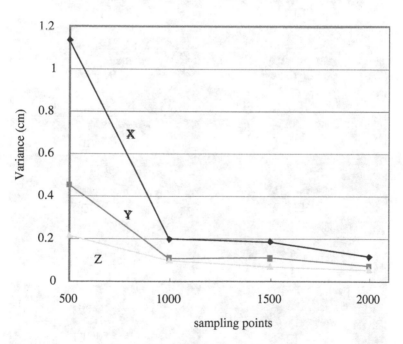

Fig. 8. Variance of position estimation

Fig. 9. Examples of sampling points: random sampling points are sparsely located and importance sampling points are densely populated

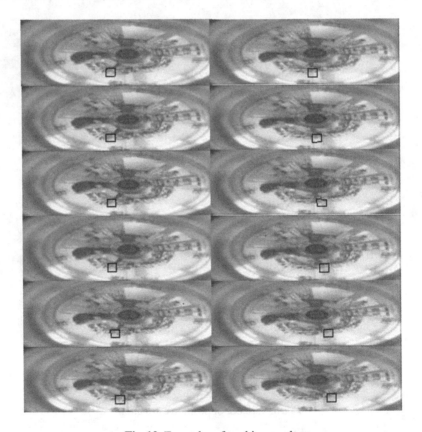

Fig. 10. Examples of tracking results

6 Conclusion

We proposed a method for hand tracking in real time using the color model with state. The proposed color model enables us to track hands in the wide range of an omnidirectional camera. In future work, we intend to improve the processing time of tracking and enhance our color model so that it can be used for an active camera. In this paper, we cannot evaluate the accuracy of depth estimation, therefore, we will compare the accuracy of our method with that of the Polhemus magnetic sensor.

References

1. Chounhong Pan and Songde Ma.: 3D Motion Estimation of Human by Genetic Algorithm. In *Proc. ICPR*, Vol. 1, pp. 159–163, 2000.
2. Christopher Wren, Trevor Darrell, and Alex Pentland.: Pfinder: Real-Time Tracking of the Human Body. *IEEE Trans. PAMI*, 19(7):780–785, July 1997.
3. T. Darrell, G. Gordon, M. Harville, and J. Woodfill.: Integrated Person Tracking Using Stereo, Color, and Pattern Detection. In *Proc. CVPR*, pp. 601–608, California, June 1998.
4. K. Yamazawa, Y. Yagi, and M. Yachida.: Omnidirectional Imaging with Hyperboloidal Projection. In *Proc. IROS*, Vol. 2, pp. 1029–1034, 1993.
5. J. Yang, L. Weier, and A. Waibel.: Skin-Color Modeling and Adaptation. In *Proc. ACCV*, pp. 687–694, 1998.
6. Y. Wu and T. S. Huang.: A CP-inference Approach to Robust Visual Tracking. In *Proc. ICCV*, Vol. 2, pp. 26–33. IEEE, 2001.
7. L. Sigal, S. Sclaroff, and V. Athitsos.: Estimation and Prediction of Evolving Color Distributions for Skin Segmentation under Varying Illumination. In *Proc. CVPR*, Vol. 2, pp. 152–159, 2000.
8. Y. Raja, S. J. McKenna, and S. Gong.: Tracking and Segmenting People in Varying Lighting Conditions Using Colour. In *Proc. Automatic Face and Gesture Recognition*, pp. 228–233, 1998.
9. Nuria Oliver, Alex Pentland, and François Bérand.: LAFTER: Lips and Face Real Time Tracker. In *Proc. CVPR*, pp. 123–129, 1997.
10. S. Birchifield.: Elliptical Head Tracking Using Intensity Gradients and Color Histograms. In *Proc. CVPR*, pp. 232–237, 1998.
11. P. Feiguth and D. Terzopoulos.: Color-based Tracking of Heads and Other Mobile Objects at Video Frame Rates. In *Proc. CVPR*, pp. 21–22, 1997.
12. W. R. Gilks, S. Richardson, and D. J. Spiegelhalter, editors.: *Markov Chain Monte Carlo in Practice*. Chapman & Hall/CRC, New York, 1996.
13. Michael Isard and Andrew Blake.: ICONDENSATION: Unifying Low-Level and High-Level Tracking in a Stochastic Framework. In *Proc. ECCV*, Vol. 1, pp. 893–908, 1998.

Recognition, Tracking, and Reconstruction of Human Motion

J. Sullivan, M. Eriksson, and S. Carlsson

Computational Vision and Active Perception Laboratory (CVAP)
KTH, SE-100 44 Stockholm, Sweden

Abstract. This paper describes a system aimed at automising the reconstruction of human motion. Human motion can be described as a sequence of 3D body postures. View based recognition of these postures forms the basis of human tracking algorithms [18]. These postures are defined by the underlying skeleton, an articulated structure of rigid links connected at rotational joints. The skeleton can be reconstructed if the rotational joints are tracked [11]. A set of posture specific key frames with pre defined joint locations are stored. Joint locations from these key frames can be mapped to actual frames once correspondence between the two shapes has been achieved. The rotational joints are in general not well defined in 2D images thus the iterative process of successively repeating point localisation and 3D reconstruction allows one to impose the geometric definition on the points. The power of the approach presented is demonstrated by the recognition, self calibration and 3D reconstruction of a tennis stroke seen from two cameras achieved without precalibrated cameras or manual intervention for initialisation and error recovery.

1 Introduction

The problem of automatic 3D reconstruction of human motion from single or multiple views has received much attention in recent years. To date no completely automated system, requiring no manual intervention at some critical stage, has been presented. The systems and algorithms in the literature typically include:

- Commercial motion capture systems using multiple pre-calibrated cameras and specific body markers.
- Manual or semi-automatic tracking of specific body locations and subsequent reconstruction from the single or multiple views tracked.
- 3D model based tracking systems using manual initialisation and error recovery.

Systems that track specific body locations require manual initialisation and usually reinitialisation after a limited number of frames [14,10]. Manual tracking of body location with self calibration has been presented in [11]. The most common method of human tracking is with the use of 3D primitives for body parts and calibrated cameras: [3,6,13,8,9,15,16,17]. Their motion in 3D is inferred indirectly from frame-to-frame tracking in images from single or multiple cameras. Impressive tracking results have been achieved, however, they require manual initialisation and can in general only recover from minor tracking failures.

F.J. Perales and E.R. Hancock (Eds.): AMDO 2002, LNCS 2492, pp. 142–154, 2002.

The key problem with these system is that once the tracking fails it cannot recover automatically. Tracking recovery and initialisation are essentially the same problem both requiring recognition of the 3D posture. Tracking algorithms have developed based upon this premise. These autonomous tracking systems require a posture to be recognised every time it occurs in an image sequence. This can be done using for instance chamfer matching [7,20] or more advanced shape matching methods [2,18]. Storing a set of posture specific key frames with pre defined body locations, allows tracking of these locations. It necessitates establishing the correspondence between the key frame and the actual frame via shape matching [12,18]. The computed correspondence being used to transfer body locations to the image sequence.

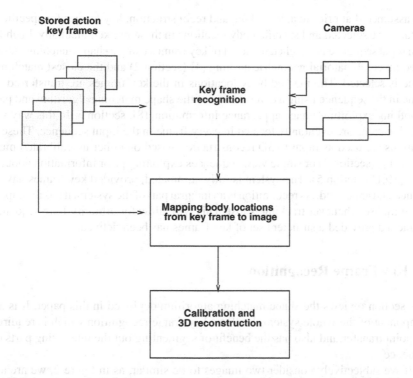

Fig. 1. This is an overview of the stages of our human motion reconstruction system. The three stages are recognition, point transfer and 3D reconstruction.

This approach has been demonstrated in the localisation of rotational joints in image sequences [18]. In the next stage of development, this method of tracking is combined with the self-calibration procedure of [11] to calibrate a two camera system and reconstruct the 3D motion. We combine automatic tracking of rotational body joints with the strict well defined geometric constraints associated with a skeletal articulated structure. This allows the identification of outliers based on epipolar geometry and thereby improve the tracking quality. This paper gives a description of each stage of the process in conjunction with results of an automatically tracked, calibrated and reconstructed 3D human motion from two camera views.

1.1 Overview

Figure 1 illustrates the stages of the complete system described for 3D reconstruction of human motion. There are three main steps:

- Selection of the closest key frame for each input frame.
- Mapping of specific body locations from key frame to actual frame.
- 3D reconstruction based on tracked body locations.

It is assumed that prior to any tracking and reconstruction, key frames for specific body postures are selected and specific body locations in these marked manually. Each frame in an input sequence is matched to the set of key frames using a shape matching algorithm based on combinatorial geometric hashing [4] (section 2) and the closest matching key frame is selected. The marked body locations in the key frames are transferred to the frame in the sequence using a combination of the shape matching algorithm and particle smoothing exploiting image appearance information[18], section 3. In this way visible body locations are eventually located in every frame in the input sequence. These body locations are used as input to 3D reconstruction based on either un calibrated multiple views [11] (section 4) or single view sequences exploiting prior information about body parts [19,1] (section 5). The system is fully automated, provided key frames have been defined and annotated. As recognition is an integral part of the system, it has the capability to reinitialise whenever tracking is lost. This will allow for arbitrary long sequences to be tracked provided a sufficient set of key frames has been defined.

2   Key Frame Recognition

This section reviews the shape matching algorithm deployed in this paper. It is a vital component of the whole system. It allows key-frame recognition which is required for the point transfer and also has the benefit of segmenting out the interesting parts of the sequence.

If we subjectively consider two images to be similar, as in figure 2, we are almost always able to map a certain point in one image to a specific point in the other. This ability, to define a correspondence field between the two images, can be taken as a starting point for defining equivalence between shapes. If the field represents a smooth deformation of one shape into the other, we are likely to consider the shapes as similar or belonging to the same category. The smaller the deformation the larger the similarity. Computing a correspondence field between two shapes enables us to measure the similarity of the shapes without any prior segmentation. The process of computing correspondence relies on the ability to define invariants, properties common to the two shapes. Since correspondence is between points on the shapes, these invariants should be computed from local pointwise information. For well defined transformations such as rigid or linear, invariants can be computed by simple algebraic manipulations. For general smooth deformations however, invariants are associated with qualitative topological shape properties. Computation of correspondence fields between shapes that are smooth deformations of each other demands computing qualitative invariants from sets of points on the shapes.

The algorithm for shape matching is based on an improved version [5] of the combinatorial geometric hashing algorithm for computing point to point correspondence between two shapes as presented in [4]. Shapes in the form of edge maps are extracted using the Canny edge detector. A certain point on a shape has a location and also a tangent direction. A complex of points and lines is formed by sampled shape points and their associated tangent lines. In figure 2 consider the complexes from two shapes when the points are in "perceptual correspondence". A certain line in one complex intersects between two points in exactly the same way in the two shapes. The order of the points $a_1 \ldots a_4$, $b_1 \ldots b_4$ is preserved as they are traversed e.g clockwise and so is the order of the line directions.

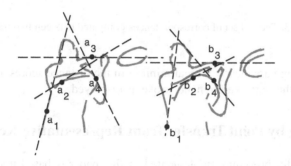

Fig. 2. Two point-line sets with the same topological type.

The three components, point order, line direction order and relative intersection of the lines and the points in a complex defines the *topological type* of the point-line complex. By selecting groups of four points in the two shapes we can build a voting matrix of correspondence between points which is updated whenever two four-point sets have the same topological type. Using a simple greedy algorithm on this matrix results in a unique point to point correspondences between the two shapes. Figure 3 shows examples of correspondences after applying this algorithm.

This correspondence field between the two shapes is used for key frame recognition and mapping of body locations. By computing the minimum residual of the field after translating the input shape, we obtain a measure of shape similarity. If the shapes are qualitatively similar, the field will in general be continuous and smooth and the residual is low. Evaluation of the matching algorithm for action recognition was made on a 30 sec sequence of tennis. The sequence essentially contains forehand and backhand strokes and many frames of the player in a stand by position. The player was automatically coarsely tracked to supply a region of interest. In the upper half of this region Canny edge detection was applied.

A specific frame (251 of the sequence) was selected as the key frame and the matching algorithm was applied to all frames in the sequence and a matching score was computed,

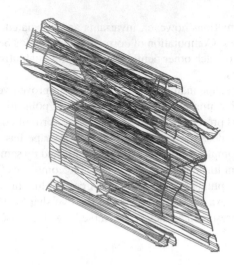

Fig. 3. The full set of correspondences computed between two frames.

see figure 4. There are clearly 9 local minima in the distance scores and each of these corresponds to the start of a forehand stroke as displayed.

3   Tracking by Point Transfer from Representative Key Frames

The point transfer procedure implemented in this paper is based upon the algorithm described in [18]. A brief synopsis is given in this section. To track specific body locations, four different key frames from a sequence of a forehand shot were prepared and body locations were marked. These are shown in figure 5

Key Frame Selection. In fig. 6 the distance scores for frames 503, 507, 510 and 513 vs. the frames in the forehand sequence 130 -140 are plotted. From this figure we can easily find the closest key frame for all frames and it can be seen that these appear in the correct order 503, 507, 510, 513 as the frames 130-140 are traversed. There is the option to impose the ordering constraint on the key frames which will simplify the key frame selection even further, which was implemented for the body localisation results.

Automatic Tracking. A brief high level synopsis of the method has already been given. We will just reiterate here that pre-defined rotational joint points, $\{P_k^R\}_{k=1}^K$, are transferred from the matched posture key-frame to the actual image using the local correspondences found between the key-frame and the image [5]. This transfer results in estimates $\{y_k\}_{k=1}^K$ of the body joint locations in the image $\{P_k\}_{k=1}^K$. These points will, in general, not all be inliers. Further colour and spatial constraints can be applied to refine these estimates. This is achieved by implementing a Monte Carlo algorithm to produce random samples from the smoothing density, $p(P_{1:K}|\mathbf{y}_{1:K})$. Figure 7 displays results achieved using this method for a forehand stroke in one of the camera views.

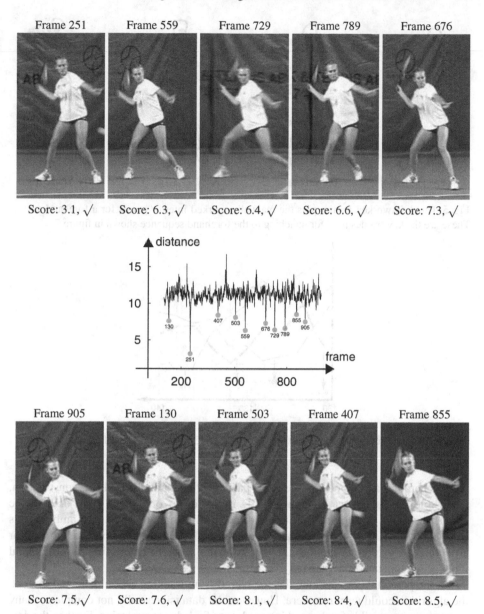

Fig. 4. Classified forehands for the sequence of the woman playing tennis. The displayed forehands correspond to the local minima of the distance scores.

4 3D Reconstruction from Two Views

When the tracking module has found the feature points in the two image sequences, the reconstruction module uses that data to compute the 3D structure of the image sequence. This is accomplished by first applying Tomasi-Kanade factorization on the

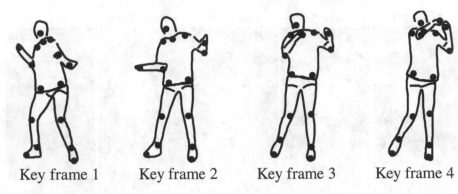

Key frame 1   Key frame 2   Key frame 3   Key frame 4

Fig. 5. Hand drawn key frames plus the manually marked interior points for a forehand stroke. These are the key frames used for matching to the forehand sequence shown in figure 7.

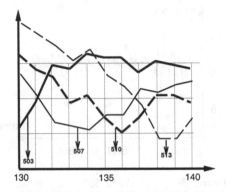

Fig. 6. Distance scores for frames 503, 507, 510 and 513 to all frames in a forehand sequence.

data, generating a 3D model as well as a pair of affine cameras. In this reconstruction, the whole time sequence of points in 3D is treated as one single rigid object. The reconstruction is correct only up to an affine transformation. The affine ambiguity is resolved by finding a rectifying transformation exploiting specific constraints valid for articulated structures in motion: the length of the segment connecting two rotational joints stays constant over time [11].

In the perfect case, when the data delivered from tracking is complete and correct, the algorithm could terminate here. However, the data is generally not complete; many features are impossible for the tracking module to find, due to occlusion. Further, the data may contain outliers. The tracking algorithm is able to identify the first case (occlusion) and returns the occluded features as unknown. However, if a point is simply erroneously tracked, it is up to the reconstruction module to catch this. This can be done, either by identifying that the point pair is inconsistent according to the computed F-matrix, or that the limb on which the point resides on is of bad length. Reconstruction follows these steps, figure 10 shows the reconstructions of the forehand stroke achieved at different stages:

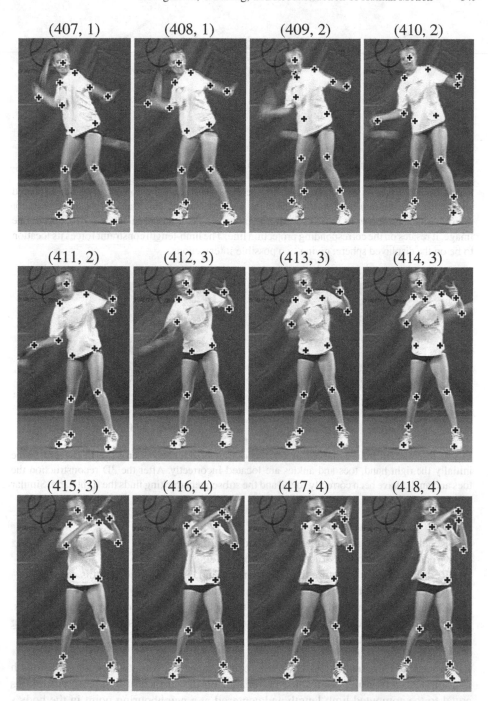

Fig. 7. Estimates of the joint locations of the skeleton after applying the point transfer and particle smoothing. The numbers displayed correspond to the frame number of the sequence and to the matched key frame displayed in figure 5.

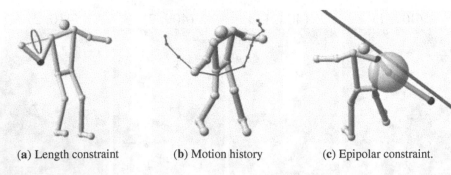

(a) Length constraint   (b) Motion history   (c) Epipolar constraint.

Fig. 8. (a) The right wrist, shoulder, and limb lengths constrain the elbow to lie on the displayed ellipse. (b) The motion trajectory of the right wrist is shown. This trajectory can be used for interpolation. (c) The right wrist's location is incorrect. As it has been accurately found in one image, it resides on the corresponding projection line. The limb-length constraint forces its location to be on the displayed sphere, giving two possible intersections.

3rd Frame   7th Frame

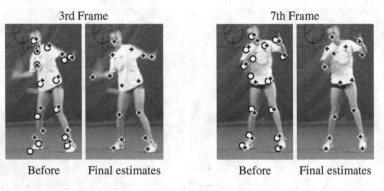

Before   Final estimates   Before   Final estimates

Fig. 9. Reprojected points marked as circles, output of tracking as crosses. In the 3rd frame initially the right hand, toes and ankles are located incorrectly. After the 3D reconstruction the toes and ankles have been correctly found and the subsequent tracking finds the right hand. Similar comments can be made for frame 7.

1. Receive data from tracking module and identify inliers.
2. Create an affine reconstruction based on inliers.
3. Rectify to metric structure using symmetry and constant limb-lengths constraints.
4. Identify outliers based on metric inconsistencies.
5. Estimate erroneous and missing points using limb-lengths and temporal constraints.
6. Reproject the reconstruction. Give the resulting 2D points back to the tracking module in order to improve the tracking.

Limb Length Constraints. After metric rectification, an estimate for each limb-length is computed. A missing point must be located on the surface of a sphere with radius equal to the computed limb-length and centered at a neighbouring point in the body's kinematic chain. This, by itself, is a fairly weak constraint, but it may be combined with others. If a missing point has two sure neighbours in its kinematic chain, its location is reduced to the circle created by the intersection of two spheres, see figure 8(a).

Temporal Constraints - 3D Interpolation. The algorithm runs without a dynamic model for the activity. However, in order to insert a missing point, the algorithm is allowed to make the assumption that each joint moves locally on a straight line in 3D space. Combined with the limb-length constraint, it can be used to generate a fairly good approximation about the position of the missing joint. The error will of course increase with the "jerkiness" of the motion, since a jerky motion invalidates the straight line assumption. The motion of the right wrist, giving the temporal constraint, is shown in figure 8(b).

Single View Constraints. Generally, a point is only occluded in one camera. Information from the other camera can be used to insert a missing point. This can be dangerous, as we are relying that this point is correct. The point has not been tested for either affine or metric consistency. If this constraint is used, the 3D point must reside on the projection line of the 2D point with regard to the computed camera. If the limb lengths are known, there are only two possible locations of the point assuming of the neighbours is known, figure figure 8(c). This can be disambiguated by using temporal constraints.

Feedback to Tracking. Once a 3D reconstruction is achieved, it can be backprojected, using the reconstructed cameras, into the images. This backprojection can then serve as the initial condition for a second iteration of the tracking. Results of this process are displayed in figure 9. In the two frames displayed the right hand is initially located incorrectly by the tracking process, but after backprojection and subsequent refinement of the estimate the right hand is accurately found.

5   Work in Progress: 3D Reconstruction from a Single View

Given the projections of rotational joints of an articulated structure, for instance a human skeleton, there is a range of possible structures in 3D. In essence a single view does not permit a unique unambiguous 3D reconstruction. However, if the length of links between rotational joints is known and the camera is calibrated, this ambiguity reduces to a twofold choice of directions in 3D for each link [19,1]. By using prior information in the form of 3D key frames for various postures, this ambiguity can potentially be resolved automatically. Figure 11 shows an example of this. The systematic use of prior information in the form of 3D key frames, is a topic of work in progress and will eventually be extended to cases where link lengths are not known.

6   Conclusions

This paper presents a shift in the traditional approach to the reconstruction of human motion. The matching process based upon the concept of *topological type* is the machinery that allows this approach to work. To improve the robustness of the point transferral, the spatial relationship of the body points and colour information is exploited. Experimental evidence has been presented which displays the power of our approach to segment out specific actions of interest, ie a forehand stroke and then to localise the body points in these highlighted frames. Therefore the need for explicit initialisation of a complicated model has been by-passed. Errors obtained in one frame do not propagate to the next frame. 3D reconstruction and the tracking are integrated using constraints from

Reconstruction Results

(a) 3D reconstruction of the forehand using manually selected points. This can be considered as ground truth.

(b) Reconstruction on the raw data points delivered from the tracking module. The occluded points are not reconstructed.

(c) Reconstruction after outlier detection and selective single view reconstruction. In the 3rd and 4th frames the right wrist is incorrectly reconstructed.

(d) Reconstruction after the second iteration of tracking. The position of the right wrist in the 3rd and 4th frames has been corrected.

Fig. 10. Displayed are the reconstructions obtained at each stage of the entire process. The quality of the reconstruction based on automatically tracked points is similar to that of the hand clicked sequence. This example demonstrates the power of combining strict geometric constraints with the more heuristic key frame mapping tracking.

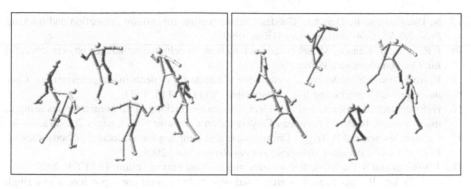

Key frame Posture   **Reconstruction**

Fig. 11. An example of reconstruction from a single camera. The left image is a panoramic view of the 3D key frame posture and the right of the reconstruction from clicked data.

epipolar geometry and articulated structures in order to verify tracking, find outliers and reconstruct despite of missing or erroneous data.

Obviously a number of issues remain unanswered and should be subject to further research. The future of the approach depends to a large extent on the ability to generate these key frames in an efficient manner and demonstrate that generic classes of motion can be tracked using a limited number of key frames.

References

1. C. Barrón and I. Kakadiaris. Estimating anthropometry and pose from a single uncalibrated image. *Computer Vision and Image Understanding*, 81(3):269–284, 2001.
2. S. Belongie, J. Malik, and J. Puzicha. Matching shapes. In *ICCV*, 2001.
3. C. Bregler and J. Malik. Tracking people with twists and exponential maps. In *CVPR*, 1998.
4. S. Carlsson. Order structure, correspondence and shape based categories. In *Shape Contour and Grouping in Computer Vision*, pages 58–71. Springer LNCS 1681, 1999.
5. S. Carlsson and J. Sullivan. Action recognition by shape matching to key frames. Workshop on Models versus Exemplars in Computer Vision at CVPR, 2001.
6. J. Deutscher, A. Blake, and I. Reid. Motion capture by annealed particle filtering. *Proc. Conf. Computer Vision and Pattern Recognition*, 2000.
7. D. M. Gavrila. Pedestrian detection from a moving vehicle. In *ECCV*, 2000.
8. D.M. Gavrila. The visual analysis of human movement: A survey. *Computer Vision and Image Understanding*, 73(1):82–98, January 1999.
9. D. Hogg. Model-based vision: a program to see a walking person. *J. Image and Vision Computing*, 1(1):5–20, 1983.
10. N. R. Howe, M. E. Leventon, and W. T. Freeman. Bayesian reconstruction of 3d human motion from single-camera video. In S. A. Solla T. K. Leen and K-R. Muller, editors, *Advances in Neural Information Processing Systems 12*, 2000.
11. D. Liebowitz and S. Carlsson. Uncalibrated motion capture exploiting articulated structure constraints. In *Proc. 8th Int. Conf. on Computer Vision*, July 2001.
12. G. Mori and J. Malik. Estimating human body configurations using shape context matching. In *Poc of European Conference on Computer Vision*, 2002.

13. N. Paragios and R. Deriche. Geodesic active regions for motion estimation and tracking. *Proc. 7th Int. Conf. on Computer Vision*, 1999.
14. J. Rehg and T. Kanade. Model-based tracking of self-occluding articulated objects. *Proc. 5th Int. Conf. on Computer Vision*, 1995.
15. K. Rohr. Towards model-based recognition of human movements in image sequences. *Computer Vision, Graphics and Image Processing*, 59(1):94–115, 1994.
16. H. Sidenbladh, M. Black, and D.J. Fleet. Stochastic tracking of 3d human figures using 2d image motion. In *Poc of European Conference on Computer Vision*, pages 702–718, 2000.
17. C. Sminchisescu and B. Triggs. Covariance scaled sampling for monocular 3d body tracking. In *Proc. Conf. Computer Vision and Pattern Recognition*, 2001.
18. J. Sullivan and S. Carlsson. Recognizing and tracking human action. In *ECCV*, 2002.
19. C. J. Taylor. Reconstruction of articulated objects from point correspondences in a single image. *Computer Vision and Image Understanding*, 80(3):349–363, 2000.
20. K. Toyama and A. Blake. Probabilistic tracking in a metric space. In *ICCV*, July 2001.

Tracking the Human Body
Using Multiple Predictors

Rui M. Jesus[1], Arnaldo J. Abrantes[1], and Jorge S. Marques[2]

[1] Instituto Superior de Engenharia de Lisboa, Postfach 351-218317001
Rua Conselheiro Emído Navarro, n⁰ 1, 1940-014 Lisboa, Portugal
{rmfj,aja}@isel.pt
http://www.deetc.isel.ipl.pt
[2] Instituto de Sistemas e Robótica, Instituto Superior Técnico
Av. Rovisco Pais, 1049-001 Lisboa, Portugal
jsm@isr.ist.utl.pt

Abstract. The objective of this work is to track the human body from a video sequence, assuming that the motion direction is parallel to the image plane. Tracking the human body is a difficult task because the human body may have unpredictable movements and it is difficult to accurately detect anatomic points in images without using artificial marks. Furthermore, self occlusions often prevent the observation of some body segments. This paper describes a tracking algorithm, which avoids the use of artificial marks. The proposed system is able to learn from previous experience, and therefore its performance improves during the tracking operation. The ability of the tracking system to gradually adapt to a particular type of human motion is obtained by using on-line learning methods based on multi-predictors. These predictors are updated in a supervised way using information provided by a human operator. Typically, the human operator corrects the model estimates several times during the first few seconds, but the corrections rate decreases as time goes by. Experimental results are presented in the paper to illustrate the performance of the proposed tracking system.

Keywords: Articulated models, Multiple predictors, Kalman filtering

1   Introduction

Tracking the human body from a video sequence is a challenging problem with applications in several areas, such as bio-mechanics and virtual reality [5]. Several attempts were made to automate this operation [2,7,8,9]. However, the problem is di cult and a robust solution remains to be found. The main di culties concern the accurate representation of the human shape and motion as well as the detection of anatomic points in the image sequence.

One way to circumvent these di culties is by using of a set of visual marks attached to the body [5]. This technique makes the tracking operation much easier but it is not possible in many applications. Another possibility, which avoids the use of arti cial marks, is to perform the analysis of the human motion

F.J. Perales and E.R. Hancock (Eds.): AMDO 2002, LNCS 2492, pp. 155–164, 2002.

manually, using a graphical editor. This is however inadequate when large video sequences are involved.

This paper proposes an interactive system to track the human body without visual marks and with the ability to learn from the corrections made by a human operator. Learning methods are used to improve the prediction of the body position and shape in future frames using multiple predictors. The paper is organized as follows: section 2 provides a system overview; section 3 describes the use of multiple predictors for tracking the human motion; section 4 presents the experimental results and section 5 concludes the paper.

2   System Overview

The tracking system described in this paper is based on three models: a body model, a motion model and a visual appearance model. A 2D articulated model is used to represent the body shape in the image (see g. 1). This model consists of 10 segments connected by 9 articulations.

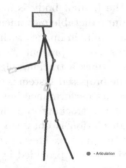

Fig. 1. Articulated model.

Each segment of the articulated model represents a body part (neck, shoulders, torso, arms, forearms, hip, thighs and legs) which is assumed to be rigid and with known length. Each articulation linking two segments is modelled by a rotation angle θ and by a translation vector t, which accounts for small displacements of the rotation center. The articulated model is therefore characterized by a set of parameters (articulation angles and displacement vectors) and some of their derivatives.

A dynamic model is used to describe the evolution of the shape parameters and allows the prediction of the human shape in the next frame using a linear predictor. However, a linear predictor is not able to represent complex motions nor motion variability. The proposed system uses two prediction mechanisms, running in parallel: a linear predictor trained from the data; and a look-up table (dictionary) containing a list of exceptions (in which the linear predictor failed).

The appearance model consists of a set of 1D and 2D RGB pro les, centered at speci c points of the imaged human body. During tracking, these features are automatically detected in the image using methods (template matching) similar to the ones adopted in [1].

The tracking algorithm performs ve steps in each frame (see g. 2):

- prediction - multiple predictors are used, in parallel, to estimate the position and shape of the body in the next frame using past information;
- feature detection - for each predicted con guration, a set of visual features is obtained from the image, using template matching;
- ltering - this step updates each predicted con guration, using the corresponding visual features obtained in the previous step; this operation is performed using the equations of the extended Kalman lter [3];
- evaluation - each model estimate is evaluated by measuring the color di erence between the appearance model and the image;
- selection - selects the model with largest matching score.

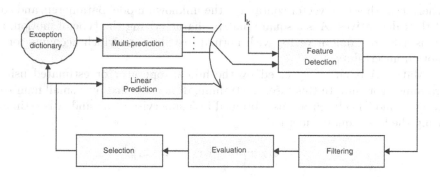

Fig. 2. Block diagram of the tracking system.

The prediction step plays a central role in this system. It is used for data fusion as usual in Kalman ltering but it is also used in feature detection and in the prediction of self occlusions (regions of the human body which can not be observed in the image). The performance of the system depends on the accuracy of the predictor. Only small errors can be corrected by the ltering step.

In order to improve the quality of the prediction results, the system needs to incorporate learning capabilities. Two learning phases are considered. The rst phase consists of training the linear dynamic model used to describe the human motion. An improved motion model is obtained after this stage. However, in general this training model still fails when unpredictable movements occur. To solve this problem, a multi-prediction technique is used. This technique consists of creating a dictionary of exceptions containing the predictors for each con g-uration of the human body in which the linear predictor failed. Whenever one of these con gurations occurs in an image, the dictionary is used to generate additional predictors.

3   Multiple Predictors

Detecting visual features and guessing which of them are occluded in the current frame are two related operations performed by the system which depend on the accuracy of the prediction stage. If the prediction error is too large, the system may not be able to recover and has to be re-initialized by the operator. In order to improve the prediction results, two types of dynamic models are used, simultaneously, by the system:

a linear model, from which a linear predictor can be obtained;
a look-up table (dictionary of exceptions), which generates additional prediction estimates.

The linear dynamic model is de ned by the stochastic equation [6],

$$x_k = Ax_{k-1} + w_k \qquad (1)$$

where x_k is the state vector containing the unknown model parameters and some of their derivatives, A is a square matrix characterizing the type of motion, and w_k is a white random vector with normal distribution, which accounts for the motion uncertainty.

Matrix A is either speci ed by the human operator or estimated using a training algorithm. In this case, the training data is de ned by a small number of previous model con gurations, obtained in a supervised way and A is estimated using the least squares method,

$$A = \arg\min_A \ _k \|x_k - Ax_{k-1}\|^2 \qquad (2)$$

This learning phase enables the linear predictor to adapt to the speci c type of motion being tracked, increasing the performance of the tracking system.

Figure 3 shows three random sequences synthesized using equation (1), after training matrix A. They all correspond to realistic human motions of the same activity. The trained dynamic model is still able to cope with motion variability but now in a very controlled way.

Unfortunately, human motion is too complex to be modelled by a linear dynamic system, even in the case of a simple activity. Typically, there are always some unexpected movements (in the sense that they are not linearly predictable), which have to be considered separately as exceptions. Consequently, the tracking system considers a second learning phase, wherein a dictionary of exceptions is dynamically created while the video sequence is analyzed in a supervised way.

Every time the automatic tracker fails, producing an erroneous estimate of the human body, the operator corrects the model. After that, the estimate obtained in the previous frame is used as a new dictionary entry, pointing to the current model con guration. Due to motion uncertainty, several predictions can be associated to the same model parameters. The dictionary of exceptions stores all model con gurations in which the linear predictor has failed as well as the

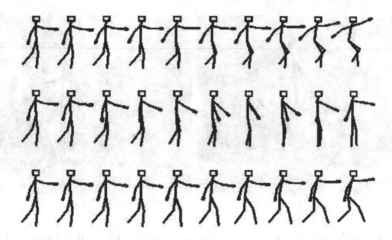

Fig. 3. Synthesized random sequences produced by the linear dynamic model after training.

Table 1. Structure of the dictionary of exceptions.

Entries ($\hat{x}_{k-1}$)	Predictors ($\hat{x}_k^-$)
$x^{(1)}$	$x^{(1,1)} x^{(1,2)} \ldots x^{(1,n_1)}$
$x^{(2)}$	$x^{(2,1)} x^{(2,2)} \ldots x^{(2,n_2)}$
.	
.	
.	
$x^{(d)}$	$x^{(d,1)} x^{(d,2)} \ldots x^{(d,n_d)}$

corresponding solutions provided by the user. Table 1 shows how the data is organized in the dictionary of exceptions: the i-th entry contains a model con guration $x^{(i)}$ and the corresponding list of predictors, where $x^{(i,j)}$ is the j-th predictor of the i-th entry.

The dictionary of exceptions is used whenever one of its entries is close to the current model con guration. Speci cally, the predictors stored in the i-th dictionary entry are used to predict the model con guration at the k-th frame if the following two conditions are veri ed,

$$i = \arg\min_n \|x_{k-1} - x^{(n)}\|, \tag{3}$$

and

$$\|x_{k-1} - x^{(i)}\| < \gamma \tag{4}$$

where γ is a given threshold.

(a)   (b)

Fig. 4. Example with 2 predictors: a) linear predictor; b) predictor provided by the dictionary of exceptions.

The tracking system uses the dictionary of exceptions as a multiple predictor generator. Whenever one of the dictionary entries occurs, multiple predictors are automatically generated and used. Multiple predictors are used when an exception is detected: the linear predictor,

$$x_k^{(0)-} = Ax_{k-1} \qquad (5)$$

and the predictors triggered by the exception,

$$x_k^{(j)-} = x^{(i,j)} \qquad (6)$$

where $j \in \{1, \ldots, n_i\}$.

The multiple predictors compete in parallel to achieve the best results. They are used in two blocks of the tracking system (see g. 2): feature detection and ltering. Di erent estimates of the body con guration (at least two) are usually obtained and a criterion is needed to automatically select the best estimate. The criterion adopted in this paper is based on color histograms. For each estimate, a set of such histograms is evaluated from the image data, using small windows centered at the speci c body points. These histograms are compared with pre-de ned histograms (stored in the appearance model) using the L_1 norm. The best predictor is selected.

Figure 4 shows an example in which two predictors are used to estimate the human body con guration. Figure 4a shows the results obtained with the linear predictor while gure 4b shows the predictor provided by the dictionary. The second predictor was chosen by the tracker.

4   Experimental Results

The tracking system proposed in this paper was used to track the human body in several activities (walking, cycling, writing on a board and running). The

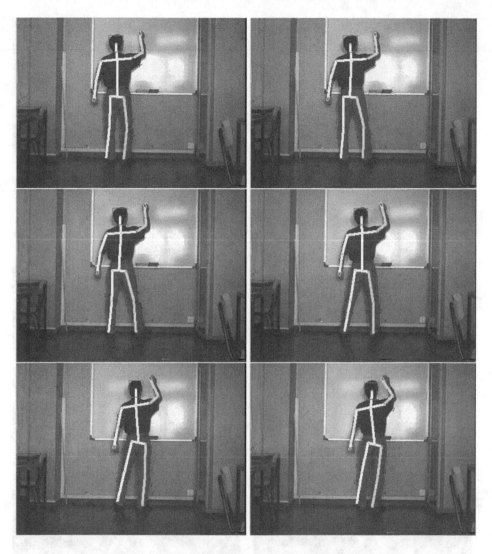

Fig. 5. Tracking results in a non-periodic activity in six consecutive frames.

images associated to the rst three types of activities were obtained with an analog camera and digitized at 13 frames/sec. The images of a person running were obtained with a digital color camera at 25 frames/sec. The motion is approximately periodic in three of the activities (walking, cycling and running), and non-periodic in the other (writing on a board).

The automatic system managed to successfully track the rst three types of activities (walking, cycling, writing on a board) without any human intervention during the second learning phase. The exception dictionary and the multi-prediction technique were needed only for the last activity (running) since

Fig. 6. Tracking results for a running sequence in six consecutive frames.

unpredictable motions occur at some running phases. Figure 5 shows the results obtained by the tracking algorithm in a non-periodic sequence of a person writing on a board. The exception dictionary was not needed in this sequence since the motion is slow. Figure 6 shows six consecutive frames of a running sequence and the tracking results obtained with the interactive system proposed in this paper. This video sequence has 200 images. Only 9 of them were manually corrected.

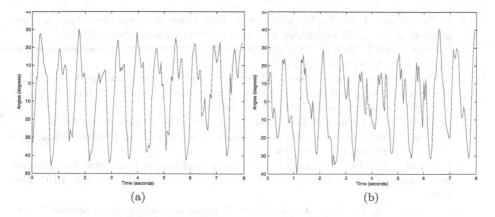

Fig. 7. Parameters evolution: a) right arm; b) left arm.

The multiple predictor technique was used 38 times: the linear predictor was chosen 8 times and the predictor given by the exception dictionary was chosen in the remaining times.

Figure 7 shows the evolution of the rotation angle associated with the arms (running sequence). As expected, the evolution is periodic and the arms are in opposing phase. It should be stressed that a large number of self-occluded segments are present in this sequence. Furthermore, the background (trees) is neither static nor homogeneous. The tracking algorithm manages to solve both di culties well in most of the frames.

5   Conclusion

This paper describes a semi-automatic system to track the human body without arti cial marks. The system has learning capability in the sense that the tracking performance improves during each experiment. Every time the user corrects the tracker output, the corrected model is stored in a dictionary. This information is then used automatically by a multi-prediction technique to correct similar cases in the future.

The main di culties associated with the automatic operation of the tracker concern unpredictable motions and the presence of moving non-homogeneous background. The system is however able to deal with both of these di culties well, most of time, as shown in the experiments described in the paper.

References

1. A. Blake and M. Isard. *Active Contours: The Application of Techniques from Graphics, Vision, Control Theory and Statistics to Visual Tracking of Shapes in Motion.* Springer-Verlag London, 1998.

2. C. Bregler and J. Malik. Tracking people with twists and exponential maps. *Proceedings of the IEEE Computer Vision and Pattern Recognition*, 1998.
3. R. Brown and P. Hwang. *Introduction Random Signals and Applied Kalman Filtering*. John Wiley and Sons, 1992.
4. J. Craig. *Introduction to Robotics Mechanics and Control*. Addison-Wesley, 1955.
5. D. Gavrila. The visual analysis of human movement: A survey. *Computer Vision and Image Understanding*, 73(1):82–98, 1999.
6. A. Gelb. *Applied Optimal Estimation*. MIT press, Cambridge, Mass, 1974.
7. D. Hogg. Model based vision: A program to see a walking person. *Image and Vision Computing*, 1(1):5–20, 1983.
8. I. Kakadiaris and D. Metaxas. Three-dimensional human body model acquisition from multiple views. *Internacional Journal of Computer Vision*, 30(3):191–218, 1998.
9. H. Sidenblabh, M. Black, and D. Fleet. Stochastic tracking of 3d human figures using 2d image motion. *European Conf. on Computer Vision*, 2000.

Motion Estimation of Articulated Objects from Perspective Views

Xiaoyun Zhang[1], Yuncai Liu[1], and Thomas S. Huang[2]

[1] Institute of Image Processing and Pattern Recognition
Shanghai Jiao Tong University, P.R. China, 200030
{xiao_yun,whomliu}@sjtu.edu.cn
[2] Beckman Institute,University of Illinois at Urbana-Champaign, Urbana, IL 61801
huang@ifp.uiuc.edu

Abstract. Motion estimation of articulated objects with two subparts from monocular images are studied in this paper for three cases: 1) one subpart translates, and the other one rotates around the joint; 2) the two rotation axes of the subparts are parallel to each other; 3) the two rotation axes of the subparts are perpendicular with each other. Three motion models are established respectively, and the conditions for a solution are discussed in detail, which shows that only 4, 5 and 6 image point correspondences are needed respectively for the three kinds of articulated motion estimation. The problem of how to distribute the points on the two subparts is also explained. Finally, a lot of simulated experiments are presented, validating the rightness and efficiency of our motion models.

Index terms: Articulated object, motion estimation, joint, point correspondence

1 Introduction

A substantial amount of work has been devoted to methods for estimating object motion based on images since the 1970 s. Most of the work [5][6] has been done under the assumption that the observed objects are rigid. However, many objects in the real world are non-rigid at all, such as human beings, animals or robots. In recent years, there has been a growing interest in the study of non-rigid motion [7][8][9], including human motion and gait analysis. One important kind of non-rigid objects is articulated objects.

By an articulated object, we mean an object consisting of rigid parts connected by joints. Articulated motion is piecewise rigid motion. The rigid parts conform to the rigid motion constraints, but the overall motion is not rigid. Prominent examples of objects, which can be approximately modeled by articulated objects, are human bodies and robot arms. Since each subpart of the articulated object is rigid, one obvious way for the articulated motion estimation would be to partition the original object into rigid subsets by some image segmentation, and thereafter use rigid-body methods to estimate the motion of each subpart independently. But, this kind of technique has two disadvantages.

F.J. Perales and E.R. Hancock (Eds.): AMDO 2002, LNCS 2492, pp. 165–176, 2002.
© Springer-Verlag Berlin Heidelberg 2002

First, segmentation itself is a di cult task, especially the correct segmentation of object subparts in di erent frames of images. The error of the segmentation would lead to the failure of motion estimation. Second, independently analyzing connected parts would ignore the very useful information provided by the interdependencies of subparts of an articulated object.

Although some work has been done in the eld of articulated motion estimation, most of them are based on strict constraints imposed on the motion type or the structure of articulated objects. John A. Webb and J .K. Aggarwal [1] did some original research based on the xed axis assumption, i.e., all movement consists of translations and rotations about an axis that is xed in direction for short periods of time. In the paper [2], a decomposition approach was presented to solve the coplanar motion with a point known or xed, where the human was modeled as an articulated object with 11 links. Coplanar multi-link motion is discussed in [3], which mainly makes use of the length invariance of each link through motion. Both [2] and [3] use joint points between links as correspondent features, which is practically di cult to obtain precisely. Paper [4] brings forward the concept of Euclidean hinge , which in fact means that the two rotation axes of the linked objects are along the same direction.

This paper explores the motion estimation of an articulated object of two rigid subparts connected by a joint in three cases: 1) one subpart translates, and the other one rotates around the joint; 2) the two rotation axes of the subparts are parallel to each other; 3) the two rotation axes of the subparts are perpendicular with each other. These three models are very common in the robots, machinery or human structure. We prove that four, ve and six image point correspondences, respectively, are needed to solve the motion of the articulated object for the three cases. This is a great improvement, because even in the motion estimation of a single rigid object, at least 5 point correspondences are required. What s more, since we solve the motion of two subparts together, it is expected to be more robust when noise are presented. Simulated experiments validate the method.

2   Notation and Camera Model

The camera used to get the images of articulated objects, is assumed to be a pinhole camera model. The coordinates of the 3D world are chosen to be xed on the camera with the origin coinciding with the center of the camera and the z-axis coinciding with the optical axis and pointing to the front of the camera. The image plane is located at $z = 1$ with its coordinates axes X and Y parallel to the axes x and y of the 3D world coordinates, respectively. Then according to perspective projection, we have

$$X = \frac{x}{z}, Y = \frac{y}{z}$$ (1)

where (x, y, z) is the 3D world coordinates of a point p, and (X, Y) is the coordinates of its correspondent image point P in the image plane.

Fig. 1 shows a model of an articulated object with two subparts. The 3D points on the subpart A and B before motion are represented by p, q, and their correspondent points after motion are noted as p', q'. The coordinates of all the 3D points p, p', q, q' are expressed in the 3D world coordinate system $o - xyz$. Accordingly, the image points are represented as P, Q, P', Q', whose coordinates are expressed in the image coordinate system $O - XY$. The 3D joint and its image are denoted as j, J, and their correspondences after motion are j', J' .

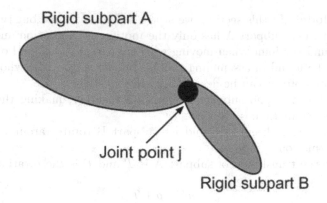

Fig. 1. An articulated object with two rigid subparts connected by a joint

3   Motion Models and Condition for Solutions

Many articulated objects, such as the robots or robot arms, do not move in a random way. Usually, there is only one degree of freedom between two links, or one link only translates or rotates, and the connected link rotates in the same or a perpendicular direction. For example, prismatic and revolute joints are the most common joints in robotics. Therefore, in the following, we will propose three kinds of model for an articulated object with two links or subparts, and present the motion models with analysis of solutions.

But before any further discussion, let s notice one important di erence between the motion models of rigid objects and articulated objects. In the previous work of motion estimation, it uses a conventional way to describe the motion as a rotation R around the origin of the 3D coordinates followed by a translation T, i.e.,

$$p' = Rp + T \tag{2}$$

As for the articulated motion, we can also adopt this motion model, but it does not make full use of the very useful articulated character of the object. The two subparts A and B do not move independently, they have a common point, i.e., the joint. Therefore, the joint point satis es both motion of the two subparts. If we contain this information in the motion equations directly, we will see that it would be easier for us to solve the problem. So in the following motion models, the motion is expressed by rotating around the joint not the origin of the coordinate system, i.e.,

$$p' = R(p - j) + j + T \qquad (3)$$

This means that the object rotates around j following a translation T.

3.1 Model 1: Subpart A Translates and Subpart B Rotates around the Joint

Motion Model. In this section, we study a kind of simple but typical articulated objects, i.e., subpart A has only the motion of translation and subpart B rotates around the joint when moving with subpart A. This kind of articulated motion can be found in assembling robots. In such a case, the whole motion of the articulated object can be decomposed in two steps:

Step 1): Subpart A and subpart B translate together, making the subpart A arrive to its destination;

Step 2): Subpart A keeps still and let subpart B rotates around the joint to another destination.

Suppose the translation of subpart A is T and R is the rotation of subpart B, then we have

$$\begin{aligned} p' &= p + T \\ j' &= j + T \\ q' &= R[(q + T) - j'] + j' \end{aligned} \qquad (4)$$

Eliminating T, we get

$$\begin{aligned} p' &= p - j + j' \\ q' &= R(q - j) + j' \end{aligned} \qquad (5)$$

When the joint j and j' are computed, translation T can be easily obtained by

$$T = j' - j \qquad (6)$$

Condition for a Solution. Since there are only image data of the object available in the given, the 3D points p, q, j and their correspondences p', q', j' in the $o - xyz$ are unknown. What we know are image points P, Q, J and P', Q', J'. In the following, suppose the image points have been matched, i.e., image point correspondences $P \leftrightarrow P'$, $Q \leftrightarrow Q'$ and $J \leftrightarrow J'$ are given, we analyze the condition for a solution, i.e., how many image point correspondences $P \leftrightarrow P'$ and $Q \leftrightarrow Q'$ are needed to get the motion parameters and depth information of the articulated object.

Expand Eqs.(4) and (5) in the coordinates of the points,

$$\begin{aligned} x'_p &= x_p - x_j + x'_j \\ y'_p &= y_p - y_j + y'_j \\ z'_p &= z_p - z_j + z'_j \end{aligned} \qquad (7)$$

$$\begin{aligned} x'_q &= r_{11}(x_q - x_j) + r_{12}(y_q - y_j) + r_{13}(z_q - z_j) + x'_j \\ y'_q &= r_{21}(x_q - x_j) + r_{22}(y_q - y_j) + r_{23}(z_q - z_j) + y'_j \\ z'_q &= r_{31}(x_q - x_j) + r_{32}(y_q - y_j) + r_{33}(z_q - z_j) + z'_j \end{aligned} \qquad (8)$$

where (x_p, y_p, z_p) are for the coordinates of p, (x'_p, y'_p, z'_p) for p', (x_q, y_q, z_q) for q, (x'_q, y'_q, z'_q) for q', (x_j, y_j, z_j) for j, (x'_j, y'_j, z'_j) for j', and $r_{ij}, i, j = 1, 2, 3$ are the components of the rotation matrix R. According to the projective projection (1), we can eliminate the unknown z'_p in Eqs.(7) to get two equations about the three unknowns z_p, z_j, z'_j

$$X'_p = \frac{x'_p}{z'_p} = \frac{z_p X_p - z_j X_j + z'_j X'_j}{z_p - z_j + z'_j}$$
$$Y'_p = \frac{y'_p}{z'_p} = \frac{z_p Y_p - z_j Y_j + z'_j Y'_j}{z_p - z_j + z'_j} \qquad (9)$$

where (X_p, Y_p) are for the coordinates of P, (X'_p, Y'_p) for P', (X_j, Y_j) for J, (X'_j, Y'_j) for J'. Similarly, combine Eqs.(1) and (8) by eliminating the depth z'_q, we can get two equations about the unknowns R, z_j, z'_j, z_q

$$X'_q = \frac{x'_q}{z'_q} = \frac{r_{11}(z_q X_q - z_j X_j) + r_{12}(z_q Y_q - z_j Y_j) + r_{13}(z_q - z_j) + z'_j X'_j}{r_{31}(z_q X_q - z_j X_j) + r_{32}(z_q Y_q - z_j Y_j) + r_{33}(z_q - z_j) + z'_j}$$
$$Y'_q = \frac{y'_q}{z'_q} = \frac{r_{21}(z_q X_q - z_j X_j) + r_{22}(z_q Y_q - z_j Y_j) + r_{23}(z_q - z_j) + z'_j Y'_j}{r_{31}(z_q X_q - z_j X_j) + r_{32}(z_q Y_q - z_j Y_j) + r_{33}(z_q - z_j) + z'_j} \qquad (10)$$

where (X_q, Y_q) and (X'_q, Y'_q) are the coordinates of Q, Q' respectively. Thus, every pair of point correspondence $P \leftrightarrow P'$ or $Q \leftrightarrow Q'$ will provide two equations about the unknowns R, z_j, z'_j, but with an additional depth unknown z_p or z_q for the point p or q.

If m pairs of image correspondences $P \leftrightarrow P'$ and n pairs of $Q \leftrightarrow Q'$ are given in subpart A and subpart B respectively, then there will totally be $2(m+n)$ equations. The number of unknown parameters are $3+2+(m+n)$, where 3 is for the matrix R since a rotation matrix introduces only 3 independent parameters, 2 is for the depth of the joint j and j', $m+n$ are for the depth of 3D points with m points at subpart A and n points at subpart B. However, the depth of 3D points can be solved from images only up to a scale factor [5]. This can be easily explained by the fact that Eqs. (9) and (10) still hold when z_p, z_q, z_j, z'_j are multiplied by any positive constant. Thus, there are in fact $4 + m + n$ unknowns to be solved. In order to get a solution, the number of equations must equal to or be larger than the number of unknowns, i.e.,

$$2(m + n) \geq 4 + m + n \qquad (11)$$

Or

$$m + n \geq 4 \qquad (12)$$

This means that with only four point correspondences, the motion of the whole articulated object can be estimated. With $m + n = 4$, we have 8 nonlinear equations about 8 unknowns, which can be solved by nonlinear least-squares.

3.2 Model 2: Subpart A and Subpart B Rotate along the Same Rotation Direction

Motion Model. There are also many articulated objects, which have only one degree of freedom between links. For example, the crus and the thigh of a human leg tend to rotate around the same direction. In robots, the rotation axes of two connective links are often designed to be parallel, such as PUMA. In this section we consider this kind of articulated motion. In a traditional way, the motion can be modeled as follows

$$p' = R_p(p - j) + j + T$$
$$q = R_p(q - j) + j + T \tag{13}$$
$$j' = j + T$$

$$q' = R_q(q - j') + j' \tag{14}$$

where Eqs.(13) means that subpart A moves to its destination, and point q on subpart B moves with subpart A together to an intermediate position q; Eq.(14) shows that q rotates around the joint j' to its destination. Eliminating T and q, we have the motion equations

$$p' = R_p(p - j) + j' $$
$$q' = R_q R_p(q - j) + j' \tag{15}$$

From the motion assumption, we know that the rotation axes n_p of R_p and n_q of R_q are the same, i.e.,

$$n_p = n_q = n \tag{16}$$

From the property of rotation matrices, the product of two rotation matrices of the same rotation axis is still a rotation with the same rotation axis, which still rotates along the same axis. For convenience, we note $R_q = R_q R_p$, then R_q rotates along n. The Eqs.(15) can be write in a simpler form

$$p' = R_p(p - j) + j' $$
$$q' = R_q(q - j) + j' \tag{17}$$

According to Eqs.(17), the motion can be explained in the following steps:
Step 1): Subpart A and B rotate around the joint respectively to the poses which are parallel to their after-motion poses;
Step 2): Translate subpart A and B together to an after-motion place.

Condition for a Solution. In the same way as the previous part, according to the number of equations and unknowns, we analyze the condition for solution.

Combining Eqs. (1) and (17) by eliminating the depth z'_p, z'_q of points p', q', each point correspondence can provide 2 equations with an additional unknown for the point depth. So if m and n pairs of image point correspondences are provided on subpart A and B respectively, there are $2(m+n)$ equations available. Accordingly, there are $4 + 2 + (m + n)$ unknowns in all, where 4 for R_p and R_q (2 for their common rotation axis n, 2 for their rotation angels), 2 for the depth of the joint j and j', $m+$ are for the depth of the m points p and n points q. However, since we cannot get the absolute depth of points from images but to a scale factor, so there are in fact $5 + m + n$ unknowns to be solved. Let

$$2(m + n) \geq 5 + (m + n) \tag{18}$$

we have

$$m + n \geq 5 \qquad\qquad (19)$$

This shows that 5 point correspondences are needed to get the motion by solving 10 nonlinear equations. Remembering that at least 5 image point correspondences [5] are needed even in the motion estimation of one rigid object, we see that it is really a great improvement to consider the two subparts of an articulated objects together than analyzing the two rigid subparts independently, which would need 10 point correspondences in all.

3.3   Model 3: Subpart A Moves in Random and Subpart B Rotates around the Joint along the Direction Perpendicular with the Rotation Axis of Subpart A

Motion Model. This is another common motion of an articulated object. For a robot, its trunk always moves with both rotation and translation, i.e., in a random way, and its arms rotate around the trunk along a direction, which is perpendicular with the rotation axis of the trunk. See Fig. 2, the rotation axes of the two subparts are perpendicular, i.e., $n_p \perp n_q$.

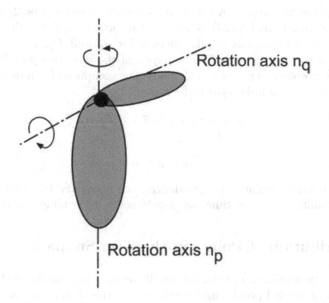

Rotation axis n_q

Rotation axis n_p

Fig. 2. An articulated object with two perpendicular rotation axes

The motion can also be implemented by two steps:

Step 1): Subpart A moves to its after-motion position, with subpart B moving together;

Step 2): Subpart B rotates around the joint to its destination.

The motion equations for the step 1) are

$$p' = R_p(p - j) + j'$$
$$q = R_q(q - j) + j' \tag{20}$$
$$j' = j + T$$

In step 2), only the point on subpart B rotates around the joint j'

$$q' = R_q(q - j') + j' = R_q R_p(q - j) + j' \tag{21}$$

Therefore, the whole motion of the articulated object can be modeled as

$$p' = R_p(p - j) + j'$$
$$q' = R_q R_p(q - j) + j' \tag{22}$$

with a constraint

$$n_p \cdot n_q = 0 \tag{23}$$

Condition for a Solution. Similar to the previous parts, here we do not describe the analysis process in detail. Given m and n pairs of image point correspondences on subpart A and B respectively, there will be $2(m + n)$ equations with a constraint Eq.(23) about the rotation axes. Accordingly, there are $6 + 2 + (m + n)$ unknowns in all, where 6 for R_p and R_q, 2 for the depth of the joint j and j', $m + n$ are for the depth of the m points p and n points q. Because the absolute depth of points cannot be computed from images, so there are in fact $7 + m + n$ unknowns to be solved. Let

$$2(m + n) + 1 \geq 7 + (m + n) \tag{24}$$

get,

$$m + n \geq 6 \tag{25}$$

Therefore, 6 image point correspondences are necessary to solve this kind of articulated motion. At this time, we should settle 13 nonlinear equations.

4   Distribution of Points in the Two Subparts

In the previous sections, we gave the condition for solutions for each model, i.e., the number of needed point correspondences on the object, $m + n$. But we have not pointed out what values m and n are respectively. Following, we show how to distribute the number of points between m and n for each model.

4.1   Model 1

From the Eqs.(5) we see that rotation R is only connected with the points on the subpart B, and R has three unknown parameters. If give only two image point correspondences $Q \leftrightarrow Q'$ on subpart B, we will get four equations about 5 unknowns (3 for R and 2 for the depth of the two correspondent 3D points), which is independent with the points on subpart A. Thus the number of the unknowns is larger than the number of the equations, the solution cannot be obtained. So, we should let $m = 1, n = 3$.

4.2   Model 2

Since the rotation R_p and R_q are related by a same rotation axis, from the Eqs.(17), we know the two subparts have only one independent unknown for rotation angle respectively. Thus, the number can be allotted in any of the following way

$$m = 1, \quad n = 4$$
$$m = 2, \quad n = 3$$
$$m = 3, \quad n = 2$$
$$m = 4, \quad n = 1$$

To balancing the e ect of the two subparts on the motion estimation, we choose $m = 2, n = 3$ or $m = 3, n = 2$.

4.3   Model 3

From the Eqs.(22), it can be seen that all unknowns appear in the equation about point q and q'. So in theory, it does not matter whether there are points on subpart A, i.e., we can let $m = 0, n = 6$. There is no constraint for the value of m. But the subpart B has two independent unknowns for its rotation R_q, so there should be at least two point correspondences on subpart B, that is

$$n \geq 2 \tag{26}$$

Therefore, there are ve choices for the distributions of m and n, from $m = 4, n = 2$ to $m = 0, n = 6$. However $m = 0, n = 6$ is not used for practical reason.

5   Simulated Experimental Results

In this section, a lot of experiments are conducted on simulated data. The 3D point data is produced by the computer, and its correspondent image data is computed according to central projection. The real motion parameters and depth of points are known in advance, which would be used to verify the rightness and e ciency of the models.

For each model, we should solve nonlinear equations, which are settled by nonlinear least-squares in our experiments. It is well known that a good initial value is important for the iterative method to get the correct solution. So, we give out the initial value to show the capability of convergence of the algorithms. And since in practice, all data are contaminated with much or less noises, it is also important for us to test the robustness of the algorithms. Supposing that

Table 1. The true, initial and estimated value in Model 1(Noise free)

Motion	True value	Initial value	Estimated value
Rotation axis n	0.666667	0.486921	0.666667
	0.666667	0.649227	0.666667
	0.333333	0.584305	0.333333
Rotation angle(degree)	45.000000	30.000000	45.000000
Joint depth	8.000000	9.500000	8.000000
	7.000000	6.000000	7.000000

Table 2. The noise effect on the solution in Model 1

Noise	Two pixels	Four pixels	Six pixels
Rotation axis n	0.665323	0.664049	0.662846
	0.669212	0.671701	0.674134
	0.330908	0.328415	0.325850
Rotation angle(degree)	44.692373	44.399520	44.121141
Joint depth	8.018327	8.036615	8.054864
	7.019393	7.038744	7.058054

the object region covers about half of the whole image of size 500×500, then in our experiments introducing 0.002 noises into the image data equals to adding about one pixels noise.

Since ir our experiments, we should deal with much about the rotation matrix R, an appropriate expression of R is important. In order to express it using least parameters, we express R with its rotation axis $n = (n_1, n_2, n_3)$ and angle θ

$$
\begin{matrix}
n_1^2 + (1-n_1^2)\cos\theta & n_1 n_2(1-\cos\theta) - n_3\sin\theta & n_1 n_3(1-\cos\theta) + n_2\sin\theta \\
n_1 n_2(1-\cos\theta) + n_3\sin\theta & n_2^2 + (1-n_2^2)\cos\theta & n_2 n_3(1-\cos\theta) - n_1\sin\theta \\
n_1 n_3(1-\cos\theta) - n_2\sin\theta & n_2 n_3(1-\cos\theta) + n_1\sin\theta & n_3^2 + (1-n_3^2)\cos\theta
\end{matrix}
\tag{27}
$$

where n is an unit vector, i.e.,

$$
n_1^2 + n_2^2 + n_3^2 = 1
\tag{28}
$$

And since the depth of 3D points can be solved only up to a scale factor, in the experiment we set one of the depth unknowns as its true value. Thus, if the obtained solution is a correct one, then the depth value are the real ones.

From Table 1,Table 3 and Table 5, we see that the correct solutions are all obtained for three models, though the initial value are a little far away from the true ones. This shows that our models and algorithm are not very dependent on the initial value, which is very important for an iterative method. Table 2,Table 4 and Table 6 show us the robustness of our algorithm. With up to six pixels noises, the algorithm still converges to the right solutions with not much de ection.

Table 3. The true, initial and estimated value in Model 2(Noise free)

Motion	True value	Initial value	Estimated value
Rotation axis n	0.666667	0.717137	0.666667
	0.666667	0.597614	0.666667
	0.333333	0.358569	0.333333
Rotation angles(degree)	30.000000	40.000000	30.000000
	36.000000	30.000000	36.000000
Joint depth	8.000000	7.00000	8.000000
	7.000000	8.000000	7.000000

Table 4. The noise effect on the solution in Model 2

Noise	Two pixels	Four pixels	Six pixels
Rotation axis n	0.668693	0.670917	0.673357
	0.670491	0.674312	0.678058
	0.321390	0.308503	0.294665
Rotation angles(degree)	30.319567	30.661064	31.026674
	36.493974	37.055839	37.694184
Joint depth	8.155326	8.303031	8.443021
	7.115209	7.223599	7.325298

Table 5. The true, initial and estimated value in Model 3(Noise free)

Motion	True value	Initial value	Estimated value
Rotation axis n_p	0.816497	0.565685	0.816497
	0.408248	0.707107	0.408248
	0.408248	0.424264	0.408248
Rotation angle	36.000000	45.000000	36.000000
Rotation axis n_q	−0.577350	−0.282166	−0.577350
	0.577350	0.451466	0.577350
	0.577350	0.846499	0.577350
Rotation angle	30.00000	27.692308	30.00000

Table 6. The noise effect on the solution in Model 3

Noise	Two pixels	Four pixels	Six pixels
Rotation axis n_p	0.825629	0.833930	0.841532
	0.403011	0.397939	0.393002
	0.394865	0.382368	0.370639
Rotation angle	35.910264	35.834414	35.771221
Rotation axis n_q	−0.564206	−0.551843	−0.540153
	0.586115	0.594454	0.602416
	0.581499	0.584888	0.587647
Rotation angle	30.803650	31.556138	32.264303

6   Conclusions and Future Work

In this paper, we consider the problem of estimating 3D motion of two link-connected articulated objects for three typical but very common models. The motion was modeled by simple equations, and very few point correspondences are needed to solve the problem. In articulated object model 1, in addition to the image of the joint, 4 image point correspondences are su cient to solve for motion; in model 2 and 3, ve and six point correspondences are respectively needed to solve the problem. Simulation experiments show our method is correct and promising.

Currently, we are studying more general cases of articulated motion estimation.

References

1. Jon A. Webb and J. K. Aggarwal, "Structure from motion of rigid and jointed motions", *Artificial Intelligence*, vol. 19, pp107-130, 1982.
2. R. J. Holt, A. N. Netravali, T. S. Huang and R. J. Qian, "Determining articulated motion from perspective views: a decomposition approach", *Pattern Recognition*, vol. 30, pp1435-1449, 1997.
3. Pan Chunhong, Chen Shen and Ma Songde, "Motion analysis of articulated objects and its application in human motion analysis", *Chinese Journal of Electronics*, vol. 9, No. 1, pp76-81, Jan. 2000.
4. D. Sinclair and K. Zesar, "Further constraints on visual articulated motions", *Proc. On CVPR*, pp94-99, 1996.
5. T.S. Huang and A.N. Netravali, "Motion and structure from feature correspondences: A review", *Proceeding of the IEEE*, Vol. 82,No. 2, February, 1994, pp. 252-268.
6. H. C. Longuet-Higgins, "A computer program for reconstructing a scene from two projections", *Nature*, vol. 293, pp133-135, Sept. 1981.
7. C. Bregler and J. Malik, "Tracking people with twist and exponential maps", *Proc. Conf. On CVPR*, pp8-15,1998.
8. H. Segawa, H. Shioya, N. Hiraki and T. Totsuka, "Constraint-conscious smoothing framework for the recovery of 3D articulated motion from image sequences", *Pro. 4th Int. Conf. On Automatic Face and Gesture Recognition*, pp476-482, 2000.
9. C. J. Taylor, "Reconstruction of Articulated Objects from Point Correspondences in a Single Uncalibrated Images", *Proc. Conf. On CVPR*, vol. 1, pp677-684, 2000.

Gesture and Posture Estimation
by Using Locally Linear Regression

Yoshio Iwai[1], Keita Manjoh[1], and Masahiko Yachida[1]

Graduate School of Engineering Science, Osaka University
1-3, Machikaneyama, Toyonaka, Osaka 560-8531, Japan
iwai@sys.es.osaka-u.ac.jp

Abstract. Many methods for measuring human motion have been proposed because they can be applied to various fields such as CG animation, virtual reality, and gesture recognition. This paper proposes a method for gesture and posture estimation which uses locally linear regression. We extract face and hand regions from stereo input images, and estimate their 3D positions by stereo matching. Performed gestures are estimated by hand position and velocity, and human posture is also estimated by using locally linear regression.

1 Introduction

The measurement of human motion is needed for various applications. Because of the widespread adoption of computers, man-machine interaction is required for a more user-friendly interface. For example, human CG animation, virtual agents, and motion capture has been researched[1]. Conventional interfaces such as mouse and keyboard require a user to be skilled. This prevents for many people from using computers. Dialogue or hand gestures which we naturally use to communicate with others in everyday life can remove the burden of using such a conventional interface. In order to use gestures as a man-machine interface, it is necessary to measure human motion.

Measurement of human motion by an image sensor[2,3,4] that does not require a user to wear sensors enables a user to observe a target without attracting attention. Many methods for posture estimation from images have been proposed[5,6]. "Model based" methods assume that the 3D articulated model of the object is given *in advance*[7]. When we use a region matching method which is relatively ambiguous compared with a feature point matching method, we need to take care when we consider the initial position of the model and computation time for searching the best parameters because incorrect determination in the early stage of the process causes worse final results. Killnig and Nagel use polyhedral models in order to match them with edge images, and use an extended Kalman filter (EKF) to estimate object motion[8]. EKF is a good estimator if the speed of object motion is slow, but that of the human hand is very fast. So, EKF is not a good estimator in such an application. MCMC (Monte Carlo Markov Chain)[9] is also used for visual tracking[10]. MCMC has the advantage that an object moving randomly can be tracked because MCMC keeps the distribution of a moving object. MCMC is based on the distribution of model parameters and probabilistic search. Thus, MCMC can hardly track a model which has many parameters.

F.J. Perales and E.R. Hancock (Eds.): AMDO 2002, LNCS 2492, pp. 177–188, 2002.
© Springer-Verlag Berlin Heidelberg 2002

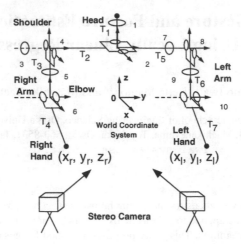

Fig. 1. Structure model of human and coordinate system

In this paper, we propose a fast algorithm for posture and gesture estimation of a human from images which uses locally linear regression. The parameters of the geometric model are calculated from human kinematics, but the image information such as the positions of the hands and head are inadequate for obtaining a unique solution of the parameters. The undetermined parameters are therefore inferred by regression.

2   Models

A typical human motion is considered as a trajectory in the model parameter space. When we can correctly trace such a trajectory, we can estimate human posture accurately and improve the computation time by using information of the motion trajectory. The parameters and the coordinate system of human posture are described in this section.

2.1   Human Structure Model

We construct a structure model of a human with a stick figure model. The operating range of joint angles in the model is restricted, as shown in table 1. The human posture is expressed by 10 parameters of joint angles, θ_i, in figure 1. A state of human posture is expressed by 20 parameters, $\Theta = (\theta_i, \dot{\theta_i})^T$. We refer to the 20-dimensional parameter space as the model parameter space (Θ-space). Here, the lengths of the links between joints, $T_1 \ldots T_7$, are given in advance. Cameras used for experiments are calibrated beforehand.

2.2   Observation

We use the velocity and position of the head and hands estimated from stereo input images of the structure model for observation data. Let $X_r = (x_r, y_r, z_r)^T$ and

Table 1. Operating range of structure model parameters

$\theta_i (deg.)$	min.	max.	$\theta_i (deg.)$	min.	max.
θ_1	-180	180	$\theta_{4,8}$	-90	90
θ_2	-15	15	$\theta_{5,9}$	-90	90
$\theta_{3,7}$	-45	180	$\theta_{6,10}$	0	180

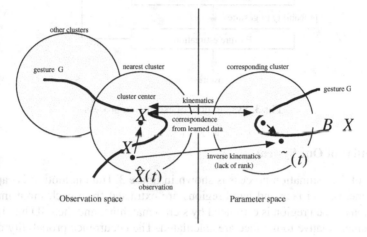

Fig. 2. Concept of posture estimation

$X_l = (x_l, y_l, z_l)^T$ be right and left hand positions relative to a face, respectively. The observation X at each time is expressed by the following equation:

$$X = (x_r, y_r, z_r, x_l, y_l, z_l, x_r, y_r, z_r, x_l, y_l, z_l)^T. \tag{1}$$

The observation X is in 12-dimensional observation space (X-space).

2.3 Locally Linear Regression

Posture estimation in this paper determines the point   in the model space by expressing the angle and angular velocity of each joint from observation X. Gesture estimation in this paper determines which learned gesture G is most similar to the observation data sequence $\{X(t)\}$.

-space is convertible into X-space by solving kinematics, but X-space is not uniformly convertible into   -space by solving inverse kinematics because the solution is not unique.

3 Gesture and Posture Estimation Algorithm

In this section, first we explain the process flow of our system and then we describe the algorithm.

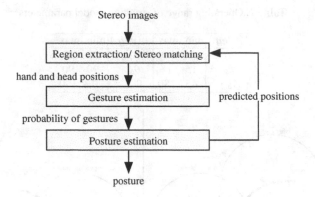

Fig. 3. System flow of estimation process

3.1 Outline of Our System

The flow of the estimation process is shown in figure 3. Human motion is captured by stereo cameras, and face and hand regions are extracted from each input image. The 3D position of each region is estimated by stereo matching, and then 3D hand positions and velocities relative to the face are calculated. The occurrence probability of gesture and human posture are calculated from the information of regions and a locally linear regression model. Finally, human posture in the next frame is predicted by a linear equation.

3.2 Gesture Model and Clustering

Clustering is an effective representation method for dealing with an enormous amount of data such as gesture data sampled at video rate. All gesture data   are classified into N clusters by using a k-mean method and each cluster is used for calculation of similarity between input data, X, and gesture data,   . Euclidean distance is used for the metric of clustering, and feature values are normalized by their variance before clustering. The results of clustering of Θ are used for clustering of X; if θ_i, θ_j belong to the same cluster in the parameter space, corresponding data x_i, x_j also belong to the same cluster in the observation space.

The advantages of clustering are that we can search for similar patterns of input data quickly and that we can calculate the occurrence probability of gestures by using the density of clusters.

3.3 Gesture Estimation

We calculate the similarity between each cluster and the input X on the observation space, and then we calculate the probability of the gesture from the most similar cluster. In this paper, N clusters, $\omega_i (0 \leq i < N)$, are generated by clustering, as described in section 3.2. The input X is most similar to the cluster ω_q which satisfies the following condition:

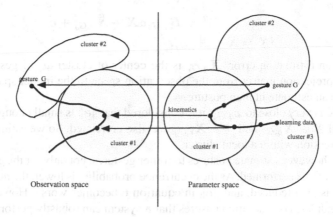

Fig. 4. Clustering

$$\omega_q = \arg\min_i D(\boldsymbol{X}, \boldsymbol{\alpha}_i), \qquad (2)$$

where D is Euclidean distance and $\boldsymbol{\alpha}_i$ is the center of the cluster ω_i. ω_q is the cluster to which an input $\boldsymbol{X}$ belongs, and ω_q contains gesture model data of each gesture G_j. The ratio of gesture model data in a cluster is considered as the occurrence probability of gestures G_j (j is a type of gesture). We calculate the occurrence probability averaged over the last K frames. We use $K = 3$ in experiments in this paper.

Let $\boldsymbol{X}(t)$ and $\omega_q(t)$ be an input and the nearest cluster at time t, respectively. The occurrence probability of each gesture, $P_t(G_j|\boldsymbol{X}(t), \ldots, \boldsymbol{X}(t-k))$, is calculated by equation 3:

$$P_t(G_j|\boldsymbol{X}(t), \ldots, \boldsymbol{X}(t-K)) = \frac{1}{K} \sum_{T=t-K+1}^{t} \frac{\#\{\boldsymbol{X}|\boldsymbol{X} \in G_j, \boldsymbol{X} \in \omega_q(T)\}}{\#\{\boldsymbol{X}|\boldsymbol{X} \in \omega_q(T)\}}, (3)$$

$$\omega_q(t) = \arg\min_{\omega_i}(D(\boldsymbol{X}(t), \boldsymbol{\alpha}_i)), \qquad (4)$$

$$G(t) = \arg\max_{G_j}(P_t(G_j|\boldsymbol{X}(t), \ldots, \boldsymbol{X}(t-K))). \qquad (5)$$

The recognized gesture $G(t)$ is selected from G_j which maximizes $P_t(G_j|\boldsymbol{X}(t), \ldots, \boldsymbol{X}(t-k))$ at time t.

3.4 Posture Estimation

3D hand positions at time t are calculated by using inverse kinematics, but this is inadequate for determining joint angles uniquely from hand and head positions. We therefore use locally linear regression to infer undetermined parameters. When an input, $\boldsymbol{X}$, is observed and the cluster to which the input belongs in X-space is determined, it is possible that the center of the corresponding cluster in Θ-space is an estimate of the input. That estimate, however, contains a large quantization error.

In this paper, to avoid a large quantization error,   is approximated by equation 6:

$$= (\ ,\ )^T = \boldsymbol{B}_{q,G_j} \delta \boldsymbol{X} + \overset{c}{\boldsymbol{X}}_{q,G_j} + \boldsymbol{e} \tag{6}$$

$$\delta \boldsymbol{X} = \boldsymbol{X} - \overset{c}{\boldsymbol{X}}_{q,G_j}, \tag{7}$$

where $\boldsymbol{e}$ is an estimation error, $\overset{c}{\boldsymbol{X}}_{q,G_j}$ is the center of cluster ω_q of gesture G_j, and $\boldsymbol{B}_{q,G_j}$ is a projection matrix from the observation space to the model space. If we get $\boldsymbol{B}_{q,G_j}$, we can estimate human posture.

When $\boldsymbol{X}$ is very close to $\boldsymbol{x}_{q,G_j}$, it is considered that $\|e\|$ is small enough to estimate posture, and $\boldsymbol{X} - \boldsymbol{X}_{q,G_j}$ and $\ - \boldsymbol{X}_{i,G_j}$ are also correlated. So we estimate $\boldsymbol{B}_{i,G_j}$ as a linear regression within a local cluster.

We also, however, estimate postures for other gestures, not only for the gesture which is most likely to be performed. As the occurrence probability is lower, the number of data in a cluster is also reduced, and $\|e\|$ in equation 6 becomes worse. However, keeping multiple candidates of a solution ensures that a system can robustly perform estimation of human posture by switching the candidates according to their occurrence probability. This is the advantage of our method and similar methods such as MCMC.

$\boldsymbol{B}_{q,G_j}$ is only dependent on the cluster ω_q and the selected gesture G_j in the posture estimation process. We can calculate $\boldsymbol{B}_{q,G_j}$ offline in advance and we can therefore reduce the computation time for regression. This is another advantage of our method.

3.5 Parameter Adjustment

Estimated posture   contains errors of estimation and gesture selection, so it is not appropriate for input images. Parameters   should therefore be adjusted to fit the image by using   as an initial value. The adjustment is evaluated by matching the structure model and a silhouette of a human region. The evaluation function C for the adjustment is expressed by the following equation:

$$C(\ ') = - \sum_{i}^{n} S \cdot P \cdot f_i(\ ') + d(\ '), \tag{8}$$

$$' = \arg \min_{\theta'} C(\ '), \tag{9}$$

where f_i is the matrix transforming feature point i in each model coordinate system into the world coordinate system, P is a projection matrix, S is an indicator function which becomes 1 if the silhouette exists on the argument position, otherwise 0. $d(\ )$ is a repelling function to keep the elbows from entering the body. Therefore, the theoretical minimum of C is the negative number of feature points, $-n$, from equation 8. When C is the minimum, all feature points are in the silhouette of the person and the elbow position is outside the body.

4   Experimental Results and Discussion

We conducted experiments using an SGI workstation (Onyx2, MIPS R12K, 400 MHz). We evaluated the performance of clustering and the accuracy of estimates by using real and simulated images. Input images were

- CG images used for learning gesture models,
- real images not used for learning gesture models.

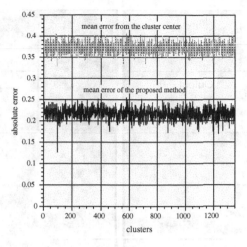

Fig. 5. Mean of quantization error and mean errors of regression

4.1 Performance of Clustering

The best cluster for the proposed method is one in which equation 6 is established with a small error, e. We evaluate an approximation error of equation 6. The mean error of estimation, e_{ω_c}, is derived from equation 6 as follows:

$$e_{\omega_c} = \frac{1}{r} \sum_{i=0}^{r-1} \left\| \omega_{c,i} - B_{c,G_j} \delta X - \hat{X}_{c,G_j} \right\|. \tag{10}$$

All data are projected from X-space into -space by equation 6. The absolute mean error of estimation, $\|e_{\omega_c}\|$, is shown in figure 5. Gray lines in the figure are mean errors between input data and corresponding clusters (mean of quantization error) and solid lines are the mean errors defined in equation 10.

As shown in figure 5, the mean absolute error of the gray lines is 0.37, and that of the solid lines is 0.22, so the size of the quantization error caused by clustering is reduced by our proposed method.

4.2 Experiment on CG Images Used for Clustering

We evaluated our system by using CG images used for clustering. The sequence contains five gestures: raising both hands (50 frames), waving the right hand (57 frames), pushing the right hand (80 frames), throwing (78 frames), and waving both elbows (62 frames). The number in parentheses represents the number of the frames for performing a gesture. Examples of experimental images are shown in figure 6.

CG images in the figure are generated from the structure model in figure 1 by giving joint angles. Face and hand regions are extracted from CG images, and then the 3D position and velocity of both hands are calculated from positions of the extracted regions.

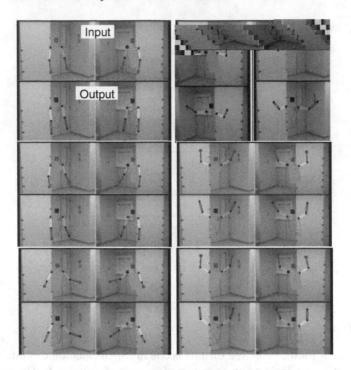

Fig. 6. Estimation results on CG images used for clustering

Occurrence Probability of Gesture. Changes in the occurrence probability of each gesture are shown in figure 7. The occurrence probability correctly changes in response to the change of gesture, as shown in the figure.

The graph which is close to a point of gesture transition from the 40th to 60th frame is shown in figure 8. The frame in which a gesture is changed is delayed by the smoothing parameter K ($K = 3$ in this experiment) in equation 3.

Posture Estimation. We evaluate errors of 3D positions between true values and estimates calculated from gestures which have the highest occurrence probability at each frame. Figure 9 shows an estimation error of the right arm. The estimation error is about 100 mm. This error was caused by using a stick model, not a volumetric model, and by the quantization error in equation 6. A large error occurred around the 130th frame because the best projection matrix B was not selected.

Posture Adjustment. The posture estimated in section 4.2 is adjusted by using the model matching described in section 3.5. The results of errors between true values and adjusted values of the 3D positions of the right arm are shown in figure 10. In this experiment, the number of features is 10 for each image and the maximum loop number is 3,000. It is clearly shown in figure 10 that the large error around the 130th frame

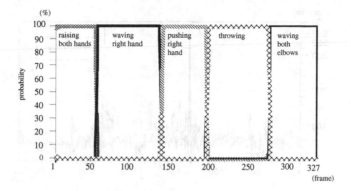

Fig. 7. Transition of occurrence probability

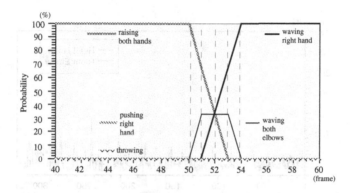

Fig. 8. Transition of occurrence probability: 40th to 60th frame

in figure 9 is reduced by posture adjustment. The estimation error of the right arm at the 240th frame became large because the adjustment process did not finish within the limitation of iteration.

4.3 Experiments on Real Images

We also evaluated our system by using real images not used for clustering. The sequence contains two gestures twice: pushing the right hand, waving the right hand. Examples of input images are shown in figure 11. We conducted the same experiments as in the previous sections. We only evaluated two results in this section because we were unable to determine fully the frame of gesture transition and true value of posture.

Occurrence Probability of Gesture. Changes in the occurrence probability of gestures are shown in figure 12. The frames of gesture transitions are around the 50th, 150th, and 200th frames. The occurrence probability correctly changes under noisy sequence, such as occurs in real images, in proportion to gesture transition.

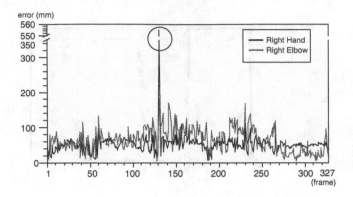

Fig. 9. Estimation errors of right hand and right elbow (learned CG images)

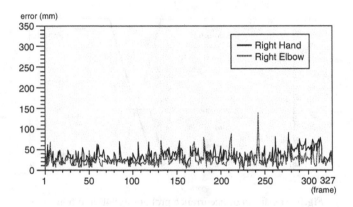

Fig. 10. Estimation error of right hand and right elbow after adjustment (learned CG images)

5   Conclusion

We proposed a method for the estimation of posture and gesture which used locally linear regression. The 3D positions of hands and head were calculated from skin color regions extracted from stereo images. The occurrence probability of gesture was estimated from the learning data which was used for locally linear regression. Posture parameters were estimated by using locally linear regression and then adjusted by model matching with a silhouette. We conducted experiments with CG images and confirmed the effectiveness of our proposed method. We conducted experiments with real images. We also confirmed that the method could estimate posture and gesture accurately. It is therefore acceptable that a locally linear regression model is viable and that it can be used in high-dimensional space.

Our proposed method can deal with many gestures and many objects by constructing clusters if the motion of objects is known in advance.

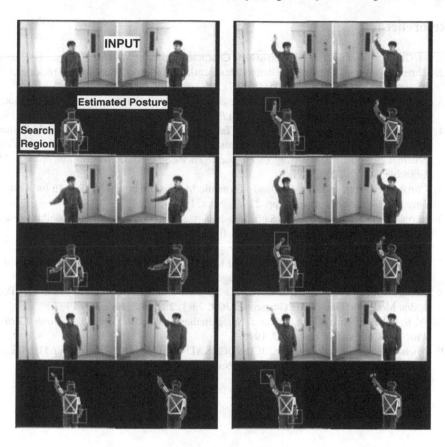

Fig. 11. Examples of estimation results

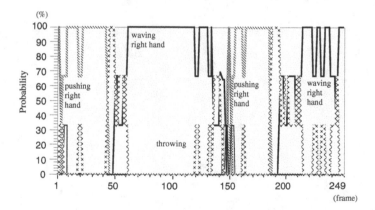

Fig. 12. Changes in occurrence probability

References

1. M. Gleicher.: Retargetting Motion to New Characters. In *Proc. SIGGRAPH*, pp. 33–42, 1998.
2. Christopher Wren, Trevor Darrell, and Alex Pentland.: Pfinder: Real-Time Tracking of the Human Body. *IEEE Trans. on PAMI*, 19(7):780–785, July 1997.
3. Ming-Hsuan Yang and Narendra Ahuja.: Extraction and Classification of Visual Motion Patterns for Hand Gesture Recognition. In *Proc. CVPR*, pp. 892–897, California, June 1998.
4. Shoichiro Iwasawa, Jun Ohya, Kazuhiko Takahashi, Tatsumi Sakaguchi, Kazuyuki Ebihara, and Shigeo Morishima.: Human Body Postures from Trinocular Camera Images. In *Proceedings of the Fourth Intl. Conf. on Automatic Face and Gesture Recognition*, pp. 326–331, Grenoble, March 2000. IEEE.
5. Christopher Wren and Alex Pentland.: Dynamic Models of Human Motion. In *Intl Conf. on Face and Gesture Recognition*, pp. 22–27, Nara, 1998.
6. Masanobu Yamamoto, Akitsugu Sato, Satoshi Kawada, Takuya Kondo, and Yoshihiko Osaki.: Incremental Tracking of Human Actions from Multiple Views. In *Proc. CVPR*, pp. 2–7, California, June 1998.
7. Yoshinari Kameda, Michihiko Minoh, and Katsuo Ikeda.: A Pose Estimation Method for an Articulated Object from Its Silhouette Image. *IEICE*, J79-D-II(1):26–25, January 1996.
8. Henner Kollnig and Hans-Hellmut Nagel.: 3D Pose Estimation by Directly Matching Polyhedral Models to Gray Value Gradients. *IJCV*, 23(3):283–308, June/July 1997.
9. W. R. Gilks, S. Richardson, and D. J. Spiegelhalter. (eds.): *Markov Chain Monte Carlo in Practice*. Chapman & Hall/CRC, 1996.
10. Michael Isard and Andrew Blake.: ICONDENSATION: Unifying Low-Level and High-Level Tracking in a Stochastic Framework. In *Proc. ECCV*, Vol. 1, pp. 893–908, 1998.

aSpaces: Action Spaces for Recognition and Synthesis of Human Actions

Jordi González, Javier Varona, F. Xavier Roca, and Juan José Villanueva

Computer Vision Center & Dept. d'Informàtica
Edifici O, Universitat Autònoma de Barcelona (UAB),
08193 Bellaterra, Spain
{poal,xaviv,xavir,villanueva}@cvc.uab.es
http://www.cvc.uab.es

Abstract. Human behavior analysis is an open problem in the computer vision community. The aim of this paper is to model human actions. We present a taxonomy in order to discuss about a knowledge-based classification of human behavior. A novel human action model is presented, called the *aSpace*, based on a Point Distribution Model (PDM). This representation is compact, accurate and specific. The human body model is represented as a stick figure, and several sequences of humans actions are used to compute the *aSpace*. In order to test our action representation, two applications are provided: recognition and synthesis of actions.

1 Introduction

Recently, computer vision research has been highly interested in the analysis of image sequences. When sequences involve humans, this task becomes challenging: human behavior analysis is still an open problem in which several issues need to be considered. We are interested in describing structured behaviors of an articulated agent in terms of its attitude and body motion, in contrast to analyze solely the location and velocity parameters of a single object. Gymnastic or yoga exercises, but also running, jumping, bending or walking provide examples.

In this paper, a taxonomy is presented in order to discuss about a classi ca-tion of human behavior in terms of knowledge: a proper de nition of the concept of human action implies to analyse and restrict our problem domain. Considering a human action as a sequence of human postures, each human posture is represented using a 2D human body model (stick gure) which is described in terms of polar coordinates in order to avoid non-linearities when the posture varies strongly. Subsequently, we present a human action model, the *aSpace*, based on a Point Distribution Model (PDM) [7]. This mathematical tool provides a compact (few parameters describe the posture), accurate (the postures which are plausible to appear in any performance of an action are included in the model) and speci c (those postures which are not presented in the action are excluded in the model) representation for human actions [9]. Several sequences of actions are used to compute the *aSpace*. Two applications are provided in order to validate our action model: recognition and synthesis of actions. Lastly, conclusions and future work is discussed.

F.J. Perales and E.R. Hancock (Eds.): AMDO 2002, LNCS 2492, pp. 189–200, 2002.
© Springer-Verlag Berlin Heidelberg 2002

2   Dealing with Humans

Our interest is centered in those applications related to humans. The aim is to describe the behavior of di erent human agents in the scene. We will call such a complex task *Dealing with Humans*. Due to the complexity of these systems, di erent reviews focus the problem of de ning a taxonomy in order to describe existing publications in terms of geometric representations [1,6,8,10]. However, in order to de ne properly the concept of *action*, we require to use a knowledge-based classi cation: we are interested describing human motion in terms of knowledge rather than in geometric terms. Thus, using a knowledge-based classi cation of motion recognition helps us to analyze the required levels of representation in order to model actions in our system.

An early approach is the taxonomy given in [12] by Nagel. A complete scheme suitable to perform generic image sequence evaluation is presented. These levels are called *change, event, verb, episode,* and *history*: a change is a discernible motion in a sequence; an event is a change which is considered as a primitive of more complex descriptions; a verb describes some activity; an episode describes complex motions, which may involve several actions; and a history is an extended sequence of related activities. These terms are more related to story understanding, because the goal is the generation of conceptual descriptions by means of natural language. However, Nagel s classi cation is mainly derived to perform reasoning, so it is not obvious how to design vision-based intermediate representations of complex human motions which can be easily embedded in his taxonomy.

Centered in humans, di erent description levels are suggested by Bobick in [2]. He described three levels: *movement, activity* and *action*. A movement is a predictable motion that can be de ned by a space-time trajectory in a proper feature space, so no knowledge other than motion is needed. An activity is composed of a sequence of movements. An action involves semantic knowledge related to the context of motion, that means, inferences rely on domain speci c knowledge. It makes explicit the requirement of deriving time and casual relations from statistics of image motion. However, inferring capabilities are limited: reasoning about the scene can only be achieved if perceptual implications are observed. Moreover, the inferences are mainly restricted to time dependencies between actions.

In this paper, a combination of both taxonomies is presented. We want to describe our approach as a human action recognition method in a generic image sequence evaluation framework. So, on the one hand, we adopt Bobick s terms in order to design intermediate representations to perform properly complex motion recognition. But, on the other hand, Nagel s classi cation will assist our system to generate semantic descriptions which are suitable to perform deep reasoning. These levels are described next and they are called *movement, action, activity* and *situation*.

A *movement* represents a change of human posture or place between consecutive frames. Movements can be characterized in terms of a space-time function, so di erent performances of the same movement recorded from the same viewpoint will have similar characterizations. No knowledge about the context is required at this point. Usually, human movement analysis publications are related to two di erent issues. First, human movement is found to be used as a constraint factor to improve the tracking of human body parts [5,13,14]. Here, an appropriate human body model is needed to be pre-de ned. Second, it is considered as the lowest stage of more complex human motion descriptions [3].

We consider a human *action* as a process of human performing that has a signi cance to our system. *Significance* means that these actions will be learned so afterwards their recognition can be properly achieved. Using the previous de nition of movement, we de ne an action as a temporal series of human movements. As a consequence, a method is required for handling time. The identi cation of an action should be independent of its temporal extent. Typical human actions are running, jumping, grasping or bending. Using conceptual terms, actions can described with *motion* verbs. No reference to the context needs to be addressed in order to characterize an action: the recognition of an action relies on the recognition of its constitutive movements. It is important to note that, at this point, the *goal* of an agent is *implicit* in the performance of an action due to the fact that the goal is not known in advance in some cases.

Activity is de ned as a sequence of one or several human actions. For example, to change a lightbulb. Di erent actions are involved in such an activity: to place the stepladder, to climb, to unscrew the lightbulb and to replace it. But no reference to the context is applied here: an activity is *generically* recognized as the consequence of the recognition of its constitutive actions. The goal is also implicit in the activity. An activity can be expressed in terms of a series of motion verbs.

Lastly, we adapt the concept of *situation* [12] to the human recognition domain. We consider the situation as an activity that acquire a meaning in a speci c scene. For example, we can model a waving arms activity. Recognizing such an activity in a football game (ball requesting) has a di erent meaning that in a subway station (help requesting). Context should be modeled suitably, in order to provide the required knowledge necessary to generate descriptions about the agent in a particular scene and to analyze and predict interactions with other people or objects in the same scene. The context will also help to determine the *goal* of the activity. If the goal is known in advance, the context will provide the required information in order to state if the goal has been successfully accomplished.

So, once the concept of action has been clearly established, we can confront the problem of modeling human actions. In the next sections, we present our method for human action representation.

3   Action Spaces

As discussed before, a movement is de ned as a change of posture. Consequently an action, de ned as a sequence of movements, is represented as a sequence of postures. So, in order to build an action space, the postures of di erent humans recorded during the performance of several actions (training examples) will constitute the basis of our action model.

It is critical the choice of a proper representation for human actions. The model should be compact, that is, it should be able to capture most of the variance of the training examples. Also, as dealing with non-rigid agents, non-linearities (due to non-linear movements of the limbs) should be handled. Furthermore, the model should be accurate, that is, the set of plausible postures that a human body can exhibit while performing the action should be modeled. However, the model of an action should be valid, in other words, it should not generate those postures which are not likely to be adopted during the performance of an action.

Point Distribution Models (PDM) are commonly used in the literature to model shape variability [4,7,9]. These statistical models are compact because it is based on PCA: a small set of deformations are found to be the most representative ones. Also, only plausible samples are generated by modifying, within limits, the principal modes of variation. These limits, related to the variance explained by each mode of variation, prevent the model to generate unallowable samples.

We adapt the PDM to represent the anatomical structure of the human body. Each training sample corresponds to a compact representation of the posture of a human skeleton, modeled as a stick gure. For each limb, polar coordinates will be used in order to represent the orientation of each limb of the stick gure. By building a PDM, the set of postures which a human body can adopt during the performance of an action are modeled. By de ning properly the limits of variation of the human posture within an action, the set of postures which are not presented in the action are excluded.

Thus, a proper model for actions is achieved by using a PDM approach. We name this representation as *aSpace*.

3.1   Point Distribution Models

A PDM is a model which describes shape variability within a set of aligned shapes in a well-de ned statistic manner. Each shape, s, is described by a vector:

$$\mathbf{x_s} = (x_1, y_1, ..., x_n, y_n)^T, \tag{1}$$

which represents the set of Cartesian coordinates specifying that shape. The set of n training vectors are aligned (translated, rotated and scaled) using a weighted least-squares algorithm and the mean shape calculated. The modes of variation are represented by using Principal Component Analysis (PCA) on the deviation of the shapes from the mean. So the covariance matrix is computed as:

$$\Sigma = \frac{1}{n} \sum_{i=1}^{n} (\mathbf{x}_i - \mathbf{\bar{x}})(\mathbf{x}_i - \mathbf{\bar{x}})^T, \tag{2}$$

where

$$\mathbf{\bar{x}} = \frac{1}{n} \sum_{i=1}^{n} \mathbf{x}_i. \tag{3}$$

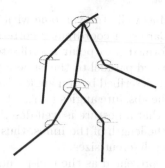

Fig. 1. General human body model, represented in terms of ten angles

Using eigenvector decomposition:

$$\lambda_i \mathbf{e}_i = \Sigma \mathbf{e}_i, \tag{4}$$

where each eigenvector, $\mathbf{e}_i$, corresponds to a mode of variation, and its corresponding eigenvalue λ_i is related to the variance explained by the eigenvector. Consequently, the smallest number m of eigenvalues which explains a large proportion of the total variance is chosen. So the m signi cant deformations of the shape are found by choosing the eigenvectors corresponding to the m largest eigenvalues. Commonly, m is much smaller than n so a very compact model is built.

Consequently, each deformed shape $\mathbf{x}$ is found as a combination of:

$$\mathbf{x} = \bar{\mathbf{x}} + \mathbf{E}\mathbf{b}, \tag{5}$$

where $\mathbf{E} = (\mathbf{e}_1, ..., \mathbf{e}_m)$ corresponds to the eigenvectors, and $\mathbf{b} = (b_1, ..., b_m)^T$ is a vector of weights. Each weight is computed within suitable limits in order to generate new allowable shapes, similar to those in the training set. The limits are related to the variance of each variation mode, so each weight b_k is restricted to lie within:

$$-3 \ \sqrt{\lambda_k} \le b_k \le 3 \ \sqrt{\lambda_k}. \tag{6}$$

Thus, the model only represents valid shapes, so all invalid shapes are excluded. Also, by using real-life training data, a realistic model of deformation is obtained.

3.2   Posture De nition

We have de ned an action as a sequence of human postures. We represent each human posture as a stick   gure composed of ten rigid body parts (torso, head, two primitives for each arm and two primitives for each leg) connected by joints in a hierarchical manner (see Fig.1).

If we build the PDM using the Cartesian coordinates of the joints, non-linear variations of these joints need to be considered [9]. Also, the lenght of the limbs is required to be modelled as well. To overcome with non-linearities, a mapping function is de ned: the Cartesian coordinates corresponding to the previously selected joints are transformed into polar coordinates. By assuming that the training actions are performed parallel to the camera plane (orthographic view), the ten rotational DOF are described by ten angles. Note that we only model the human body in terms of the absolute angles (w.r.t. the world coordinate system) of the limbs. We consider that a posture is well-described by means of angles: it is no necessary to model the length of the limbs, thus allowing to generalize our representation to people of di erent sizes.

So, each stick gure, represented as the end-points of the limbs[1]:

$$\mathbf{p_s} = (x_1, y_1, ..., x_{11}, y_{11})^T, \tag{7}$$

is reparameterized as follows. As described previously, the human posture is modeled as series of jointed segments. Consider a limb l described by its end-points (x_i, y_i) and (x_j, y_j). The absolute angle of the limb is computed as:

$$\theta_l = \tan^{-1} \frac{y_i - y_j}{x_i - x_j}. \tag{8}$$

So the orientation of the ten limbs of our stick gure consists of ten angles:

$$= (\theta_1, \theta_2, ..., \theta_{10})^T. \tag{9}$$

Using this representation, we can model the relative motion of the human body, that means, the motion of the limbs with respect to the center of coordinates of the body (in our case, the hip). In order to model the global motion of the human body, the Cartesian coordinates of the hip, $\mathbf{u} = (u, v)$, are also considered. Thus, we can analyse the motion of the whole body. So a posture is represented as:

$$\mathbf{x_s} = (\mathbf{u}, \quad)^T. \tag{10}$$

That is, our posture model is de ned in terms of twelve parameters: ten angle values, , and the hip center coordinates, $\mathbf{u}$. Note that we consider the stick gure as a hierarchical tree, with the root located at the hip. This is important when building a new stick gure from the parameters of $\mathbf{x_s}$.

3.3   Building Action Spaces

Once the representation for each posture of an action has been computed, the *aSpace* is built. An action A is described by a sequence of n postures, $A = \{\mathbf{x}_1, ..., \mathbf{x}_n\}$, where n represents the complete set of postures corresponding to several performances of di erent people doing the same action, and where $\mathbf{x}_i$ represents the posture (the orientation of the ten limbs and the position of the hip) at frame i recorded during the performance of the action A (see Fig. 2).

---

[1] Current implementation requires of a manually selection of the end-points of the limbs. This will be avoided in further releases.

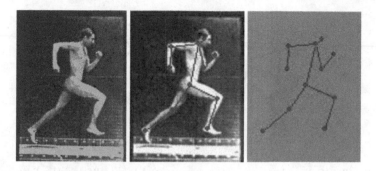

Fig. 2. Posture representation: once the joints are selected, the stick figure is built and the orientation of the limbs is computed

First, the mean posture for that action, $\bar{\mathbf{x}}$, is substracted from each sample:

$$A = \{\mathbf{x}_1 - \bar{\mathbf{x}}, ..., \mathbf{x}_n - \bar{\mathbf{x}}\}. \tag{11}$$

Then, we find the covariance matrix as:

$$\Sigma = AA^T. \tag{12}$$

The eigenvalues λ_i and eigenvectors $\mathbf{e}_i$ of Σ are calculated by solving the eigenvector decomposition equation of Eq. (4), where each eigenvector $\mathbf{e}_i$ corresponds to a mode of variation of the posture during the execution of the action, and its corresponding eigenvalue λ_i is related to the variance explained by the eigenvector. The smallest number m of eigenvalues which explains a large proportion of the total variance of the sequence of postures is chosen.

Consequently, each posture of the action can be expressed using Eq. (5) as a combination of the mean body human posture $\bar{\mathbf{x}}$, the eigenvectors $\mathbf{E}$ and the vector of weights $\mathbf{b}$ restricted to lie within the limits of Eq. (6).

Thus, our action model is the compact representation called *aSpace* which consists of the eigenvectors and the mean posture of that action:

$$A = (\mathbf{E}, \bar{\mathbf{x}}). \tag{13}$$

Note that when the range of angle values measured lies near 360° and 0°, PCA gives bad results due to the angle discontinuity problem. As presented in [9], in order to avoid this problem, each angle is computed twice, once in the range $0^o \leq \theta < 360^o$ and once in the range $-180^o \leq \theta < 180^o$. Next, we compute the standard deviation of the angles for both ranges. A boundary crossing has happened if the standard deviation is larger for one range. In this case, the angles of the other range is used to build the PDM.

3.4 Examples

The control points of the PDM (in our case, these points correspond to the *joints* of the skeleton) should be selected accurately. For this reason, these control

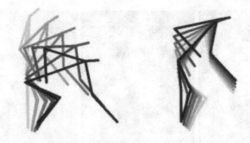

Fig. 3. Bending Space: human postures generated by modifying the first and second eigenvectors

Fig. 4. Jumping Space: human postures generated by modifying the first, second and third eigenvectors

points will be annotated manually in order to check our method by avoiding errors in the training data which would corrupt the reliability of the *aSpace* representation.

We selected three actions in order to test our method: bending, jumping and punching. Five different people (of different sizes) performed four times these actions. During the bending action, the posture varies strongly, but the polar representation prevents of non-linearities in the *aSpace*. During the jumping action, the position of the hip is demonstrated to be useful in the representation of postures. During the punching action, only the angle of the arm is strongly modified during any performance. However, the punching and jumping actions contain quite similar limb orientations. The idea is to analyse whether the *aSpace* representation can distinguish between actions with similar (but not equal) postures.

In Figs. 3 and 4 the principal modes of variation of the posture for the bending and jumping actions are shown. Once the three *aSpaces* are computed, these figures are built from the postures generated by varying the vector of weights of the Eq. (5) within the limits of Eq. (6).

4   Recognition

Once the *aSpace* is built, we pose the problem of human action recognition as a distance function applied to each eigenspace. Consequently, in order to achieve recognition, the likelihood function de ned in [11] is applied. The authors present a distance de nition as a su cient statistic for characterizing the probability that our posture representation, $\mathbf{x}$, belongs to an action space:

$$d(\mathbf{x}) = \sum_{i=1}^{m} \frac{y_i^2}{\lambda_i} + \frac{\epsilon^2(\mathbf{x})}{\rho}, \tag{14}$$

where $\mathbf{y} = (y_1, ..., y_m)$ is the sample projection in the *aSpace*, λ_i are the eigenvalues, and m is the number of dimensions of the reduced eigenspace. $\epsilon^2(\mathbf{x})$ is the distance from feature space (DFFS), which is computed as

$$\epsilon^2(\mathbf{x}) = \sum_{i=m+1}^{n} y_i^2 = \| \mathbf{x} \|^2 - \sum_{i=1}^{m} y_i^2, \tag{15}$$

where $\mathbf{x}$ is the posture $\mathbf{x}$ mean normalized (by subtracting the mean), and n is the original dimension of the image space.

Finally, ρ is a weight that is found by minimizing a cost function,

$$\rho = \frac{1}{n-m} \sum_{i=m+1}^{n} \lambda_i. \tag{16}$$

So once the *aSpaces* have been computed, a new sample $\mathbf{x}$ is projected onto all the action spaces. In each *aSpace*, the distance is computed and the *aSpace* which minimum distance is chosen as the most likely one. In Fig. 5, the distance function is shown for two new action performances. The bending action is easily recognized, but the jumping and punching actions are similar. This is because the postures for both actions have characteristics in common (like the standing posture). In Fig. 5.(a) a new jumping performance was detected. Despite the similarity between jumping and punching, these two actions are successfully recognized. In Fig. 5.(b), the bending performance is detected easily, due to the fact that the postures of the bending action are quite di erent from those of the other two actions.

5   Synthesis

We can recover the human posture by building a synthetic human body model (with prede ned length limbs). In order words, the angle values are reparameterized back into Cartesian coordinates. For example, considering the hip coordinates (u, v) and the torso angle θ_1, the coordinates of the joint corresponding to the neck can be found as follows:

$$x_{neck} = u + r\,cos(\theta_1),$$
$$y_{neck} = v + r\,sin(\theta_1), \tag{17}$$

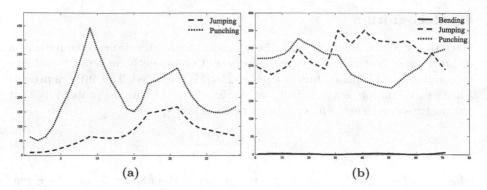

Fig. 5. (a): distance function for a new performance of the jumping action. Jumping and punching contain quite similar postures, but detection is achieved. (b): a new bending performance is easily detected

where r is the prede ned length of the torso of our synthetic model. Subsequently, we can found the end-points of the limbs corresponding to the head, left and right forearms. Note that the order in which the stick gure is built up is important: the stick gure is de ned as a hierarchical tree, where the root is at the hip coordinates.

In order to generate new actions by means of merging postures of di erent actions, we build a multi-action space. Here, the training data is composed of the complete set of human postures presented in all the actions. So a PDM is built, where each posture can be expressed in terms of:

$$\mathbf{x}_M = \mathbf{\hat{x}}_M + \mathbf{E}_M \mathbf{b}_M, \tag{18}$$

where $\mathbf{E}_M$ corresponds to the eigenvectors of the multi-action space, and $\mathbf{b}_M$ is the vector of weights. Note that the vector of weights $\mathbf{b}_M$ include the projections of the postures.

Our goal is to determine which projections of postures belonging to di erent actions are close to each other in the multi-action space. Similar projections indicate postures which are similar, so they can be used to switch between actions, thus generating new mixed sequences. As a result, a sequence is displayed in Fig. 6, where the jumping and punching actions are mixed.

6   Conclusions

First, the concept of human action should be established by means of a taxonomy suitable to be applied when dealing with humans. The basis of our method is the posture, described in terms of the orientation of the limbs of the human agent and the coordinates of the hip. The set of posture of di erent humans performing several times the same action constitutes the training examples for our *aSpace*. This model for human actions is based on a PDM which encapsulates

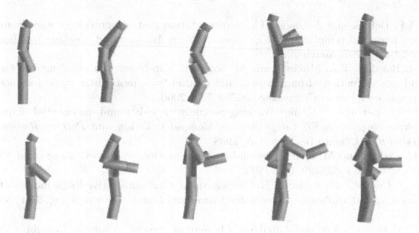

Fig. 6. Synthetic sequence generated by switching between the jumping and punching actions

the plausible postures for a given action. Using the *aSpaces*, recognition and synthesis can be achieved.

Future work relies on improving the stick model by using 3D information. Thus, we will test our approach in more complex environments and the multiple views issue can be posed. Also, the manual selection of the joints of the stick gure should be avoided in order to be selected automatically. For example, by selecting manually the joints at the rst frame, which can be tracked during the rest of the sequence. Consequently, large occlusions should be handled. At present, we are calculating the orientations of the limbs using relative angles (the orientation of each limb with respect to its parent). Lastly, a proper set of actions should be selected in order to build a large action library. What is required is a public human action database, likewise the existing face databases, in order to compare existing methods and evaluate their performance and reliability. We consider this issue as critically necessary.

Acknowledgements

This work has been supported by project TIC2000-0382 of spanish CICYT.

References

1. J.K. Aggarwal and Q. Cai. Human motion analysis: A review. *Computer Vision and Image Understanding*, 73(3):428–440, 1999.
2. A.F. Bobick. Movement, activity and action: The role of knowledge in the perception of motion. In *Royal Society Workshop on Knowledge-based Vision in Man and Machine*, volume 352, pages 1257–1265, London, England, 1997.

3. A.F. Bobick and J. Davis. The representation and recognition of movement using temporal templates. *IEEE Trans. Pattern Analysis and Machine Intelligence*, 23(3):257–267, march 2001.
4. R. Bowden, T.A. Mitchell, and M. Sahardi. Non-linear statistical models for the 3d reconstruction of human pose and motion from monocular motion sequences. *Image and Vision Computing*, 18:729–737, 2000.
5. C. Bregler and J. Malik. Tracking people with twists and exponential maps. In *Proceedings of IEEE Conference on Computer Vision and Pattern Recognition (CVPR'98)*, Santa Barbara, CA, 1998.
6. C. Cédras and M. Shah. Motion-based recognition: A survey. *Image and Vision Computing*, 13(2):129–155, 1995.
7. T.F. Cootes, C.J. Taylor, D.H. Cooper, and J. Graham. Active shape models - their training and application. *Computer Vision and Image Understanding*, 61(1):39–59, 1995.
8. D.M. Gavrila. The visual analysis of human movement: A survey. *Computer Vision and Image Understanding*, 73(1):82–98, 1999.
9. T. Heap and D. Hogg. Extending the point distribution model using polar coordinates. *Image and Vision Computing*, 14:589–599, 1996.
10. T. Moeslund and E. Granum. A survey of computer vision based human motion capture. *Computer Vision and Image Understanding*, 81(3):231–268, March 2001.
11. B. Moghaddam and A. Pentland. Probabilistic visual learning for object representation. *IEEE Trans. Pattern Analysis and Machine Intelligence*, 19(7):696–710, 1997.
12. H.-H. Nagel. From image sequences towards conceptual descriptions. *Image and Vision Computing*, 6(2):59–74, 1988.
13. S. Watcher and H.-H. Nagel. Tracking persons in monocular image sequences. *Computer Vision and Image Understanding*, 74(3):174–192, June 1999.
14. C.R. Wren and A.P. Pentland. Dynamic models of human motion. In *Proceedings of Third International Conference on Automatic Face and Gesture Recognition*, Nara, Japan, 1998.

Face Recognition
Based on Efficient Facial Scale Estimation

Takatsugu Hirayama[1], Yoshio Iwai[1], and Masahiko Yachida[1]

Graduate School of Engineering Science, Osaka University
1-3, Machikaneyama, Toyonaka, Osaka 560-8531, Japan
hirayama@yachi-lab.sys.es.osaka-u.ac.jp
{iwai,yachida}@sys.es.osaka-u.ac.jp

Abstract. Facial recognition technology needs to be robust for arbitrary facial appearances because a face changes according to facial expressions and facial poses. In this paper, we propose a method which automatically performs face recognition for variously scaled facial images. The method performs flexible feature matching using features normalized for facial scale. For normalization, the facial scale is probabilistically estimated and is used as a scale factor of an improved Gabor wavelet transformation. We implement a face recognition system based on the proposed method and demonstrate the advantages of the system through facial recognition experiments. Our method is more efficient than any other and can maintain a high accuracy of face recognition for facial scale variations.

1 Introduction

Currently, the main medium of human-computer interaction is textual. However, it is reported that only 7% of the messages in human-to-human communication are transmitted by language, while as much as 55% of the messages are transmitted by facial expression[1]. Therefore, a human interface using a facial image would seem to be effective for human-computer interaction. Based on this assumption, much work has been done developing methods for recognizing a face in an image.

A facial appearance changes according to facial pose, expression, lighting, and age. In initial work, some researchers proposed methods such as template matching[2], "Eigenface" algorithms[3], and "Fisherface" algorithms[4]. These methods are effective for recognizing a face normalized for position, scale, direction, and expression under the same illumination. To attain a more useful human interface, it is desirable to develop a face recognition method which relaxes the above constraints.

In recent work, researchers have mainly proposed facial recognition methods which are robust for various facial appearances. A method using face graphs and Gabor wavelet transformation (GWT)[5] has the highest recognition performance of those methods. In this method, the nodes which construct the graph are positioned according to facial feature points (FFPs). Each node is labeled with Gabor features, which are extracted by GWT at the FFPs locations. GWT can extract sufficient information to represent facial features by using Gabor wavelets with several different scales (frequencies) and directions. The Gabor features are also robust for illumination variations. As for the method's demerit, the computational cost of GWT is very high and increases in proportion to the

F.J. Perales and E.R. Hancock (Eds.): AMDO 2002, LNCS 2492, pp. 201–212, 2002.

number of wavelets. In order to construct a real-time human interface, the efficiency of the facial recognition method must be improved.

An elastic matching method[6][7] and our flexible feature matching method[8][9] have been proposed to match a face reference graph with a facial image. These methods can robustly recognize faces with small variations because the matching processes are performed by using non-rigid graphs. Large variations, however, decrease accuracy of face recognition. As a first step to further improve accuracy of face recognition, we take account of facial scale and propose a face recognition method robust for facial scale variations. The method is based on the above matching methods.

The elastic matching method can cope with large variations of facial scale by preparing several reference graphs with various scales and by selecting the best reference graph for the facial image[7][10]. This method, however, has to prepare many reference graphs in order to increase the matching accuracy, which requires much memory and a high computational cost. Krüger et al. regard this high cost as a problem[10]. A method for preprocessing the elastic matching was also proposed, which models a face by using an ellipse and then estimates the facial scale[11]. However, this method also has a high computational cost because the ellipse model is deformed into a proper one by an iterative operation. Thus, the first problem we must solve is the trade-off problem between accuracy and efficiency.

It is necessary to normalize the Gabor features to scale in order to obtain optimum performance because the spatial frequency of facial images changes in proportion to facial scale. This is the second problem. In previous work, multiple Gabor features were generally extracted by using multiple scales of Gabor wavelets to cope with facial scale variations[6][7][8][9][10][12][13][14]. The shapes of the Gabor wavelets, however, were not optimally changed for facial scale variations. Therefore, the face recognition rate decreased[11]. For this problem, Lades et al. computed optimum features for facial scale by using interpolation between the multiple features[15]. However, as interpolation resulted in a low accuracy, a method which could normalize the facial image to scale was proposed[11][16]. However, this normalization method omits information from the image and can decrease the recognition rate.

Our proposed method is more efficient than the above methods and can maintain a high face recognition rate. For the first problem, we propose an efficient procedure called scale conversion. This procedure probabilistically estimates the facial scale of an input image by using only a reference graph and then converts the graph to the proper one to scale. For the second problem, we propose a procedure that normalizes Gabor wavelets for facial scale. Information on the scale is obtained by using the scale conversion. And the Gabor wavelets can optimally extract Gabor features. This procedure is more efficient than normalizing images and can maintain a high recognition rate even though the scales of the Gabor wavelets are reduced. This scale reduction seems to increase efficiency. In order to process this normalization efficiently, we propose an improved formula for Gabor wavelet transformation. We showed the outline of the proposed method and the results of preliminary experiments in [17]. In this paper, we describe the proposed method and new experiments in detail.

The proposed method is more efficient than any other for the following three reasons: (1) the method is based on the flexible feature matching method[8][9] which is more

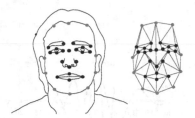

Fig. 1. Face representation. Gray nodes on contour, black nodes on facial organ.

efficient than the elastic matching method, (2) the method uses only a few scales of Gabor wavelets because these wavelets are normalized for facial scale and can optimally extract Gabor features, and (3) the facial scale is estimated by a simple method called scale conversion. Our method is also robust for scale variations because we use the optimum scale of Gabor wavelets for Gabor features extraction and the proper scale of face graph for the matching procedure. We implement a face recognition system based on the proposed method and demonstrate the advantages of the system through facial recognition experiments.

2 Face Representation

2.1 Facial Features

A face is represented as a graph where 30 nodes are placed on the FFPs (Fig. 1). Each node has the Gabor features extracted by GWT at the corresponding location. Each node also has a Euclidean distance to other nodes.

2.2 Gabor Wavelet Transformation

The Gabor feature representation allows description of spatial frequency structure in the image while preserving information about spatial relations. General GWT is the convolution of the image with a family of Gabor wavelets:

$$\psi_{j,\theta} = \frac{1}{4\pi a^{2j}\sigma} \exp\left(-\frac{x^2 + y^2}{2a^j\sigma^2}\right) \cdot$$

$$\exp\left(\frac{iu\left(x\cos\theta + y\sin\theta\right)}{a^j}\right) - \exp\left(-(u\sigma)^2\right),$$

$$j = 1, \cdots, N_j, \qquad \theta = \frac{\kappa\pi}{N_\theta} \text{ with } \kappa = 0, \ldots, N_\theta - 1. \tag{1}$$

The first factor in equation (1) is the normalized Gaussian window. The scale of Gabor wavelets is controlled by parameters a, σ, and j (a, σ : const.). The second factor is the sinusoidal component of the wavelets. The (x, y) term is projected in the θ direction to determine the complex exponential. Parameter u controls the frequency. Since these wavelets are compensated for their DC values by the second term in the bracket of

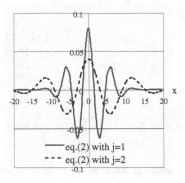

Fig. 2. Shapes of equation (2).

equation (1), the Gabor features have robustness for variations of illumination. GWT can extract sufficient information to represent facial features by using wavelets with several scale factors j and direction factors θ. GWT also produces complex features for every scale and direction. The magnitude information slowly varies with position and the phase information quickly varies. We use only the magnitude information because the phase information taken from image points only a few pixels apart has a very different value despite representing almost the same local feature.

It is a little complex to transform the scale of the Gabor wavelets because equation (1) has nonlinearity for factor j. We propose a new Gabor wavelets equation in order to simply extract the Gabor features normalized for facial scale.

$$\psi_{j,\theta} = \frac{1}{4\pi a^2 j^2 \sigma} \exp\left(-\frac{x^2 + y^2}{(2aj\sigma)^2}\right) \cdot$$

$$\exp\left(\frac{iu\left(x\cos\theta + y\sin\theta\right)}{aj} - \exp\left(-(u\sigma)^2\right)\right). \tag{2}$$

In equation (2), multiplying the factor j by an elastic ratio s_{opt} $(j \leftarrow j \times s_{opt})$, the scale of the wavelets become directly proportional to facial scale (s_{opt} is the scale ratio of face image to reference graph and is defined in section 3.3). We can thus simply extract the Gabor features corresponding to facial scale. Equation (2) has $1/20$ as much computational cost as equation (1). The shapes of equation (2) for $j = 1$ and 2 are shown in Fig. 2.

3   Face Recognition System

3.1   System Overview

The proposed system is summarized in Fig. 3. The system is composed of face detection, FFPs detection, and face identification procedure. The FFPs detection stage is composed of the scale conversion and the flexible feature matching procedure. Many model images

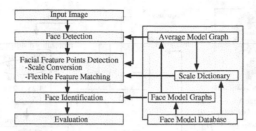

Fig. 3. Overview of the system.

are registered in the face model database. The faces in these images are nearly equal to each other in scale. Model graphs, an average model graph, and a scale dictionary are made from those images. The scale dictionary is used in the scale conversion procedure.

3.2 Face Detection

The face detection procedure begins with generation of the average model graph from available model graphs. The average model graph is generated by taking the average information of the Gabor features and the Euclidean distances of the available model graphs. The average model graph is used as a reference graph for the matching process. Then, by applying a sparse scanning of the reference graph through the Gabor features of the input image and by computing the Euclidean distance between the Gabor features of the input image and the reference graph, we can find the position of the face. The position with the smallest distance is considered as the estimated face position. This matching method is called fixed matching because it is done keeping each node's spatial relationships of the reference graph.

3.3 Facial Feature Points Detection

Scale Conversion. The scale conversion procedure efficiently estimates the facial scale of the input image and converts the reference graph (average model graph) to the proper one to scale by using the scale dictionary. The scale dictionary is made when the system is built.

First, we explain how to make the scale dictionary. N_t training images are used, whose scale is as large as that of the reference graph. Then, shadow graphs are generated by mapping elastic reference graphs with various scales (elastic ratio s_T) to the face position in each training image. The shadow graph represents a hypothesis for positions of FFPs. The appropriateness of the hypothesis can be measured from network response O:

$$O(G) = \sum_{m \in G} [\|W_{m,j} - I_{m,j}\| + u_m \sum_{n \in G-m} \|v_{mn} - e_{mn}\|]. \tag{3}$$

The network responses O of shadow graphs are registered in a database called the scale dictionary. These network responses are training data which indicate the unity level

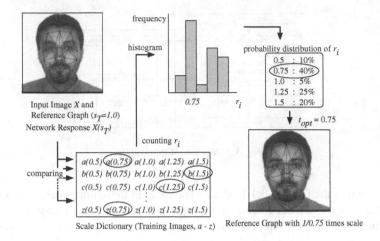

Fig. 4. Scale conversion process.

between the scale of face image and reference graph. A total of these network responses is N_t (number of training images) $\times$ T (step number of s_T).

G in equation (3) expresses the node of a graph. $W_{m,j}$ is the vector of the reference graph and the elements are the Gabor features that belong to scale j and node m. $I_{m,j}$ is the vector of the shadow graph G. v_{mn} is the Euclidean distance between node m and n on the reference graph and e_{mn} is that on the shadow graph G. u_m is a multiplicative weight. For generating the scale dictionary, u_m is set at 0.

The scale conversion is probabilistically performed using this scale dictionary. This process begins with generation of shadow graph G by mapping the original (non-elastic) reference graph G_{ref} at face position in the input image. The face position is estimated by the face detection procedure. Then, r_i are derived by the following equation:

$$r_i = \arg\min_{s_T}[O(G) - O(G_{ref} \times s_T)] \quad \text{for training image } i,$$
$$i = 1, \ldots, N_t, \quad T = 1, \ldots, T. \tag{4}$$

The second term, $O(G_{ref} \times s_T)$, in the bracket of equation (4) is the network response (the training data) in the scale dictionary. $G_{ref} \times s_T$ expresses the reference graph scaled by s_T. After the derivation of r_i, a probability distribution of r_i is calculated from statistics on r_i. We estimate facial scale according to this distribution, i.e., a scale ratio t_{opt} is r_i with the highest probability. A shadow graph with the proper scale is generated using the elastic ratio s_{opt} (=$1/t_{opt}$). In fact, r_i with the highest probability is not necessarily optimal. We must choose some candidates (t_{cand}) for t_{opt} in order to curry out the scale conversion accurately. We generate candidates for the shadow graph by using elastic ratios ($1/t_{cand}$) based on each t_{cand} and match these graphs with the input image. The elastic ratio of the best matching graph is used as s_{opt}. This process is summarized in Fig. 4.

Flexible Feature Matching. After the scale conversion procedure, we have rough positions of FFPs. These positions are used as initial information for finding the exact positions. First, Gabor wavelets are normalized by s_{opt} and GWT is performed. And an initial network response O_{norm} is computed.

$$O_{norm}(G) = \sum_{m \in G} \|W_{m,j} - I_{m,j \times s_{opt}}\| + u_m \sum_{n \in G-m} \|v_{mn} - \frac{e_{mn}}{s_{opt}}\| . \quad (5)$$

The Gabor features and the Euclidean distance in the equation (5) are normalized by s_{opt} for the facial scale. Then, by activating neighborhood connections around the nodes of the shadow graph, a candidate for a new shadow graph is created and the network response O_{norm} is computed. If the network response O_{norm} of the candidate graph is smaller than that of the shadow graph, the candidate graph becomes the new shadow graph. The flexible feature matching procedure repeats this process by using the random diffusion process. u_m in equation (5) is defined as

$$u_m(t) = u_{ini} \frac{u_{fin}}{u_{ini}}^{\frac{t}{t_{max}}} . \quad (6)$$

This monotonically decreases as the matching process runs. Here, u_{ini} is the distance of node movement at the initial step in the matching process and u_{fin} is that at the final step. t is the current step number and t_{max} is the maximum step number. The distance of node movement decreases according to equation (6). In order to prevent the node from moving to a strange position, this procedure moves the node according to a simple constraint. This constraint is defined by general knowledge of the facial component.

This matching method can robustly extract the FFPs from a person unregistered in the model database because the average model graph is used as the reference graph. Moreover, the method also works nicely on face images distorted by facial accessories because it uses spatial relationships.

3.4   Face Identification

The most valid shadow graph can be considered to be an accurate representation of the face in the input image. Face identification is performed by comparing the shadow graph with every model graph in the database. The network response O_{norm} (equation (5)) is evaluated for every model. Here, $W_{m,j}$ in equation (5) is the Gabor features vector of the model graph. $v_{m,j}$ is the Euclidean distance on the model graph. The model with the minimum network response is judged to be of the person matching the input face. If the network response is smaller than a certain threshold, the system accepts the identification.

4   Experimental Results

We conducted face recognition experiments to verify whether our system is effective. The system for the experiments was constructed on Onyx2 (CPU R12000 300MHz,

MEMORY 4GB, OS IRIX6.5.10m). The experiments were performed on 100 images (one image per person, 256×256pixel, 8bits gray scale) from the Purdue University's AR face database[18]. The faces of each image are expressionless and in frontal pose. Of these images, 50 images were registered as models in the database; the others were unregistered. The registered face images are nearly equal to each other in scale. The FFPs of models were manually extracted. Test images consisted of the following 500 images: the above 100 original images and 400 images which were scaled to 80, 90, 110, and 120% of their original size. Scaling of images was carried out by Graphic Converter 3.8.1 on MacOS 9.2. The parameters of the scale dictionary were: $N_t = 20$, $T = 11$ and s_T ranges from 0.5 to 1.5 by 0.1. The parameters of u_m in equation (5) were $u_{ini} = 4$, $u_{fin} = 1$, and $t_{max} = 200$. GWT was performed using 16 Gabor wavelets ($N_j = 2$, $N_\theta = 8$), with parameters $\sigma = 1$, $a = 2.5$ and $u = \pi$. The general face recognition method uses 40 Gabor wavelets ($N_j = 5$, $N_\theta = 8$).

We compared the performance of our system with that of the following two systems. The first system uses eleven reference graphs (50, 60, 70, 80, 90, 100, 110, 120, 130, 140, and 150% scale of the average model graph). This system estimates the facial scale by matching these graphs with an input image. The best matching reference graph is used in the FFPs detection procedure (i.e., the previous flexible feature matching procedure[8][9]). We call this system, previous system 1. The second system normalizes the input image to scale. The only reference graph is the average model graph. This system makes eleven images of the input image (scaled to 1/50, 1/60, 1/70, 1/80, 1/90, 1/100, 1/110, 1/120, 1/130, 1/140, and 1/150% of their original size). This system matches the reference graph with these images. The best matching image is used in the FFPs detection procedure (i.e., the previous flexible feature matching procedure). This system has an extra computational cost for scaling the image. We call this system, previous system 2.

4.1   Performance of Scale Conversion

We compare performance of the scale conversion procedure with that of the facial scale estimation (general procedure) used by the previous system 1. We represent a processing time for the former procedure as $t_c + c \times t_n$ and that for the latter procedure as $T \times t_n$. Here, t_c is a processing time to choose t_{cand}, t_n is the time to match a graph with an image, c is the number of t_{cand}, and T is the number of reference graphs used by the previous system 1. T is also the step number of s_T in the scale conversion procedure. t_c increases in proportion to T. t_n includes a processing time to compute GWT and the network response O. Through the experiments, an actual measurement of t_c and t_n was 13 ms and 470 ms respectively. t_c can be disregarded for t_n because t_c is much smaller than t_n. The comparison between the processing time needed by the both procedures is dependent on c and T. T was 11 through the experiments.

We set c by using statistics shown in Fig. 5. The statistics cumulate the probability of r_i. As the statistics indicate, the cumulative probability from the first candidate to the fifth candidate exceeds 90%. We confirmed that an optimal scale ratio was included in the five candidates. Therefore, we set c to 5. The scale conversion procedure ($c = 5$) is more efficient than the general procedure ($T = 11$).

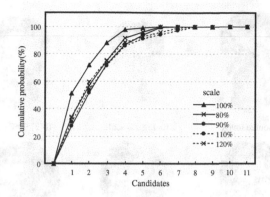

Fig. 5. Cumulative probability of candidates for optimal scale ratio.

Table 1. Differences between the Gabor features of the model and those of the input image.

image scale	80%	90%	110%	120%
equation (2)	0.37	0.35	0.37	0.32
equation (1)	0.62	0.43	0.48	0.54

4.2 FFPs Detection Accuracy

Examples of FFPs detection are shown in Fig. 6. Each position of the FFPs in an image does not completely correspond with a position in the other images even though our system normalizes the Gabor features for facial scale. We consider the cause of this discrepancy in Table 1. Table 1 shows mean difference between the Gabor features of the model graph and those extracted by equations (1) and (2) from the facial image which corresponds to the model. We extracted the FFPs on all models manually. We multiplied the scale factor j in equation (2) by the elastic ratio of the image in order to normalize Gabor wavelets. It is obvious that the Gabor features extracted by equation (2) are not affected by variations of spatial frequency because the mean differences for equation (2) in Table 1 are almost constant. However, as these values are not zero, the normalization is not completely correct. We believe this result occurs because of a degradation of the image caused by scaling the image. The degradation causes incomplete normalization and thus there is discrepancy between the FFPs positions.

Accuracy of FFPs detection is measured by the position error (average pixel per node) between the most valid shadow graph and the model graph corresponding to the face of the input image. The spatial relationships of the shadow graph are normalized according to equation (5). The level of accuracy achieved is shown in Table 2. The proposed system maintains a high accuracy for every scaled image. As for the previous systems, the accuracy deteriorates for scaled input images. This occurs because previous system 1 does not normalize the Gabor features and previous system 2 degrades an image by scaling the image. There is a difference in accuracy between the three systems for source images (100% scale). This occurs because faces of these images are not same scale (though the faces are nearly equal scale). In other words, the difference results

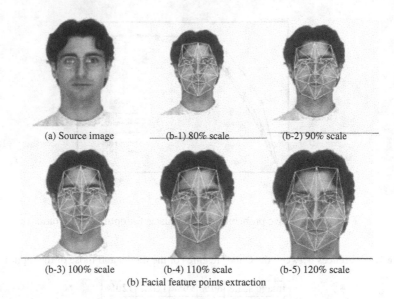

(a) Source image   (b-1) 80% scale   (b-2) 90% scale

(b-3) 100% scale   (b-4) 110% scale   (b-5) 120% scale
(b) Facial feature points extraction

Fig. 6. Detection results.

Table 2. FFPs detection error (pixel).

image scale	80%	90%	100%	110%	120%
Proposed system	4.43	4.77	4.20	4.73	5.40
Previous system 1	9.34	6.12	4.49	5.52	7.05
Previous system 2	9.78	6.02	4.50	5.91	8.78

from that the scale conversion and normalization of the Gabor features are applied to source images.

4.3   Face Identification Accuracy

Accuracy of face identification is represented by the ROC curve in Fig. 7. The curve connects identification rates with thresholds to judge whether the system accepts the identification result. The identification rate of an unregistered person (the vertical axis in the figure) is the rate of which the system rejects the identification result. The accuracy of the proposed system is higher than that of the previous systems and remains good for variations of facial scale. The accuracy of the previous systems is degraded for the reasons described in section 4.2.

5   Conclusions

We proposed a face recognition method robust for variations of facial scale. Such a method can contribute to the construction of a human interface to realize more natural computer communication. The proposed method efficiently estimates the facial scale

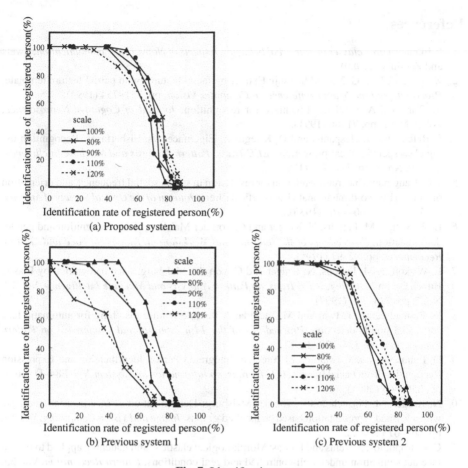

(a) Proposed system

(b) Previous system 1

(c) Previous system 2

Fig. 7. Identification rate.

and extracts the Gabor features which are normalized for scale. The matching method is based on the flexible feature matching method. We implemented the face recognition system using the proposed method and tested the system through facial recognition experiments. The results demonstrated that the system can robustly detect the FFPs and maintain a high accuracy of person identification for face scale variations. The results also demonstrated that normalizing Gabor wavelets in order to normalize the Gabor features is more useful than normalizing the input image. Moreover, we could construct a system which used only a few scales of Gabor wavelets. As the computational cost of GWT is very high and increases in proportion to the number of the wavelets used, our system is very efficient in comparison.

This paper shows results for images scaled to 80, 90, 110, and 120% of their original size. The system can deal with every variation of facial scale. A model graph of an unregistered person can be automatically registered in the database because its facial image is accurately recognized. In future work, the proposed method will be applied to variations in facial pose and occlusion of facial parts.

References

1. P. Ekman: *Three classes of nonverbal behavior, Aspects of Nonverbal Communication*, Swets and Zeitlinger (1980).
2. X. Song, C. Lee, G. Xu and S. Tsuji: Extracting facial features with partial feature template, *Proceedings of the Asian Conference on Computer Vision*, pp. 751–754 (1994).
3. M. Turk and A. Pentland: Eigenface for recognition, *Journal of Cognitive Neuroscience*, Vol. 3, No. 1, pp. 71–86 (1991).
4. P. Belhumeur, J. Hespanha and D. Kriegman: Eigenfaces vs. Fisherfaces: Recognition using class specific linear projection, *IEEE Trans. Pattern Analysis and Machine Intelligence*, Vol. 19, No. 7, pp. 711–720 (1997).
5. J. G. Daugman: Uncertainty relation for resolution in space, spatial frequency, and orientation optimized by two-dimensional visual cortical filters, *Journal of the Optical Society of America A*, Vol. 2, pp. 1160–1169 (1985).
6. L. Wiskott, J. M. Fellous, N. Krüger and C. von der Malsburg: Face recognition and gender determination, *Proceedings of the International Workshop on Automatic Face and Gesture Recognition*, pp. 92–97 (1995).
7. L. Wiskott, J. M. Fellous, N. Krüger and C. von der Malsburg: Face recognition by Elastic Bunch Graph Matching, *IEEE Trans. on Pattern Analysis and Machine Intelligence*, Vol. 19, No. 7, pp. 775–779 (1997).
8. D. Pramadihanto, Y. Iwai and M. Yachida: A flexible feature matching for automatic face and facial points detection, *Proceedings of the 14th International Conference on Pattern Recognition*, pp. 324–329 (1998).
9. D. Pramadihanto, Y. Iwai and M. Yachida: Integrated Person Identification and Expression Recognition from Facial Images, *IEICE Trans. on Information and System*, Vol. E84–D, No. 7, pp. 856–866 (2001).
10. N. Krüger, M. Pötzsch and C. von der Malsburg: Determination of face position and pose with a learned representation based on labelled graphs, *Image and Vision Computing*, Vol. 15, pp. 665–673 (1997).
11. C. Kotropoulos, A. Tefas and I. Pitas: Morphological elastic graph matching applied to frontal face authentication under well-controlled and real conditions, *Pattern Recognition*, Vol. 33, pp. 1935–1947 (2000).
12. M. Lades, J. C. Vorbruggen, J. Buhmann, J. Lange, C. von der Malsburg, R. P. Wurtz and W. Konen: Distortion invariant object recognition in the Dynamic Link Architecture, *IEEE Trans. Comput.*, Vol. 42, pp. 300–311 (1993).
13. D. Pramadihanto, H. Wu and M. Yachida: Face Identification under Varying Pose Using a Single Example View, *The Transactions of the Institute of Electronics, Information and Communication Engineers D–II*, Vol. J80–D–II, No. 8, pp. 2232–2238 (1997).
14. M. J. Lyons, J. Budynek, A. Plante and S. Akamatsu: Classifying Facial Attributes using a 2–D Gabor Wavelet Representation and Discriminant Analysis, *Proceedings of the International Conference on Automatic Face and Gesture Recognition*, pp. 202–207 (2000).
15. M. Lades: *Invariant Object Recognition Based on Dynamical Links, Robust to Scaling, Rotation and Variation of Illumination*, Ruhr Universität, Bochum, Germany (1995).
16. K. Okada, J. Steffens, T. Maurer, H. Hong, E. Elagin, H. Neven and C. von der Malsburg: *The Bochum/USC Face Recognition System: And How it Fared in the FERET PhaseIII Test*, Springer-Verlag, Sterling, UK (1998).
17. T. Hirayama, Y. Iwai and M. Yachida: Person Identification System Robust for Facial Scale Variants, *IEEE International Workshop on Cues in Communication*, No. 11 (2001).
18. A. M. Martinez and R. Benavente: The AR face database, CVC Technical Report 24 (1998).

Eyebrow Movement Analysis over Real-Time Video Sequences for Synthetic Representation

Ana C. Andrés del Valle and Jean-Luc Dugelay

Institut Eurécom, Multimedia Communications Department,
2229, route des Crêtes B.P. 193 – 06904 Sophia Antipolis cedex – France
Tel: +33 (0)4.93.00.{29.21}{26.41}; Fax: +33 (0)4.93.00.26.27
{ana.andres,jean-luc.dugelay}@eurecom.fr
http://www.eurecom.fr/~image

Abstract. To study eyebrow behavior from video sequences we utilize a new image analysis technique based on an anatomical-mathematical motion model. This technique conceives the eyebrow as a single curved object (arch) that is subject to the deformation due to muscular interactions. The action model defines the simplified 2D (vertical and horizontal) displacements of the arch. Our video analysis algorithm recovers the needed data from the arch representation to deduce the parameters that deformed the proposed model. The present technique is meant to suit real-time requirements and to work under uncontrolled environments: without specific known lighting or special markers on the face, by using only computer vision and image processing methods.

1 Introduction

Face animation has become a need for those multimedia applications where human interaction with virtual and augmented environments enhances the interface. It is also a solution for face image transmission in low bit rate communications, video-telephony, virtual teleconferencing, etc.

To synthesize the speaker's face expression in real-time communications, we must develop video image analysis techniques robust to any environment, lighting conditions by not imposing any physical constraints. Most of the existing face expression analysis techniques are not really suitable for practical purposes. The most performing analysis systems utilize the synthesis of head models. DeCarlo and Metaxas [1] have developed a technique based on optical flow constraints to analyze and interpret face motion. Eisert and Girod [2] use a similar approach in their teleconferencing system. Their research results are very encouraging but their analysis algorithms work under many environmental restrictions.

In our previous work about virtual teleconferencing environments [3, 4], we have developed a video analysis framework where we artificially separate pose tracking from face expression analysis. To understand face expression motion, we develop some dedicated analysis techniques to apply on eyes, eyebrows and mouth. Our analysis algorithms generate face animation parameters used to synthesize feature motion in 3D. Other approaches, e. g. Y. Tian et al. [5], study more face features; the given solutions are usually too complex to be utilized in real-time. T. Goto at al. describe in [6] a complete real-time system also based on different feature image analy-

F.J. Perales and E.R. Hancock (Eds.): AMDO 2002, LNCS 2492, pp. 213–225, 2002.
© Springer-Verlag Berlin Heidelberg 2002

sis techniques. They give few details about the image processing algorithms involved in the analysis of the eyebrows. In general, we have not found in the literature a formal description of analysis algorithms to study eyebrow behavior, even though eyebrows play an active role in emotional face expression.

We utilize a two step process to develop our image analysis algorithms. First, we design image-processing techniques to study the features extracted from a frontal view of the face. Faces show most of their expression information under this pose and this allows us to verify the correct performance of the image processing involved. Second, we adapt our algorithms to analyze features taken at any given pose. To do so, we use the pose parameters predicted during face tracking and the 3D model synthesis of the speaker's clone. This approach has already been successfully tested to analyze the eye feature [7].

To study the eyebrow behavior we have developed an anatomical-mathematical motion model that can easily be used to derive the parameters describing 2D (vertical and horizontal) eyebrow movements. Our technique is here tested for a frontal view and works under no environmental constraint, besides fixing the head pose. As briefly explained in Section 4, in our future perspective, we will adapt the algorithm to couple pose and expression information.

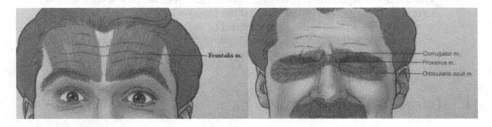

Fig. 1. Several muscles generate the eyebrow movements. Upward motion is mainly due to the Frontalis muscle and downward motion is due to the Corrugator, the Procerus and the Orbicularis Oculi muscles[1]

Table 1. Notation conventions used in formulae

x_n, y_n: real coordinate values of the eyebrow in their neutral position.

$x_n[i]$, $y_n[i]$: coordinate value of the pixel obtained from the video image analysis of the eyebrow in its neutral position at position i.

x, y: real coordinate values of the eyebrow in their current (analyzed frame) position.

$x[i]$, $y[i]$: coordinate value of the pixel obtained from the video image analysis of the current frame eyebrow at position i.

x, y : real coordinate difference between the current eyebrow arch and the neutral arch x_{frame} $x_{neutral}$, y_{frame} $y_{neutral}$ respectively.

$x[i]$, $y[i]$: real coordinate difference between the pixels from the current eyebrow arch being analyzed and those from the neutral arch at position i.

[0], [N] and [max] indicate the computed values for the first point ($x = 0$), the last point ($x =$ last) and the point with the maximum vertical value ($x : y =$ max) on the arch.

[1] Images and information based on data from www.oculoplastic.co.uk/eyebrows/anatomy.html

2   Anatomical-Mathematical Eyebrow Movement Modeling

To model the eyebrow movement, we define some mathematical expressions that superficially follow the muscular behavior and interaction when eyebrow motion exists.

Basically, four muscles control the eyebrow movement:
(i)   *Frontalis* (F): that elevates them.
(ii)   *Corrugatori* (CS): that pulls them downwardly, produces vertical glabellar wrinkles.
(iii)   *Procerus*: that lowers the eyebrows downwardly.
(iv)   *Orbicucularis oculi*(OO): that closes eyes and lowers eyebrows.

Although the shape is slightly dependent on the anatomy of the person, eyebrow motion is more general. This enables us to represent eyebrows as arches, whose shape is specific to the person but whose motion can be mathematically modeled. We parameterize the arch movement as the displacement in the x, y and z-axis of each of its points compared to the initial neutral position (when no force acts). ($x = x_{frame}$ $x_{neutral}$, $y = y_{frame}$ $y_{neutral}$ and $z = z_{frame}$ $z_{neutral}$). All notation conventions can be found in Table 1.

Two different behaviors exist in eyebrow motion, one when the expression goes upwards and another when the expression goes downwards. Different muscular action is involved for each of them and therefore different models control them. These expressions have been derived from the observation of the muscular motion of the eyebrows and the empirical study of the optical flow behavior of the eyebrow area observed on real video sequences and adapting the parameters involved to the anatomical shape of the eyebrow.

Eyebrow Motion Expressions:

UPWARDS:

$$x = Ff_x \ e^{(\ x_n / \ )} \tag{1}$$

$$y = Ff_y + Ff_y'e^{(\ x_n / \ )} \tag{2}$$

DOWNWARDS:

$$y = \ Fcs_y \ Foo_y \ (|x_n| \ )^2 \tag{3}$$

If $x_n <$
$$x = \ Fcs_x \tag{4a}$$

If $x_n >$
$$x = Foo_x \ (\ x_n) \ Fcs_x \tag{4b}$$

Ff, Fcs and *Foo* are the magnitudes associated to the force of the Frontalis muscle, Corrugator muscle and the Orbicucularis Oculi respectively. The action of the Procerus muscle, being close and highly correlated to the one from the Corrugator, is included in the *Fcs* term. $_x$ and $_y$ indicate the different components,

$= 2 \dfrac{w}{3}$ and $= \dfrac{w}{2}$. All coordinates relate to the eyebrow local coordinate system. Figure 2 depicts the coordinate axis for the left eyebrow; the right eyebrow is symmetrical over an imaginary vertical line between the eyebrows.

$z = f(\ x,\ y)$, quite more difficult to model, does not provide critical information regarding the eyebrow expression. z is never well estimated from a frontal point of view. If we want to realistically synthesize 3D eyebrow motion with information obtained from image analysis under these conditions, we may estimate the z movement by assuming that the eyebrow motion follows the front surface, thus, simulating its natural behavior. The *"displacement of texture coordinate"* synthetic animation technique described in [3] illustrates this concept. This procedure simulates the eyebrow skin sliding motion on the skull. Changing the texture coordinates vertically and horizontally generates the animation; the model 3D coordinates remain unchanged, thus leaving the skull shape untouched.

Applying the formulae over two rounded arches with different parameter values, we obtain deformations that correspond to the expected eyebrow deformation due to those forces. Figure 3 shows the simulation of extreme modeled movement (*downwards* and *upwards*) on both eyebrows.

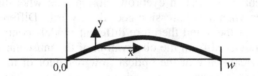

Fig. 2. Eyebrow model arch for the left eye and its coordinate reference. The origin for the analysis algorithm it is always situated at the inner extreme of the eyebrow (close to the nose) and defined for the eyebrow in its neutral state

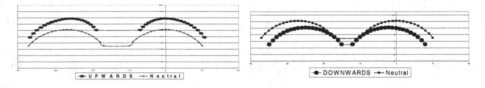

Fig. 3. The action of the eyebrow behavior model applied over the neutral arch results on a smooth deformation. The graph on the left depicts eyebrow rising motion (*upwards*) for positive values of Ff_x, Ff_y and Ff_y'. The graph on the right represents eyebrow frowning (*downwards*) for positive values of Fcs_x, Foo_x, Fcs_y and Foo_y

3   Image Analysis Algorithm: Deducing Model Parameters in a Frontal Position

We achieve two goals by modeling the eyebrow movement. On the one hand, we simplify the eyebrow motion understanding to a point where we can derive its movements on images by comparing image data with the model parameters. On the other hand, this model is complete enough to generate the required information to create synthetic eyebrow expressions.

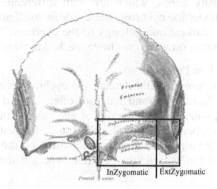

Fig. 4. The eyebrow changes its hair density as it goes away from the inner extreme. The bone structure of the skull determines the shading difference along the eyebrow. We set two different binarization thresholds: Th1 for the *InZygomatic* zone and Th2 for the *ExtZygomatic*

The developed image analysis algorithm tries to reduce the image of the eyebrow down to the proposed model in order to study the distribution of the points on the eyebrow arch. Then, it deduces the strength of the parameters involved. The analysis compares data extracted from the current video frame against the data obtained from the frame where the eyebrow is in a neutral position or *neutral frame*.

Algorithm procedure:

Binarization: Eyebrows and skin are normally easy to separate in terms of hue, and with less accuracy, intensity. Under 'regular' although 'not controlled' lighting conditions we can differentiate eyebrows from skin and therefore binarize the feature image. We consider 'normal, not controlled' lighting any illumination over the face that permits the eyebrow visual differentiation on the video frame.

Due to the anatomical nature of the head, eyebrows do not present the same aspect all over their arch. The area situated on the inner part of the *Superciliary* arch is generally better defined and easier to differentiate from the skin than the eyebrow arch that goes towards the joint with the *Superior Temporal Line*, because this last one is usually more sparse. Our analysis algorithm needs to detect the complete eyebrow because we are interested in studying the overall shape behavior. We have developed a binarization algorithm that analyzes the eyebrow in two different zones. One zone includes from the center of the face up to the point which is half way between the *Foramen* and the *Zygomatic* process (point where the eyebrow usually changes shape direction and texture) and the other zone goes from there to the external end of the eyebrow. We refer to Figure 4 to locate the different parts.

To perform the binarization we apply two different thresholds, one per zone. Each threshold is obtained by analyzing the histogram distribution of the corresponding area. The eyebrow is taken as the darkest part on the video image being analyzed.

$$Th_i = \min_i + \frac{\max_i\ \min_i}{3} \tag{5}$$

If pixel_value<Th_i, the pixel is considered as part of the eyebrow. The threshold has been chosen to be at a third of the intensity distribution because the analysis area covers three major intensity zones, which are well differentiated in most lighting conditions: the eye zone under the eyebrow, the eyebrow itself and the front zone over the eyebrow. Usually the darkest one belongs to the eyebrow. Figure 5-a shows the histogram of one of the zones, on which we have marked the three different zones.

Results of the Binarization Process:
This binarization algorithm correctly detects the eyebrow even if in some cases it also introduces some artifacts. Eyes and hair are often labeled as being part of the eyebrow (see Figure 5-b, where eye is marked as eyebrow). Both, eye and hair must not be taken into account when analyzing the Region of Interest (ROI) to extract the eyebrow arch. Due to their predefined and fixed situation on the ROI, we have easily adapted the thinning algorithm to avoid the possible expected artifacts.

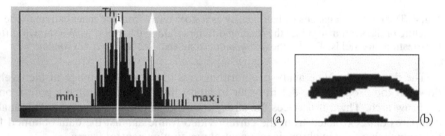

Fig. 5. The eyebrow 'two part' binarization leads to good determination of the eyebrow area but it also may introduce artifacts by labeling eyes or hair as part of the eyebrow. In the current eyebrow binary image we see how the eye has also been detected

Thinning: We perform a vertical thinning over the binarized image to obtain the rounded arch that will define the eyebrow. This vertical thinning delineates the eyebrow arch by choosing the pixels located in the vertical middle of the binarized eyebrow shape. Figures 7 and 8 show some thinning results.

Expression choice: To establish the correct parameters, we first deduce the eyebrow main action. We compute the average vertical value (y_{avg}) of the eyebrow for each frame and we compare it to the average vertical value computed when the eyebrow was in its neutral position. If the new average is greater, we will deduce that we have an *upward* expression; if it is smaller, we will deduce that we have a *downward* expression. The average value for the *neutral* expression arch is computed from the analysis of a frame previously labeled as neutral, on which the speaker did not move its eyebrows.

Parameter deduction: Depending on the general expression we obtain the mathematical model parameters. They are deduced from comparing the thinned arch at the current frame against the arch of the eyebrow in a neutral position.

Parameter expressions:

UPWARDS:

$$Ff_x \quad x[0] \quad e^{(x_n[0]/\ )} \quad x[0] \tag{6a}$$

$$Ff_y' \quad \frac{y[N] \quad y[0]}{(e^{(\ x_n[N]/\ )} \quad 1)} \tag{6b}$$

$$Ff_y \quad y[0] \quad Ff_y' \tag{6c}$$

DOWNWARDS:

$$Fcs_x \quad x[0] \tag{7a}$$

$$Foo_x \quad \frac{x[N] + Fcs_x}{x_n[N]} \tag{7b}$$

$$Fcs_y \quad \frac{y[0] \quad y[N]}{2} \tag{7c}$$

$$Foo_y \quad \frac{Fcs_y \quad y[\max]}{2} \tag{7d}$$

4   Verifying the Analysis Technique over Video Sequences

To our knowledge, it does not exist a database of face images that completely suits the needs of our tests. Nevertheless, we have tried to test our procedure over more than one speaker; and specifically, we show the results from the analysis of three individuals of different eyebrow characteristics taped under uncontrolled lighting conditions.

To test the correct behavior of the model and its application for eyebrow motion analysis, we applied the binarization-thinning technique over the left eye on the frames of several video sequences. Then, we deduced the model parameters contrasting the frame arch against the *neutral position arch*. To verify that the obtained parameters actually correspond to the eyebrow behavior, we have plotted the thinning results of each frame together with the obtained arch from applying the model over the *neutral position arch*, this resulting arch is the *modeled arch*. Figure 8 shows this arch comparison for the frames presented in the sequence of Figure 6; they also include the *neutral position arch*.

The best way to evaluate the performance of our techniques is to visually compare arch results; unfortunately, this procedure is not suitable to be applied over a large amount of data. To interpret the performance correctness of our approach, we have defined two different measurements:

(i)   a *pseudo-area*:

$$\tilde{a} = \quad \left| y_k[i] \quad y_m[i] \right| \tag{8}$$
$$\phantom{\tilde{a} =}_i$$

which can be understood as the area contained in-between arch k and m and it denotes the shape similarity between them; the closer $\tilde{a}$ is to 0 the more alike they are. We apply this measurement to check if the eye shape modeled by the extracted motion parameters follows the expected eyebrow obtained from the action;

(ii) a *mean difference comparison*: where we compare the mean (average vertical value of the arch) difference between the *current frame arch* and the *neutral position arch* against the mean difference between the *current frame arch* and the *modeled arch*. This information helps us to evaluate if the analysis procedure was not even able to detect the right eyebrow general action: up/down and it also provides information on the shape behavior of the *modeled arch*, by studying the sign of the measurement that gives a vertical location estimation.

We consider that the algorithm has worked right if the *pseudo-area* comparison shows that the *modeled arch* is closer to the *current frame arch* than the *neutral position arch*. Completely understanding the performance of this technique would also imply generating the synthetic eyebrow expression over a 3D head model of the speaker for a more detailed visual inspection. We will be able to perform this kind of tests when the pose coupling adaptation of the algorithm will be done and the tests will be performed on the complete analysis-synthesis of pose and expression system.

Test conclusions:

Results show that this analysis technique positively deduces the eyebrow behavior. We are able to analyze video images and extract the few needed parameters to understand and to later synthesize eyebrow motion.

From the visual inspection of our results we conclude that errors come more from the image processing performance of the analysis than from the motion model used. Correct binarization and later thinning are critical to obtain accurate motion parameters. Figure 9 plots the measurement results of three different tests. The percentage of estimation success (better measurements over the *modeled arch*) is around 85% for those sequences where image quality and environment lighting conditions are standard. For low quality video input performance drops to around 50%. We must point out that the worst estimation usually happens for low expression movements, where the inaccuracy of the situation of the analysis area (the speaker may slightly move) is large enough to mislead the average results. In this case, like the *average difference* measurement shows, we may interpret an *up* movement as being *down* or vice versa.

Looking at Figure 7-b we realize how important the correct and precise definition of the eyebrow analysis area is. The graph plots the results of one analyzed sequence along with the neutral analyzed frame of another sequence where head location and size were not exactly the same. Motion not due to the eyebrow expression but to the overall head pose leads to mistaken results. Our tests have been performed accepting that the head pose on the video sequence is known and frontal. This is an unrealistic assumption if practical use of the algorithms is desired. Section 5 briefly explains which will be our next steps to adapt our algorithm to any given pose and to be able to use it within the telecom context exposed in the introduction.

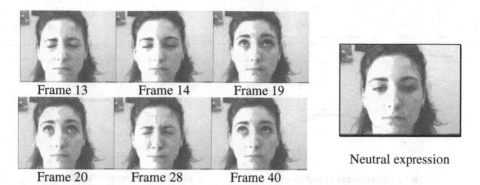

Frame 13   Frame 14   Frame 19

Frame 20   Frame 28   Frame 40

Neutral expression

Fig. 6. Our tests were performed over video sequences where the lighting over the face was not uniform. No environmental conditions were known besides the exact location of the ROI including the eyebrow feature, which remained unchanged through the sequence. Here we present the frames analyzed to obtained the results presented in Figure 8

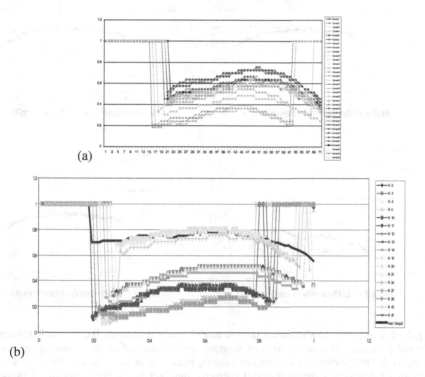

(a)

(b)

Fig. 7. Correct binarization and thinning clearly gives the data from which to extract the model parameters. Graph (b) plots the mixed results from the analysis of two different video sequences. **Neut. Seq.2** is the analysis of a frame where the eyebrow was relaxed taken from a sequence different from the **Fr sequence**. This comparison simulates what would happen if the pose of the speaker changed during the analysis. The pose motion would cause the movement of the eyebrow but the algorithm would interpret it as a local eyebrow expression (being *upwards* when in reality it is neutral) We must control the pose of the user to completely exploit the algorithm in practical applications

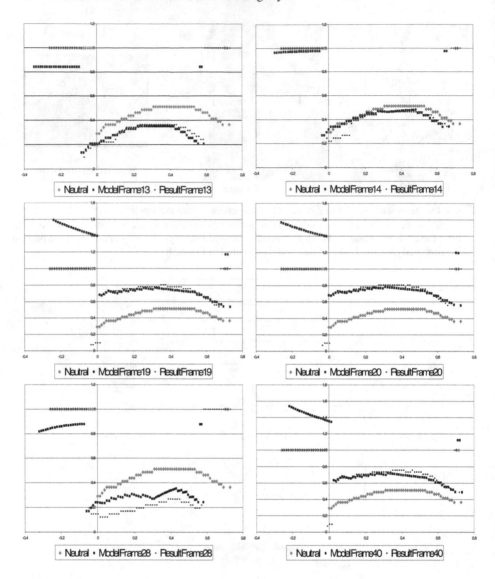

Fig. 8. The anatomic-mathematical motion model nicely represents the eyebrow deformation. We see on frame 28 how the strange thinning result obtained at the beginning of the arch, probably due to the eyebrow-eye blending during binarization, worsens the algorithm accuracy. Although the obtained parameters still correctly interpret the general downward movement, showing fair robustness, they are no longer able to express the exact motion intensity

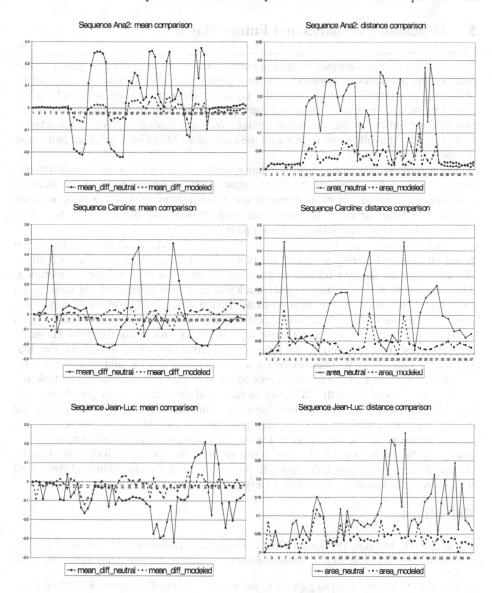

Fig. 9. These plotted results from three different sequences: Ana2, Caroline and Jean-Luc illustrate the analysis behavior of the algorithm under different conditions. The algorithm proves to detect the right movement (the mean difference decreases) and to estimate the motion parameters correctly (the area decreases). We observe the best behavior for extreme eyebrow expressions. Ana2 sequence success rate: 90.71%, Caroline sequence success rate: 78.38% and Jean-Luc sequence success rate: 82.26%

5   Concluding Remarks and Future Work

The eyebrow motion analysis technique herein proposed has proved to give positive results. The animation parameters obtained represent eyebrow behavior and can be utilized to generate 3D-motion synthesis. To do so, these parameters need to be interpreted by some animation system and may have to be adapted to face animation parameter "semantics" of the animation engine. We have started to develop the adaptation procedure that allows us to generate the equivalent MPEG-4 FAP (face animation parameters).

The algorithms presented show two major weaknesses. First, we need to define one *neutral position frame* out of the video sequence from which we start the analysis comparisons. Second, all measurements are taken assuming that the pose remains unchanged along the time. In communication applications the analyzed face will freely move and such restriction will disappear.

In our complete analysis framework we have developed a head-tracking algorithm based on Kalman Filtering to predict the pose of the person. We also utilize a realistic 3D model of the speaker (clone) to generate an analysis by synthesis cooperation. This framework allows us to correctly track the region of interest of the features on each frame and to adapt our 'near-to-front' image analysis algorithms to any given pose after having verified their correct performance under the pose that gives the most expression information. We adapt these algorithms by redefining them on 3D using data extracted from the clones. We have already done this adaptation to the eye feature image analysis we had developed for a frontal position [7, 8] and we are currently developing and testing the adaptation procedure over the eyebrow analysis technique.

The use of highly realistic 3D head models will also allow us to get all the data taken for the *neutral position frame* from the analysis of synthesized images of the clone. The binarization process we have presented is suitable for white skin people with average eyebrows, but it may not work for people with very dark skin or almost unappreciable eyebrows. An 'a priori' color study of the speaker's skin as well as the choice of the most suitable color space to perform the binarization skin/eyebrow could let us extend the complete procedure to any given case.

References

1. DeCarlo, D., Metaxas, D.: Optical Flow Constraints on Deformable Models with Applications to Face Tracking. In *International Journal of Computer Vision* (July 2000) 38(2) 99-127
2. Eisert, P., Girod, B.: Analyzing Facial Expressions for Virtual Conferencing. In *IEEE Computer Graphics & Applications* (September 1998) 70-78
3. Valente, S., Dugelay, J.-L.: Face Tracking and Realistic Animations for Telecommunicant Clones. In *IEEE Multimedia Magazine* (February 2000) 34-43
4. Dugelay, J.-L., Andrés del Valle, A. C.: Analysis-Synthesis Cooperation for MPEG-4 Realistic Clone Animation. In Proceedings of the *Euroimage ICAV3D* (June 2001)
5. Tian, Y., Kanade, T., Cohn, J.: Recognizing Lower Face Action Units for Facial Expression Analysis. In Proceedings of the *4th IEEE International Conference On Automatic and Gesture Recognition* (March 2000) 484-490
6. Goto, T., Escher, M., Zanardi, C., Magnenat-Thalmann, N.: MPEG-4 Based Animation with Face Feature Tracking. In Proceedings of the *Eurographics Workshop on Animation and Simulation* (September 1999) Springer-Verlag 89-98

7. Andrés del Valle, A. C., Dugelay, J.-L.: Eye State Tracking for Face Cloning. In Proceedings of the *International Conference on Image Processing* (October 2001)
8. Andrés del Valle, A. C., Dugelay, J.-L.: Facial Expression Analysis Robust to 3D Head Pose Motion. In Proceedings of the *International Conference on Multimedia and Expo* (August 2002)

Software Laboratory for Physical Based Human Body Animation

Francisco Rojas[1], Sandra Baldassarri[2], and Francisco J. Serón[2]

[1] Area de Electrónica y Nuevas Tecnologías
Instituto Tecnológico de Aragón, María de Luna 8, 50018
frojas@ita.es
[2] Grupo de Informática Gráfica Avanzada. Dep. de Informática e Ingeniería de Sistemas
Centro Politécnico Superior – Universidad de Zaragoza, María de Luna 1, 50018
{sandra,seron}@posta.unizar.es

Abstract. New applications in virtual reality, robotics and medicine are impelling the dynamics-based methods for the human body simulation. The dynamics allows to establish global solutions of motion in virtual autonomous agents, in the locomotion of biped robots and in the development of intelligent prosthesis for motor disabilities recovery. This paper presents the conceptual design of a software laboratory for the study, development and verification of dynamic-techniques of motion control and human body representation. The main idea of this work is the use, as basic pattern of motion, of the direct solution of very simple dynamic models governed by a finite state machine. These models are developed, specializing, linked and solved using empirical laws of the real movement. The visualization improved the final result, applying kinematics over the basic pattern of motion. As an example of laboratory application, this paper describes the previous work, developments and results obtained in the simulation of human locomotion. The whole set of software tools, derived from the laboratory concept design, has been completely developed and implemented. These tools could be modified and customized in some of the suggested future works.

1 Introduction

Biomechanics is a discipline that involves from empirical studies that statically describe only one functional parameter to detailed microscopic models of the muscular fiber chemistry. This area includes experiments of corpse muscular stiffness and laboratories specialized in data obtained by motion-capturing systems. Moreover, biomechanics studies the motion control looking for the patterns of involuntary behavior that allows the movements of humans. The used techniques deal with multi-articulated inverted pendulum considering the active stiffness (activated muscles) and passive stiffness (mechanics of tendons and ligaments). In [1] the construction of a dynamic simulator of locomotion for finding the best combination of electrical stimulation and the development of prosthesis for the rehabilitation of paraplegic patients is presented. [2] emphasizes the role of the elastic energy of the postural muscles and column and pelvis joint systems in the beginning of the walk.

F.J. Perales and E.R. Hancock (Eds.): AMDO 2002, LNCS 2492, pp. 226–240, 2002.
© Springer-Verlag Berlin Heidelberg 2002

The same main idea of using actives and passive dynamic controls in Biomechanics is developed in detail in Robotics. The control passive systems minimize the energetic consumption while the active ones increase it, but can be controlled better. The active control of biped robots has, as obliged reference, the work of Raibert [3]. The passive systems are inspired in McMahon [4]. [5] describes and develops the mechanic equations of motion and control according to a constant equivalent to the potential energy of the system. [6] simulates a biped robot with less energy consumption synchronizing passive and active dynamics.

On the other hand, Computer Graphics deals with more general problems of human body animation. The first "software laboratory" dynamics-based animation is the DYNAMO system [7]. There, Lagrange multipliers are used for considering generic constraints in the motion equations. [8] and [9] are complementary reviews that present the evolution of computer animation of the human body. [10] outlines the difficulties of the rigid solid articulated systems with his "translational" dynamics. [11] approximates the dynamic of articulated rigid bodies by the dynamic of particle systems. *Jack* [12], a *virtual agent*, is guided by natural language instructions in simulations that affect its own *virtual world.* [13] uses a finite state automaton that controls the simple dynamic of "clockwork toys". A dynamic model governed by a control-system based in a state automaton and PD[1] regulators is used in [14] for simulating "Olympic" fancy dives.

In this Section some *software laboratories* of the related literature has been introduced. Section 2 explains the conceptual design of human locomotion model. As an example of the laboratory application, Section 3 describes the previous work, developments and results obtained in the simulation of human locomotion. Finally, in Section 4 the conclusions and the possible future works are presented.

2   Conceptual Design

The comprehension of the subconscious pattern that guides the human decisions, based in an intrinsic knowledge of the human body mechanics, allows to obtain the parameters about how a person moves. In order to get the motion equations, the problem must be *modeled*, that is, a reduced model that represents the general system must be found. Moreover, the system ought to react in the same way with the same extern impulses. This is a hard process and requires the use of "trail and error" techniques.

The laboratory tools that aid this process involves: to analyze the real dynamic behavior, to unify criteria and geometric references, to incorporate as reference simple subsystems with well-known physical properties (like springs and dampers) and to correctly understand and to use a basic set of mathematical tools, either analytical as numerical. In this way, the laboratory *concept design* helps to reduce the system complexity splitting the system in independent subsystems that use extremely simplified models. Inserting boundary conditions extracted from experimental studies in each phase, force values that optimize the dynamic results can be numerically found. These results establish the basic pattern that follows all the kinematic movements that constitute the final visualization.

---

[1] PD - *Proportional and Derivative.* Other controls are also used in Robotics (P, PID)

3   Laboratory Test: Simulating Human Locomotion

The use of direct kinematics for walking skeleton animation requires the skills of the animator to overcome the movement discontinuities, like the support of the foot in the ground. An improvement could be the use of rotoscopy techniques, in order to capture the data of an actor in movement and to use them in the model. An easiest way could be to get the positions of the key frames from tabulated data. [15] presents a simple kinematic approach with parameters obtained from tables of normalized experimental data. The model allows real-time interaction of the animator, considering temporal and spatial parameters. In [16] procedural systems specified by high-level parameters are proposed. Both systems work generating a basic pattern of locomotion, either in a procedural way or interpolating the control parameters of the average curves. The tabulated data are discrete and arise from persons with different body measures and of different sex, walking at different speed. The principal drawback of these systems is that only the dynamic effects gathered from data capture are considered.

The direct dynamics-based systems require to know a priori the "motor" force values, the constraints and the moment of inertia of each element of the model. They generate equation systems very difficult to solve and not much intuitive for the animators to use. Nevertheless, it can be presupposed that the basic patterns of motion, calculated from a dynamic simulation, correspond better, in a global way, to the real movement. [17] combines control by dynamics with high-level description of the motion system obtained from the empirical knowledge of the locomotion. The dynamics generates a pattern that is improved a posteriori by kinematics, according with the control goals. [18] presents a locomotion method, called SPEEDY, that uses inverse dynamics to balance the locomotion and keeps the forces and torques in a moderate range. In [19] the locomotion is obtained considering the less muscular effort. The interpolation of the movements captured by rotoscopy systems is corrected with dynamic models [20] of the muscles and tendons of the hip and the lower limbs.

3.1   Biomechanics of the Human Locomotion

The locomotion is a subconscious process modeled by basic patterns of behavior (sequences of nervous impulses that active muscles for obtaining a rhythmic and efficient frequency of steps) and by events that perturb them with small variations from sensorial signals (for example, reflex acts to avoid obstacles).

Two consecutive steps form the *human locomotion cycle*. Persons can walk by alternating these steps, which are symmetric. Therefore, only the step of one leg has to be studied in detailed. During the walk there are two phases: *the stance phase* and *the swing phase*.

In the *stance phase*, while the foot is in contact with the ground, the forces that allow the human body to move forward are generated. This phase can be divided in:
1. *Contact:* begins with the contact of the heel to the ground and ends when the remainder of the foot touches the ground. This sub-phase lasts 15% of the locomotion cycle.
2. *Midstance:* begins when the entire foot has contacted the ground. The body weight is supported by the leg, which changes from being a mobile adaptor to a rigid lever in order to propel the body forward during 15 % of the cycle.

3. *Propulsion:* begins after the heel leaves the contact with the ground and ends with toe off. This sub-phase is constituted by the *heel take off*, that lasts 25% of the cycle and *instep take off*, that lasts 5%.
4. *Double stance phase:* is produced between the *instep take off* of one leg and the periods of *heel support and midstance* of the other. In this phase both legs are in the ground. It lasts 10% of the locomotion cycle and is a very important parameter because it's directly related with the *gait frequency*.

The *swing phase* is the time period when the foot is in the air, rotating forward. It begins when the toes leave the contact with the ground and ends when the heel touches the ground again. This phase lasts 40% of the human locomotion cycle and can be divided in:

1. *Acceleration:* it lasts 10 % of the swing phase and represents the acceleration of the leg movement in order to leave the ground and put it front the body.
2. *Midswing:* it lasts 80% of the swing phase. The leg rotates to put itself in front of the body and must be brought back enough in order to avoid the collision with the ground.
3. *Deceleration:* it lasts 10% of the swing phase and it's characterized by the loss of speed for controlling the position of the foot before the heel support.

Other empirical knowledge of human locomotion are:

Timing of phases: the proportion between stance and swing phase changes if the speed increases. The time of *double stance* decreases as the step frequency increases. This period vanishes when a person runs.

Symmetry in double stance: at the moment of the heel support, the relative orientation of both hips is constant. When the feet are completely in the ground, the legs and the ground form an isosceles triangle with the step length as the base.

Energetic minimization: to be stand up implies a great energetic cost but it's a profitable way of locomotion. The gravity center of the upper body is 5cm in front of the third lumbar vertebra *(L3)*, so that the back muscles are activated in order to avoid the blend of head and shoulders. The leg supporting the body acts as the body swing center, converting the potential energy in kinetic energy because of the ground reaction *(inverse pendulum)*. The opposite movements of the legs are alternated for controlling the gravity center and for not falling forward or backward. The pelvis wide and the circle arc over one of the hips determine the step length. For minimize the muscular energetic cost, the human body exploits the elastic properties of joints *(spring-damper)*.

3.2 System Description

Our articulated model is a hierarchical structure of 48 segments corresponding to the main muscle-skeletal joints of a person, in which the principal element is the *pelvis*. If the pelvis makes a translational or a swing movement, the entire body moves.

The system calculates the whole locomotion cycle instead of eliminating the second step because of the step symmetry and the phase lag of the previous movement. Each step is characterized by global parameters set by the animator, like the walk speed.

The main loop corresponds to a finite state machine that first solves the dynamic equations of a simplified model of the *support leg*, to produce the *basic pattern of motion* of the *support hip*. The generalized forces are searched recursively (direct dynamics) until the experimental laws of human locomotion are satisfied.

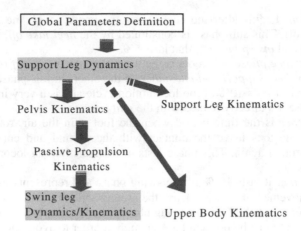

Fig. 1. Scheme of the calculus loop of a step in the locomotion cycle. The dynamic phase of the *swing leg* is solved considering a simplified model that "hangs" directly from the previously calculated movement of the hip.

The movements of the main model are visualized by *kinematics*, according to articular groups: the pelvis and the M.C.[2], the support leg, the swing leg, the upper body, the superior limbs and the head.

3.3   Dynamics-Based Control

There is not only one equation system of motion. Instead, a simplified dynamic model is used for each phase of the human locomotion cycle. The control and the numerical process of integration are simplified because:

The dynamic model is constrained to the two dimensions of the walk plane.

The support leg is a telescopic segment controlled by an axial force. The swing leg is a double articulated segment that includes the weight and the position of the foot in its moment of inertia. The superior body is modeled as only one rigid solid articulated in the hip.

All the segments are supposed symmetric and with constant mass. The mass and the length of each segment are proportional to the total mass and height.

A dynamic active-passive balance is simulated with actuators and dampers elements placed in series.

The simulation of the support leg is separated from the simulation of the swing leg, disregarding the mass of the swing leg against the total weight of the body.

The simulation of each leg is divided in phases that simplify the number of motion equations by the action of kinematics joints. So that an extra work in the characterization and derivation of the motion equation is produced.

The movement remains continuous applying the energy conservation between phases. In the collisions, the actions of the external forces are supposed instantaneous.

---

[2] Mass Center

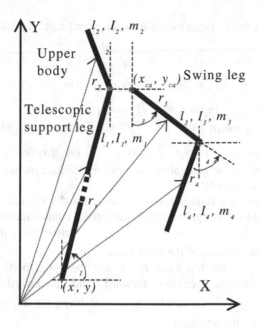

Fig. 2. Dynamic model of the stance and swing legs

In the system a *Lagrange-Euler method* is utilized. This method is used in the design of *control laws* in Robotics for deducing the motion equations. The energy of the system allows the identification of the *interaction and coupling forces* presented according to each generalized coordinate q :

$$\vec{F}_q = \frac{d}{dt}\frac{T}{\dot{q}} - \frac{T}{q} + \frac{U}{q} \qquad \begin{array}{l} T \quad \text{Kinematic energy} \\ U \quad \text{Potential energy} \end{array} \tag{1}$$

The method produces a *multivariable system of second-order differential equations, nonlinear and strongly coupled* which expression is $[A]\ddot{\vec{q}} = B(\vec{q},\dot{\vec{q}})$ with

$$\vec{q} = \begin{array}{l} 1 \\ 2 \end{array} \quad \text{for the support leg and} \quad \vec{q} = \begin{array}{l} 3 \\ 4 \end{array} \quad \text{for the swing leg.}$$

The *energy* expression of the simplified model of the *support leg* is (with g – *gravitational constant*):

$$\begin{aligned} T_a &= \frac{1}{2}m_2 \, {}^{\cdot 2} + \frac{1}{2}(I_1 + m_1 r_1^2 + m_2 \, {}^2)\, \dot{}_1^2 + \frac{1}{2}(I_2 + m_2 r_2^2)\, \dot{}_2^2 + \\ &\quad + m_2 r_2 \, {}_2 \left[\dot{} \sin(\, {}_1 - \, {}_2) + \, {}_1 \cos(\, {}_1 - \, {}_2) \right] \\ U_a &= m_1 g(y + r_1 \sin \, {}_1) + m_2 g(y + \sin \, {}_1 + r_2 \, {}_2 \sin \, {}_2) \end{aligned} \tag{2}$$

Developing the general expression for each coordinate, the following equations are obtained:

$$F = m_2 \ddot{\,} + m_2 r_2 \ddot{\,}_2 \sin(\,_1 \quad _2) \quad m_2 \ \dot{\,}_1^2 \quad m_2 r_2 \ \dot{\,}_2^2 \cos(\,_1 \quad _2) + m_2 g \sin \,_1$$

$$F_1 = (I_1 + m_1 r_1^2 + m_2 \ ^2)\ddot{\,}_1 + 2m_2 \ \dot{\,}_1 + m_2 r_2 \ddot{\,}_2 \ \cos(\,_1 \quad _2)$$

$$m_2 r_2 \ \dot{\,}_2^2 \sin(\,_1 \quad _2) + (m_1 r_1 + m_2 \ )g \cos \,_1$$

$$F_2 = (I_2 + m_2 r_2^2)\ddot{\,}_2 + m_2 r_2 \ddot{\,} \sin(\,_1 \quad _2) + 2m_2 r_2 \ \dot{\,}_1 \cos(\,_1 \quad _2) +$$

$$+ m_2 r_2 \ddot{\,}_1 \cos(\,_1 \quad _2) \quad m_2 r_2 \ \dot{\,}_1^2 \sin(\,_1 \quad _2) + m_2 g \ r_2 \cos \,_2$$

(3)

The expressions of the generalized forces are deduced including the active control systems of the biped robots:

The longitudinal generalized force F simulates the flexion and extension of the knee and the ankle. It supplies the characteristic sinusoidal movement of the M.C. The expression is: $F = \quad (l_1 + p_a \quad) \quad \dot{\,}$ where p_a is the *position actuator*, an active control element of the axial force value.

The torque respect the hip joint, F_2, keeps the upper body upright and gives a smooth characteristic rocking forward and backward. It expression is: $F_2 = \quad _2(\,_2 \quad _{2\_des}) \quad \dot{\,}_2 \,_2$, with $\,_{2\_des} \quad 0$ being the angle respects the vertical that can be set by the animator.

The torque F_1 represents the muscular actions that, during 20% of the locomotion cycle, produces the rotation of the support leg that makes the body move forward. F_1 is a constant, determined in a recursive way, so that the generalized coordinate $\,_1$ can reach an objective value.

In the case of the *swing leg energy* is obtained that:

$$U_g = m_3 g \,(y_{ca} + r_3 \sin \,_3) + m_4 g (y_{ca} + l_3 \sin \,_3 + r_4 \sin(\,_3 \quad _4))$$

$$T_g = \frac{1}{2}(m_4 l_3^2 + I_4 + m_4 r_4^2 + 2m_4 l_3 r_4 \cos \,_4 + I_3 + m_3 r_3^2)\,\dot{\,}_3^2 +$$

$$+ m_4 r_4 (\,_3 \quad _4)(\dot{y}_{ca} \cos \,_3 \quad _4) \quad \dot{x}_{ca} \sin(\,_3 \quad _4))$$

(4)

$$(I_4 + m_4 r_4^2 + m_4 l_3 r_4 \cos \,_4)\,\dot{\,}_3 \,_4 + \frac{1}{2}(m_3 + m_4)(\dot{x}_{ca}^2 + \dot{y}_{ca}^2) +$$

$$+ \frac{1}{2}(I_4 + m_4 r_4^2)\,\dot{\,}_4^2 + (m_3 r_3 + m_4 l_3)\,\dot{\,}_3(\dot{y}_{ca} \cos \,_3 \quad \dot{x}_{ca} \sin \,_3)$$

From the general expression for each coordinate, the following equations are deduced:

$$F_3 = (m_3 r_3 + m_4 l_3)(\ddot{y}_{ca} \cos \,_3 \quad \ddot{x}_{ca} \sin \,_3) + m_4 g (l_3 \cos \,_3 + r_4 \cos(\,_3 \quad _4)) +$$

$$+ (m_4 l_3^2 + I_4 + m_4 r_4^2 + 2m_4 l_3 r_4 \cos \,_4 + I_3 + m_3 r_3^2)\ddot{\,}_3 + m_3 g r_3 \cos \,_3$$

$$(I_4 + m_4 r_4^2 + m_4 l_3 r_4 \cos \,_4)\ddot{\,}_4 \quad m_4 l_3 r_4 \ \dot{\,}_4(2 \,_3 \quad _4)\sin \,_4 +$$

$$+ m_4 r_4(\ddot{y}_{ca} \cos(\,_3 \quad _4) \quad \ddot{x}_{ca} \sin(\,_3 \quad _4))$$

(5)

$$F_4 = (I_4 + m_4 r_4^2 + m_4 l_3 r_4 \cos \,_4)\ddot{\,}_3 + (I_4 + m_4 r_4^2)\ddot{\,}_4 + m_4 l_3 r_4 \ \dot{\,}_3^2 \sin \,_4$$

$$m_4 r_4(\ddot{y}_{ca} \cos(\,_3 \quad _4) \quad \ddot{x}_{ca} \sin(\,_3 \quad _4)) \quad m_4 g \ r_4 \cos(\,_3 \quad _4)$$

During the dynamic phase of swing, the value of the generalized forces F_3 and F_4 depends on the sub-phase of calculus. Simplifying, these values would represent the motor actions produced by the calf of the leg.

If these values are obtained in a recursive way, they take the following exponential expression: $F_{3,4} = Be^{(At)^2}$ and $A = \dfrac{max\_lp}{\sqrt{2}\,lp\,0.5\,t_{swing\_phase}}$ where the constant B is the unknown value of the iterative problem.

In other case, they are deduced like in the stance phase and the expression is $F_{3,4} = k_{3,4}\left(\dot{\theta}_{3,4\,swing\_phase} - \dot{\theta}_{3,4}\right)_{3,4}\;\theta_{3,4}$ with $\dot{\theta}_{3,4\,swing\_phase}$ configurable by the animator.

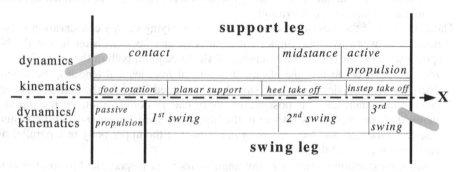

Fig. 3. Timing of the periods in which the stance and swing phase are divided

3.4   Phases in the Resolution of the Dynamic Model

The resolution of the motion equations of the *support leg* is divided in three sub-phases that correspond with those of the biomechanics: *contact, midstance and propulsion*. The last one is also divided, in *active propulsion* and *passive propulsion*.

1. *contact*: this sub-phase lasts approximately 15% of the *locomotion cycle*. The equation systems can be simplified if the telescopic leg is too long before the hip passes by the ankle vertical. In this case, the elongation is blocked and the equation of the generalized coordinate w is removed.
2. *midstance*: the duration of this phase depends on if the telescopic leg is longer than a fixed length experimentally determined. The longitudinal actuator is transformed in order to simulate the action of the ankle extension.
3. *active propulsion*: In this phase the final control condition is evaluated. The motion equations are simplified according to the inverted pendulum.
4. *passive propulsion*: this phase coincide with the *double support phase*, where the other leg begins its stance dynamic phase. Hence the system is simplified transferring the weight and control of the body from one dynamic phase to the other, calculated from the kinematics.

The *swing phase* is recursive in each of the three sub-phases it is divided in. As the dynamic model coincides with the global hierarchical model, the results of the simulation are incorporated directly into the kinematics visualization.

1. *1st swing sub-phase*: it lasts 50% of the total time of the *swing phase*. A recursive
   search is done over torque F_3. When a polynomial trajectory [21] experimentally
   obtained is applied to the ankle, the motion equation of the coordinate $_4$ is removed. The expression is a *4th order Hermite polynomial* [22] and $_4$ must be updated step by step. It is solved numerically by *Newton-Raphson*, optimizing the
   calculus by the *Horner* method.
2. *2nd swing sub-phase*: it lasts 35% of the total time of the *swing phase*. The value
   of the torque applied in the knee, F_4, is considered unknown. The leg rotates by
   the muscular action until $_4$ reaches an experimental limit.
3. *3rd swing sub-phase*: the expression of F_3 and the resolution method are identical
   to those of the *1st sub-phase*. In this case, the leg blocks the knee like an inverted
   pendulum. The initial value of the generalized coordinate $_3$ is obtained applying
   angular momentum conservation.

The continuity of the movement must be assured applying energy conservation in two
transitions between dynamic models: the inelastic the heel collision in the double
support phase and the end of the extension of the knee joint, both of the swing leg.

Heel support: because of the elastic structure of muscles and tendons, the kinetic
energy of the collision leg can be stored and returned later. As the collision is considered instantaneous, it is possible to apply energy conservation to: the *angular
moment* of the upper body respect to the hip, the *angular moment* of all the system
respect to the heel and the *amount of movement* of the upper body in a parallel direction to the axis of the support leg.

Complete extension of the knee: the angular moment respect the hip joint is con-
served.

3.5   Numeric Resolution

Motion is governed directly by the generalized forces *(direct dynamics)* which expressions are based in biomechanical principles of the *passive dynamics*. The value of
each generalized force is calculated recursively verifying, at the end of each step, if it
fulfilled some boundary conditions. These conditions are constructed from the biomechanics concepts of phase timings, energetic minimization and double support symmetry.

Once the values of the anthropometrical constants (gender, height and corporal
mass) are introduced, at least one of the three intuitive global parameters must be set:
speed, step frequency or step length. Individuals present two strategies to accelerate
the walk that relate these parameters between each other: either make longer steps or
increase the step frequency. The duration of one step is deduced from the parameters.
The experimental relation between the duration of one step and the double support
phase allows the calculus of the other dynamic *phase timings*.

The trajectory followed by the M.C. goes up and down, and moves from left to
right. This sinusoidal movement minimizes the *energetic consumption* and affects the
step length and the hip kinematics.

In the double support phase the legs and the ground represent an isosceles triangle,
so that the boundary conditions of the generalized coordinates that control the dynamics can be directly deduced.

Considering the possible instability of the *rigid* system, the numerical resolution method implemented [22] is a multi-step n-dimensional *predictor-corrector* algorithm with *adaptative control* of the integration step. An *Adams-Bamsford* algorithm is used as *predictor* and a *Moulton-Adams* algorithm is used as *corrector*. The system is initialized with a 4th order *Runge Kutta* method.

3.6   Kinematics-Based Visualization

The visual appearance of the articulated model is improved by kinematics. A specific timing of the movements, much closer to the biomechanical experimental principles is developed. Kinematics constraints are applied to the movement of all those segments and angles of the articulated model that are not direct result of the dynamic simulation (particularly, all the transverse to the walking plane). The constraints can fit to values extracted from anthropometric measures, either experimental or aesthetic, that allow the characterization of each animation individually.

By linear interpolation of the different sub-phases, the kinematics of the *swing leg* is reduced to complete the foot movement. The kinematics of the *support leg* reflects the biomechanical performance of the knee and the ankle. They absorb the collision of the heel, soften the transition between the *swing* and *stance* states and keep the major possible height of the *M.C.* The trajectories of the hip and the ankle are deduced from the dynamics. The kinematics of the support leg is divided in:

1. *foot rotation over the heel:* this sub-phase ends in the moment in which the dynamic leg pass over the vertical. The calculus of the ankle is directly interpolated and the knee angle is deduced later by inverse kinematics.
2. *planar support*: this sub-phase ends when the dynamic leg reaches a value greater than the real length of the leg or when the joint of the kinematic ankle reaches an anatomic limit of 15°. Two kinematic chains are solved: one from the hip to the ankle and other from the ankle to the toe on the ground.
3. *heel take off:* the beginning of the *double support phase* marks the end of the progressive elevation of the heel while the instep remains on the ground. The algorithm gets the ankle position as the intersection of circumference arcs centered in the involved joints.
4. *instep take off:* the end of the dynamic *stance phase* determines the end of the progressive elevation of the instep while the toe remains in the ground. The algorithm of kinematic calculus reduces to experimental values the linear interpolation of the angle between the knee and the ankle. The position of the hip is taken from the dynamic phase of the support leg of the next step.

The most important movement of the pelvis is the *pelvic rotation* produced in the transverse plane and that increases the *step length*. In the coronal plane the *pelvic balancing* occurs, which produces one hip to be higher than the other. The *lateral displacement* is perpendicular to the walking plane and transfers part of the body weight to the support leg. In the heel support, the *pelvic rotation* is maximum, and the *lateral displacement* and the *pelvic balancing* disappear. There is no rotation in the *midstance* but the displacement is maximum. The greater difference of height between the hips occurs at the beginning of the swing phase.

Our model of the upper body kinematically simulates all the vertebral column, gathering the movements according to *lumbar, thoracic and cervical vertebras*. Each vertebra only makes rotation movements with respect to the previous one. The *lumbar vertebras* absorb, in a proportional way, the angular movement of the generalized coordinate of the dynamic model and the pelvic balancing. The pelvic rotation and the rotation of the shoulders in the opposite direction are compensated along the vertebral column in such a way that the head always remains in the walking direction. In the transverse plane, the shoulders rotate in an opposite direction and proportionally to the *pelvis*. In the walking plane, instead, the *arms* rotate proportionally to the "dynamic" angle of the *hip* of the opposite leg and the *forearms* are directly interpolated between the experimental values.

3.7   Results

The laboratory presents two main modules: the *calculus module* and the *visualization module*, both programmed in C. The *visualization module* employs external OpenGL libraries, optimized for the use of graphic accelerators.

Table 1. Calculation times at a 12 MFLOPS workstation according the number of steps. In all the cases the system converges with a natural step at 5 km/h (the swing phase presents a superior calculation time, but less time of real simulation) and with different integration step

$h_{max} = 0,01$	Simulated	Frames	C.P.U.
3 steps	1,27 sec	62	330 msec
4 steps	1,81 sec	89	510 msec
5 steps	2,37 sec	117	580 msec
6 steps	2,93 sec	145	680 msec

Some graphical outputs of our application are shown below.

4   Conclusions and Future Work

The main objective of the paper is to show the work done, up till now, for carrying out a software laboratory for the study, development and verification of dynamic techniques of motion-control and human body representation. The principal idea of this work is the use, as basic pattern of motion, of the direct solution of very simple dynamic models governed by a finite state machine. These models are developed, specialized, linked and solved using empirical laws of the real movement. The visualization improved the final result, applying kinematics over the basic pattern of motion. These tools could be modified and customized in some of the suggested future works.

An extensively studied test case, the simulation of the human locomotion, was used for tuning the system. The main characteristics of this application example developed in the laboratory are:

Allow the realistic simulation of the locomotion of individuals with different anthropomorphic characteristics without the animator operation.

Make the motion control dynamically, in a simple and intuitive way, from global parameters like *speed* or *step frequency*.

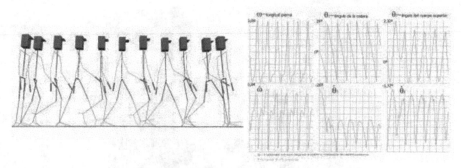

Fig. 4. Left: 5-step global model sequence. Right: generalized coordinates of the dynamic model of the support leg. Three cycles of locomotion are represented: telescopic leg, $_1$ hip, $_2$ upper body (down, 1st derivative)

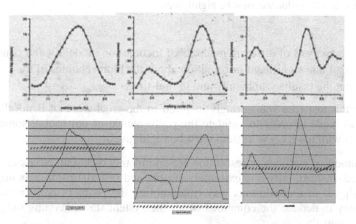

Fig. 5. Comparison of the simulation of a *natural step* of one person with *80 Kg* and *1,80 m* and the *experimental* graphics. The similarity between the inferior and superior limits, the growth intervals and the slopes can be observed for a natural step at 5 km/h. From left to right: hip, knee and ankle angles

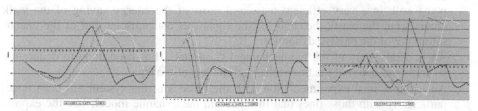

Fig. 6. Variation of the global control parameters. The sequences representing different step length and step frequency (0,64 m - 130,2 steps/m, 0,77 m - 107,7steps/m and 0,90 m -92,6 steps/m) . From left to right: hip, knee and ankle angles

Fig. 7. Variations of the anthropometric data: individuals with different weights (65 Kg, 80 Kg and 120 Kg) walking at the same speed (5 km/h). The changes produced in the heel support by means of the gravity influence must be highlighted

Favor the analysis of different methods of locomotion modeling and controlling.
Allow to obtain significant information about the biomechanics of the problem.
Represent the results graphically and in real-time.

Although this test case was strongly inspired in the great work of Bruderlin [17] (the choice was made in order to validate the performance of our tools), some important differences with his KLAW system must be highlighted:

The numerical methods of resolution are completely different. No external libraries are used. Instead, only one extremely simple and fast algorithm was implemented. For using it in a continuous way (maintaining the problem convergence), it was necessary to deduce the equations of all the system states keeping only one reference system.

The calculus of the moments of inertia had been improved (it can be said that the "humans" of KLAW have a greater muscular mass).

In our laboratory, active and passive elements are differentiated: the animals don't use only the active feedback in their mechanisms of control of the movement. Humans walk in a very efficient way, and most of the energy saving of the walk comes from the elastic behavior of the ligaments and muscles and of the unconscious use of the passive dynamics.

An in-depth study of the biomechanical "constants" has been done to deduct the stiffness and damp of the biomechanical models of the legs.

An in-depth final experimentation with the physics of the system has been done, particularly with those ones that influence in the dynamic model, like the expressions and duration of the muscular actions or in the simulation of special dynamic behaviors (change in the constant of gravity: g).

As final consideration, an in-depth in the Mechanics of the system has been realized. Even though, it is proved that the KLAW system is robust and adaptable, and is capable of absorbing these "deviations" in the dynamics and presenting excellent results. However, our system is more efficient and versatile.

About the future work, three lines can be distinguished:

Implementation of New Dynamic Problems in Locomotion. The boundary conditions, the phases and the parts of the model can be redefined for simulating other cases in human locomotion: Running, Going up or down stairs, Sloping planes, Taking Loads, No rectilinear trajectories, Modified gravity environments, Variations of the system stiffness (ground and muscular). A special interest must be dedicated to calculate the beginning parameters by passive dynamic control in order to minimize the energetic consumption and to improve the stability of the problem.

Improvements According to the Biomechanical Point of View. If the biomechanical behavior is studied in depth, the possible open work lines of the system could be: More exact calculation of the model from the mass and height parameters, Characterization of the bones, muscles and tendons for developing physical modes of the principal joints, Calculation of the mass and inertia values from real data, Extraction of the dynamic data for the design of "intelligent" prosthesis, Verification of the model comparing the results with rotoscopy systems.

Extension of the Laboratory Scope. Other future lines of work are framed in the extension of the laboratory: Verification of the muscular deformation by means of finite elements, Inclusion of complex dynamic models of specific joints, Inclusion of other forms of biped locomotion, Test laboratory for dynamic simulation of clothes, Optimization of the code: multithreading and sharing memory, Use of VRML and the H-Anim specification, Dynamic of the Olympic rowing, Biomechanics analysis of autonomous dynamic agents in computer games.

References

1. Van de Belt D., Simulation of Walking Using Optimal Control, Ph. Thesis of Univ. of Twente, Nederlands (1997).
2. Bordoli P. D.: Biomecánica de la columna vertebral y Locomoción humana. Boletin Digital Factores Humanos, Telefónica I+D, n° 17 (1998)
3. Raibert M. H.: Legged Robots. Communications of the ACM, Vol. 29 (1986) 6:499-514
4. Garcia M., Chatterjee A., Ruina A., Coleman M.: The Simplest Walking Model: stability, complexity, and scaling ASME Journal of Biomechanical Engineering, (1997)
5. Kajita S., Yamaura T., Kobayashi A.: Dynamic walking control of a biped robot along a potential energy conserving orbit. IEEE Transactions on Robotics and Automation, Vol 8, n°4, (1992) 431-438
6. Ahmadi M., Buehler M.: Stable Control of a Simulated One-Legged Running Robot with Hip and Leg Compliance. IEEE Transactions on Robotics and Automation, Vol 13, n° 1, (1997) 96-104
7. Isaacs P. M., Cohen M. F.: Controlling Dynamic Simulation with kinematic constrains, behavior functions and inverse dynamics. ACM Computer Graphics, Vol 21, n° 4, (1987)
8. Tost D., Pueyo X.: Human Body Animation: a survey. The Visual Computer, Vol 3 (1988) 254-264
9. Cerezo E., Pina A., Serón F. J.: Motion and behaviour modelling: state of art and new trends. The Visual Computer, Vol 15, (1999) 124-146
10. Girard M.: Constrained Optimization of Articulated Animal Movement in Computer Animation. Make then Move, Addison-Wesley, (1990) 209-232

11. Van Overveld C. W. A. M.: A Simple Approximation to Rigid Body Dynamics for Computer Animation. The Journal of Visualization and Computer Animation, Vol 5, (1994) 17-36
12. Badler N. I., Phillips C.B., Webber B. L.: Simulating Humans. Computer Graphics Animation and Control. Oxford University Press, (1993)
13. Van de Panne M.,: Parameterized Gait Synthesis. IEEE Computer Graphics and Applications, (1996) 16: 40-49
14. Wooten W. L., Hodgins J. K.: Animation of Human Diving. Computer Graphic Forum, Vol 15, (1996) 3-13
15. Boulic R., Magnenat Thalmann N., Thalmann D.: A global human walking model with real-time kinematic personification. The Visual Computer, Vol 6, (1990) 344-358
16. Bruderlin A., Teo C. G., Calvert T.: Procedural Movement for Articulated Figure Animation. Computer & Graphics, Vol 18, (1994) 453-461
17. Bruderlin A., Calvert T.W, Goal-Directed: Dynamic Animation of Human Walking, Computer Graphics ACM, Vol 23, (1989) 233-242
18. Ko H., Badler N. I., Animating Human Locomotion with Inverse Dynamics. IEEE Computer and Graphics, (1996) 16: 50-59
19. Komura T., Shinagawa Y., Kunii T., Creating and retargeting motion by the musculo-skeletal human body model. The Visual Computer, Vol 16, (2000) 254-270
20. Chen D., Zeltzer D.: Pump It Up: Computer Animation of a Biomechanically Based Model of Muscle Using the Finite Element Method. (SIGGRAPH'92 Proceedings), Computer Graphics, Vol 26, (1992) 89-98
21. Beckett R., Chang K., An Evaluation of the kinematics of gait by minimum energy J. Biomechanics, Vol 1, (1968) 147-159
22. Burden R., Faires D., Numerical Analysis. PWS, Boston, (1985)

Computer Visual System Analyzing the Influence of Stimulants on Human Motion

Ryszard S. Choras[1] and Michal Choras[1]

[1] Institute of Telecommunication, University of Technology and Agriculture
ul. Prof. Kaliskiego 7, 85-792
Bydgoszcz, Poland
choras@mail.atr.bydgoszcz.pl

Abstract. In many situations determining the fact if human is under the influence of any stimulants (fi. alcohol or medicaments of any kind) can be crucial. The knowledge of how those stimulants (activators) influence the human motion and in what way, is of a great importance. Images of five markers situated on a moving person are analyzed. The vector of features characterizing the image of a marker (marker motion) is calculated and than compared to the reference vector. The reference vector describes the motion of a person not influenced by any stimulants. The features parameters calculated in the proposed method are: moments, kurtosis, skewness, normalization coefficients, moments coefficients, coefficient of the main axis of the region, orientation angle and 7 Hu Invariant Moments. The analysis of presented parameters is efficient enough to detect the existence of stimulant and to determine the exact kind of the stimulant applied to the examined person. Furthermore, the proposed method can specify the approximate amount (dose) of the stimulant.

1 Introduction

In many situations determining the fact if the person is under the influence of any stimulants is necessary. In some medical cases, it is also important to know what is the influence of those stimulants on the motion abilities of human being. The system of computer vision enables to specify the state of the moving person from the distance without the need of any action (fi. taking the blood). Such system also enables to determine the approximate amount of taken substance.

Stimulants influence the functioning of the brain parts responsible for controlling the motion process. The analysis of human motion can determine information if the moving person is under the influence of such stimulant. The examined person walks along the mechanical race-track with the average velocity of 70 steps per minute. Five markers are placed respectively on head, shoulder, elbow, knee and foot. The images of markers motion are obtained by a camera situated as shown in Figure 1. The image obtained by the camera is presented in the Figure 2a. The images of markers motion without and with the applied stimulant are shown in the Figures 2b and 2c respectively.

F.J. Perales and E.R. Hancock (Eds.): AMDO 2002, LNCS 2492, pp. 241–250, 2002.

Obtained images are than the subject of preliminary processing: images are threshold first in order to obtain binary image and the operation extracting the area of the markers motion is carried out next. We consider the sequence of 640 images, therefore we theoretically consider 640 points, each characterizing the location of the single marker in the image. The morphological operation *opening* enables to obtain the image of the markers motion area. The image of the marker motion area is described by the feature vector consisting of parameters describing for instance location and orientation of the image region, or global and local region parameters. The feature vector is later compared with the reference vector and basing on this comparison, decision if the person is or is not under the influence of any stimulants is made. The estimation of the amount of taken stimulant can be also made.

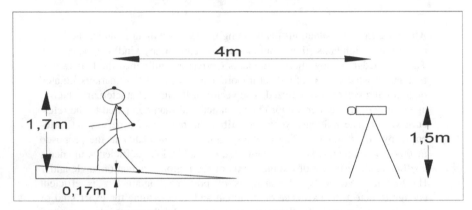

Fig. 1. Basic parameters of our experimental environment.

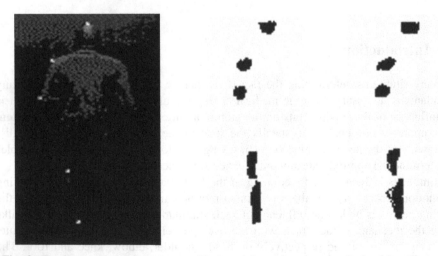

Fig. 2. The image of moving person with the markers placed on head, shoulder, elbow, knee and foot (left). The image of markers motion for the case without any stimulants (middle). The image of markers motion representing the case with the stimulant applied to examined person (right).

2   Preliminary Processing

There are following steps of preliminary processing:
- threshold,
- extraction of images corresponding to particular markers,
- morphological operation *opening*.

2.1   Threshold

If the marker image and the background, on which the marker is placed, differ considerably in luminance, we come across two distinct and remote (distant) maximums plotted on the luminance histogram curve. The value of luminance, corresponding to minimum between those maximums on the histogram, determines the threshold value of the luminance. Usually, we do not come across such an ideal case and in order to find the threshold value we proceed in the following way:

- we find two largest local maximums (peaks) of the luminance histogram, such that the second maximum is lesser than the main maximum of $K\%$ and such that those two maximums are distant of the luminance value d,
- we find the absolute minimum point between those maximums. The luminance value corresponding to that minimum becomes the threshold value th. All the elements of the image with the luminance values lesser than th are classified as the background. All the other regions are classified as the marker image.

We obtain:

$$b(i, j) = \begin{matrix} 1 & if & p(i, j) \geq th \\ 0 & if & p(i, j) < th \end{matrix} \qquad (1)$$

Proceeding in the described manner, we can obtain five marker images, each corresponding to different marker.

Afterwards, we use the morphological operation *opening* in order to obtain the image of the marker motion area. The operation *opening* is defined as:

$$o(X, B) = [X \ominus B] \oplus B, \qquad (2)$$

and consists of operation *erosion*:

$$[X \ominus B] = \bigcap_{x \in B} T(X; x), \qquad (3)$$

where $T(X; x)$ is translation of X about the vector x, $-B$ means mirroring of B and B is a structural element.

Moreover   indicates the operation *dilation* defined as:

$$A \quad B = \bigcup_{x \ B} T(A; x) = \bigcup_{x \ A} T(B; x). \tag{4}$$

Below, we present images of marker motion and images of marker motion area (after operation *opening*) for the case without and with the stimulant (alcohol).

Fig. 3. The image of marker motion area: the case without any stimulants (left), the case with the influence of alcohol (right).

3   Feature Extraction

We first overview the theory of moments and the features used in the classification techniques.

In feature extraction, the aim is to represent the image in terms of some quantifiable measurements that may be easily used in the classification stage. Extracted features must minimize the within class pattern variability and maximize the between class pattern variability in order to provide sufficient discrimination among the different marker motion areas. The performance of the recognition system highly depends on this stage.

Two dimensional moments provide features for classification. For a digital image the moment of order $(p + q)$ is given by:

$$m_{pq} = \sum_i \sum_j i^P j^q b(i, j) \qquad p, q = 0, 1, 2, \ldots, \quad . \tag{5}$$

The central moments of image are given by:

$$\propto_{pq} = \sum_i \sum_j (i \quad \bar{i})^P (j \quad \bar{j})^q b(i, j), \tag{6}$$

where $\bar{i} = \dfrac{m_{10}}{m_{00}}$, $\bar{j} = \dfrac{m_{01}}{m_{00}}$ are the coordinates of the centroid of the image.

The normalized central moments of an image are given by:

$$\eta_{pq} = \frac{\alpha_{pq}}{\alpha_{00}^{\gamma}}, \tag{7}$$

where $\gamma = \dfrac{p+q}{2} + 1$, $p+q = 2,3,\ldots$.

We used features derived from combinations of moments:

- kurtosis, which describes the flatness of the region:

$$K_1 = m_{04} / m_{02}^2, \tag{8}$$
$$K_2 = m_{40} / m_{20}^2, \tag{9}$$

- skewness, which describes asymmetry of the region:

$$S_1 = m_{03} / (m_{02})^{1.5}, \tag{10}$$
$$S_2 = m_{30} / (m_{20})^{1.5}, \tag{11}$$

- normalization coefficients:

$$R_1 = \frac{S_1}{(K_1)^{0.75}}, \tag{12}$$

$$R_2 = \frac{S_2}{(K_2)^{0.75}}, \tag{13}$$

- moments coefficients:

$$M_1 = m_{01} / m_{10}, \qquad M_2 = m_{02} / m_{20}, \qquad M_3 = m_{04} / m_{40}, \tag{14}$$

- coefficient of the main axis of the region:

$$e = \frac{2(m_{20} + m_{02}) + 2[(m_{20} - m_{02})^2 + 4m_{11}^2]^{1/2}}{2(m_{20} + m_{02}) - 2[(m_{20} - m_{02})^2 + 4m_{11}^2]^{1/2}}, \tag{15}$$

- orientation angle:

$$\varphi = 1/2 \;\; \arctan \frac{2m_{11}}{m_{20} - m_{02}} + n\frac{\pi}{2}. \tag{16}$$

- Hu moment invariants based on moments up to the third order:

$$\phi_1 = (\eta_{20} + \eta_{02})$$

$$\phi_2 = (\eta_{20} - \eta_{02})^2 + 4\eta_{11}^2$$

$$\phi_3 = (\eta_{30} - 3\eta_{12})^2 + (3\eta_{21} - \eta_{03})^2$$

$$\phi_4 = (\eta_{30} + 3\eta_{12})^2 + (\eta_{21} + \eta_{03})^2$$

$$\phi_5 = (\eta_{30} - 3\eta_{12})(\eta_{30} + \eta_{12})[(\eta_{30} + \eta_{12})^2 - 3(\eta_{21} + \eta_{03})^2]$$
$$+ (3\eta_{21} - \eta_{03})(\eta_{21} + \eta_{03})[3(\eta_{30} + \eta_{12})^2 - (\eta_{21} + \eta_{03})^2]$$

$$\phi_6 = \{(\eta_{20} - \eta_{02})[(\eta_{30} + \eta_{12})^2 - (\eta_{21} + \eta_{03})^2] +$$
$$+ 4\eta_{11}(\eta_{30} + \eta_{12})(\eta_{21} + \eta_{03})\}$$

$$\phi_7 = \{3\eta_{21} - \eta_{03})(\eta_{30} + \eta_{12})[(\eta_{30} + \eta_{12})^2 - 3(\eta_{21} + \eta_{03})^2]$$
$$(\eta_{30} - 3\eta_{12})(\eta_{21} + \eta_{03})[3(\eta_{30} + \eta_{12})^2 - (\eta_{21} + \eta_{03})^2]\}$$

$$(17)$$

where η_{pq} is given by Eq. (7).

4   Recognition and Decision Making

To make a reference feature vector for the marker motion area for a person v $(v = 1,...,V)$ one takes a vector. Vector F_v is built-up from N (in our case $N = 18$) features F_v $(\mu = 1, N)$ of the marker motion area – kurtosis, skewness, moments, coefficient e, orientation angle, and Hu moment invariants.
The reference vector F^{ref} have components given by:

$$\overline{F}_\mu = \frac{1}{V} \sum_{v=1}^{V} F_v .$$

$$(18)$$

$\overline{F}_\mu$ is the arithmetic mean of single feature eg. $\overline{F}_1$ is the arithmetic mean of features K_1 obtained for v persons without any stimulants, $\overline{F}_2$ is the arithmetic mean of features K_2 obtained for v persons without any stimulants etc. and finally $\overline{F}_{18}$ is the arithmetic mean of features ϕ_7 obtained for v persons without any stimulants. In our case $V = 50$.

We have got two vectors: the first one (the reference vector) is the vector of parameters calculated for the person not influenced by any stimulants (F^{ref}), and the second one is the vector of features obtained for the person being under influence of some stimulants (alcohol, medicaments).
We have obtained:

$$F^{ref} = \left[\overline{K}_1^{ref}, \overline{K}_2^{ref}, \overline{S}_1^{ref}, \overline{S}_2^{ref}, \overline{R}_1^{ref}, \overline{R}_2^{ref}, \overline{M}_1^{ref}, \overline{M}_2^{ref}, \overline{M}_3^{ref}, \overline{e}^{ref}, \overline{}_i^{ref}, \overline{}_i^{ref} \right]$$

and (19)

$$F = \left[K_1, K_2, S_1, S_2, R_1, R_2, M_1, M_2, M_3, e, \quad , \quad _i \right].$$

is the vector obtained for a person requiring classification.

Some values of the feature vectors, for the examples of the marker motion shown in the Figure 3, are presented below.

Table 1 presents the feature parameters for person not influenced by any stimulants. Table 2 presents parameters calculated for person influenced by alcohol, and finally Table 3 shows parameters characterizing person influenced by another stimulant (of a medical kind).

Table 1. Feature parameters for person not influenced by any stimulants.

Normalized Central Moments			
1.0E+000	0.0E+000	3.1E-004	3.7E-007
0.0E+000	1.2E-006	-6.9E-008	0.0E+000
4.8E-004	1.8E-007	1.4E-007	0.0E+000
-3.1E-007	0.0E+000	0.0E+000	0.0E+000

Hu Invariant Moments						
7.9E-004	3.0E-008	3.7E-014	4.4E-013	-1.6E-026	-2.8E-017	5.3E-026

Parameters	
Kurtosis	7.17
Skew	-3.03

Table 2. Feature parameters for person under the influence of alcohol.

Normalized Central Moments			
1.0E+000	0.0E+000	3.2E-004	-3.8E-007
0.0E+000	-2.7E-006	-1.3E-007	0.0E+000
4.9E-004	-1.5E-007	1.5E-007	0.0E+000
-5.9E-007	0.0E+000	0.0E+000	0.0E+000

Hu Invariant Moments						
8.1E-004	3.1E-008	5.3E-014	8.0E-013	3.1E-027	3.7E-017	-1.6E-025

Parameters	
Kurtosis	5.54
Skew	-2.75

Table 3. Feature parameters for person influenced by another stimulant (of a medical kind).

Normalized Central Moments			
1.0E+000	0.0E+000	3.4E-004	6.4E-007
0.0E+000	-9.7E-007	1.4E-008	0.0E+000
5.1E-004	2.3E-007	1.6E-007	0.0E+000
-4.2E-008	0.0E+000	0.0E+000	0.0E+000

Hu Invariant Moments						
8.5E-004	2.9E-008	1.1E-014	7.7E-013	-4.6E-026	-1.3E-017	-5.3E-026

Parameters	
Kurtosis	3.09
Skew	-2.26

Features of the unknown person are compared to the reference features. In this stage we use the Euclidean distance measure and cross correlation function. The Euclidean distance measure is given by:

$$d(F^{ref}, F) = \sqrt{\sum_{=1}^{N}(F^{ref} \quad F\quad)^2}, \tag{20}$$

where F^{ref} is the   th feature of the reference and F is the   th feature of the unknown person under consideration. The smallest Euclidean distance is produced when any unknown person is identified with the reference vector.

Another function, which we use in the process of classification, is the cross correlation defined as:

$$CC = \frac{\sum_{=1}^{N} F^{ref} \, F}{\sqrt{\sum_{=1}^{N} F^{ref\,2} \sum_{=1}^{N} F^{\,2}}}, \tag{21}$$

where F^{ref} and F have the same definitions as in Eg. (20).

Fig. 4 illustrates the performance of the system. It shows that the cross correlation measure based classifier performs better than classifier based on Euclidean distance.

The performance of the classifier that uses 18 elements in the feature vector is different than performance while using smaller number of elements. Intuitively, the performance of the classifier should improve with addition of more elements to the feature vector. Fig. 5 illustrates the performance of the cross correlation classifier that uses: a) 18 elements in feature vector, b) 11 elements in feature vector (feature vector without Hu moment invariants) and c) 7 elements in feature vector (feature vector with only Hu moment invariants).

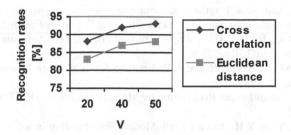

Fig. 4. Performance of the system.

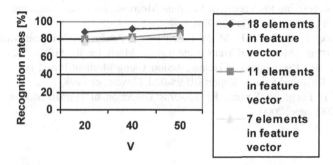

Fig. 5. Performance of the system vs. number of elements in the feature vector.

5   Conclusions

In article, we presented the method of analyzing the images of the markers placed on human body in order to determine if the examined person is under the influence of any stimulants (activators). The system uses combinations of statistical moments. Also the two classifiers were implemented. The classifier based on cross correlation measure produce the best recognition results. The implementation of more features leads to better recognition performance but the computational expense is higher. Increasing numbers of Hu moment invariants from 7 to 32 improves the recognition rates by about 2%.

The analysis of presented parameters is efficient enough to detect the existence of stimulant and to determine the exact kind of the stimulant taken by the examined person. Furthermore, the proposed method can specify the approximate amount (dose) of the applied stimulant.

References

1. Aggarwal, J.K, Cai, Q: Human Motion Analysis: A Review, Computer and Vision Research Center, The University of Texas at Austin.
2. Belkasim S., Shridhar M., Ahmadi M.: Pattern Recognition with Moment Invariants: A Comparative Study and New Results, Pattern Recognition, 12 (1991) 1117-1138.

3. Choras R., Andrysiak T. (et all): Komputerowy system wizyjny do oceny wplywu lekow na wybrane elementy motoryki czlowieka, Internal Report (not published).
4. Hodgins, J.K., Brogan, D.C., Wooten, W.L., O'Brien, J.F.: Animating Human Athletics, Proceedings of SIGGRAPH'95.
5. Hogg D.: Model-Based Vision: A Program to See a Walking Person, Image and Vision Computing, 1 (1993) 5-20.
6. Hu, M.K.: Visual Pattern Recognition by Moment Invariants, IRE Trans. Inform. Theory, IT(8), 1962.
7. Leung M., Yang Y.H.: Human Body Motion Segmentation in a Complex Scene, Pattern Recognition, (1987) 55-64.
8. Leung M., Yang Y.H.: A Region Based Approach for Human Body Motion Analysis, Pattern Recognition, (1987) 321-339.
9. Li Y.: Reforming the Theory of Invariant Moments for Pattern Recognition, Pattern Recognition Letters, 7 (1992) 723-730.
10. O'Rourke J., Badler N.I.: Model-Based Image Analysis of Human Motion Using Constraint Propagation, IEEE Trans. Pattern Anal. Mach. Intell., (1980) 522-536.
11. Rosales, R.: Recognition of Human Action Using Moment-Based Features, Boston University Technical Science Report BU 98-020, November 1998.
12. Song, Y, Feng, X., Perona, P.: Towards Detection of Human Motion, Proceedings of CVPR'00, June, 2000.

Recovering Non-rigid 3D Shape
Using a Plane+Parallax Approach

Nicolás Pérez de la Blanca* and Antonio Garrido

Department of Computer Science and Artificial Intelligence
University of Granada, 18071 Granada, Spain
nicolas@ugr.es, agarrido@decsai.ugr.es

Abstract. The recovering of 3D shape from video sequences has been one of
the most important computer vision problems in the last ten years. For the case
of rigid scenes, linear and factorization approaches have been developed. However, for non-rigid scenes only factorization methods for parallel projection,
based on the Tomasi-Kanade's factorization method, have been proposed. In
this paper we study the case of perspective cameras for non-rigid scenes. Our
approach makes use of recent results of the plane+parallax representation for
rigid scene. We show that it is possible, from a reference system defined on a
particular plane of the scene, to estimate the 3D Euclidean coordinates of the
moving points and the camera center.

1   Introduction

This paper proposes a technique for recovering 3D non-rigid shape models from image sequences that have been recorded by a single camera. We recover the non-rigid
3D structure and the camera parameters from a set of image key-point tracked
throughout the image sequence. The Tomasi-Kanade's factorization method and its
subsequent extensions [11][3], allows us to recover the 3D pose and 3D shape of one
or several rigid objects, but only under parallel projection. For rigid objects under
perspective projection, factorization methods have also been proposed [10][4], although the estimation problem is much more complex since the projective depths of
the points must be fixed before applying factorization on the measurement matrix.
Unfortunately, due to the underlying rigidity hypothesis, these approaches are no
longer valid for the case of non-rigid shapes.

Recovering non-rigid 3D shapes from image sequences is a very active field of research. One of the most successful approaches has been the use of the Principal
Component Analysis [1][5][14]. Bascle and Blake [1], for instance, have proposed a
solution to separate facial expressions and pose during tracking, although they required a set of basis images as learning set before starting the factorization process.
More recently, Bregler at al. [2][12] have developed a technique that does not require
any prior knowledge on the set of basis images, since they describe the shape of a
non-rigid object as a key-frame basis set which selection is included as part of the

---

* This work has been financing by the Grant IT-2001-3316 from the Spanish Ministry of Science and Technology

F.J. Perales and E.R. Hancock (Eds.): AMDO 2002, LNCS 2492, pp. 251–256, 2002.
© Springer-Verlag Berlin Heidelberg 2002

estimation problem. However, they only study the parallel projection case. In this paper we approach the case of general perspective camera by using some interesting properties of the plane+parallax representation of rigid scenes.

For rigid shape multi view reconstruction, it is shown that the bilinearity of the camera and structure estimation problem can be reduced to a linear formulation using the knowledge of a common reference 3D plane in all views [7][8][4]. The aligning of all images in the sequence using the projection of the common plane makes the camera and structure estimation problem independent of the calibration and orientation parameters. In this paper we will start transforming the non-rigid problem to a rigid one and then solve this problem using the linear technique suggested in [7].

2 Technical Approach

2.1 Point and Camera Coordinates

Let us consider the following five points $\{(1,0,0,0), (0,1,0,0), (0,0,1,0), (0,0,0,1), (1,1,1,1)\}$ as a proyective reference system of the 3D space. We assume that there is a reference plane containing the following four points $\{(1,0,0,0), (0,1,0,0), (0,0,1,0), (X,Y,Z,0)\}$, there of them from the 3D space basis and the fourth one any other collinear point. In this situation it is shown in [7][8] that it is possible to define a mapping among the four points in the 3D plane and the image plane basis in the way that the projection relations can be rewritten as linear constraint equations in terms of the points and camera center non-homogeneous coordinates. It can be noted that the chosen reference plane is at infinity, but this does not imply any additional problem in the estimation problem.

The mapping between the 3D reference plane and the image plane is defined by

$$
\begin{array}{cccc|c}
P_1 & P_2 & P_3 & P_4 & Q \\
- & - & - & - & - \\
1 & 1 & 0 & X & A \\
0 & 0 & 0 & Y & B \\
0 & 0 & 1 & Z & C \\
0 & 0 & 0 & 0 & D
\end{array}
\qquad
\begin{array}{cccc|c}
p_1 & p_2 & p_3 & p_4 & q \\
- & - & - & - & - \\
1 & 0 & 0 & 1 & 0 \\
0 & 1 & 0 & 1 & 0 \\
0 & 0 & 1 & 1 & 0
\end{array}
\tag{1}
$$

In this setting the parameterization of the camera matrix will be given by

$$
\mathbf{P} = \left(u\mathbf{I}_{3x3} \quad \mathbf{c} \right)
\tag{2}
$$

where $(\mathbf{c}, u)^\mathsf{T}$ is the coordinate vector of the projection center and $\mathbf{I}$ the identity matrix. We use a projective representation for points, although will be assume that cameras lie out of the reference plane and therefore they are scaled affinely, i.e. $u=1$. Thus, cameras are only parameterized by non-homogeneous 3-vector $\mathbf{c}$. Expression (2) shows that this particular 3D reference system induces a proyective geometry equivalent to translating, calibrated cameras.

The projection of a 3D point $\begin{matrix} \mathbf{x}_i \\ w_i \end{matrix}$ on the k-th image plane is given by

$$_{ki}\mathbf{x}_{ki} = \mathbf{P}_k\mathbf{X}_i = \begin{pmatrix} \mathbf{I} & \mathbf{c}_k \end{pmatrix}\begin{matrix} \mathbf{x}_i \\ w_i \end{matrix} = \mathbf{x}_i \quad w_i\mathbf{c}_k \tag{3}$$

$_{ik}$ being the unknown projective depth of the point.

2.2   Recovery Algorithm

Let $\mathbf{S}$ be a 4xQ matrix of Q projective points coordinates representing the shape of a non-rigid surface at any time instant. We assume that each observation, $\mathbf{S}_t$, can be expressed as a linear combination of M fixed 4xQ basis shapes $\mathbf{S}_i$.

$$\mathbf{S}_t = \sum_{i=1,M} l_{ti}\mathbf{S}_i \tag{4}$$

Each basis matrix $\mathbf{S}_i$ is defined, by column, by the coordinates of Q unknown key-points. The problem is to estimate $\{\mathbf{S}_i\}, \{l_{it}\}$, M and the camera parameters $\{\mathbf{c}_k\}$ from a coordinate matrix of Q points tracked throughout a sequence of F-images. We assume a perspective camera with fixed and unknown internal parameters. According to (2) and (4) the measurements matrix in the plane+parallax framework for all the Q tracked points can be expressed by

$$\mathbf{W} = \begin{matrix} _{11}\mathbf{x}_{11} & \cdots & _{1Q}\mathbf{x}_{1Q} \\ _{21}\mathbf{x}_{21} & \cdots & _{2Q}\mathbf{x}_{2Q} \\ \vdots & \vdots & \vdots \\ _{F1}\mathbf{x}_{F1} & \cdots & _{FQ}\mathbf{x}_{FQ} \end{matrix} = \begin{matrix} l_{11}\mathbf{P}_1 & \cdots & l_{1M}\mathbf{P}_1 & \mathbf{S}_{11} & \cdots & \mathbf{S}_{1Q} \\ l_{21}\mathbf{P}_2 & \cdots & l_{2M}\mathbf{P}_2 & \mathbf{S}_{21} & \cdots & \mathbf{S}_{2Q} \\ \vdots & \cdots & \vdots & \vdots & \vdots & \vdots \\ l_{Q1}\mathbf{P}_F & \cdots & l_{QM}\mathbf{P}_F & \mathbf{S}_{M1} & \cdots & \mathbf{S}_{MQ} \end{matrix} \tag{5}$$

where $\mathbf{P}_k=(\mathbf{I}\ -\mathbf{c}_k)$ is the matrix of the k-th camera, and $\mathbf{S}_{ij}$ represents the j-th point of $\mathbf{S}_i$. The dimensionality of the matrices in equation (5) is (3FxQ)=(3Fx4M)x(4MxQ). We assume Q>>4M. A solution for the parallel cameras case has been given in [2]. A direct generalization of this technique to the perspective case is much more complex since the $_{ij}$ parameters have to be estimated before applying any factorization algorithm. Other possible approach is using an iterative upgrading approach starting from the solution of the parallel case. However, as pointed out in [7], knowing four coplanar reference points on all the views, cameras and points can be estimated without needing the $_{ij}$ parameters. Taking into account the equation (5), and for a fixed M value we apply the SVD decomposition to the measurement matrix

$$\mathbf{W}=\mathbf{U}\mathbf{D}\mathbf{V}^\mathsf{T}=\mathbf{T}_{(3Fx4M)}\mathbf{B}_{(4MxQ)}, \tag{6}$$

where $\mathbf{T}=\mathbf{U}_{(3F\times 4M)}\mathbf{D}^{1/2}_{(4M\times 4M)}$ is the matrix containing the information on the cameras and $\mathbf{B}^{T}=\mathbf{V}_{(Q\times 4M)}\mathbf{D}^{1/2}$ is the matrix associated to the basis vectors. This factorization is not unique, since from any global projective transformation of the 3D projective space we can calculate a different decomposition.

Let us denote that each three consecutive rows of $\mathbf{T}$ allow us to estimate the l_{ij} parameters associated to each different view. Reordering the three rows of $\mathbf{T}$ associated to the i-th view we can write

$$\mathbf{W}_{i\,(M\cdot 12)} = \begin{matrix} l_{i1} \\ l_{i2} \\ \vdots \\ l_{iM} \end{matrix} \; \mathbf{P}_{(1x12)} \tag{7}$$

where $\mathbf{p}$ is the row vector associated to the i-th camera matrix. Since $\mathbf{W}'_{(Mx12)}$ is the product of two range one matrices, its range is also one. Using its SVD decomposition and applying the range condition,

$$\mathbf{W}'_{i\,(Mx12)}=\mathbf{U}_{i1(MxM)}\mathbf{D}_{i1(MxM)}\mathbf{V}_{i1}^{T}{}_{(Mx12)} = \mathbf{U}_{i1(Mx1)}\mathbf{D}_{i1(1x1)}\mathbf{V}_{i1}^{T}{}_{(1x12)} = \mathbf{L}_{i(Mx1)}\mathbf{C}_{i(1x12)}, \tag{8}$$

where $\mathbf{L}_i=\mathbf{U}_{i1}\mathbf{D}_{i1}^{1/2}$ and $\mathbf{C}_i^{T}=\mathbf{V}_{i1}\mathbf{D}_{i1}^{1/2}$ and calculate the $\{l_{ij}\}$ values from the $\mathbf{L}_i$ vectors. Of course, the $\{l_{ij}\}$ values are not unique since exits an indetermination among the $\{l_{ij}\}$ and the $\{\mathbf{S}_{ij}\}$ values fitting the $\mathbf{S}$ values. Once we know the $\{l_{ij}\}$ values, equation (5) can be expressed as

$$\hat{\mathbf{W}} = \begin{matrix} \hat{\mathbf{x}}_{11} & \cdots & \hat{\mathbf{x}}_{1Q} \\ \hat{\mathbf{x}}_{21} & \cdots & \hat{\mathbf{x}}_{2Q} \\ \vdots & \vdots & \vdots \\ \hat{\mathbf{x}}_{F1} & \cdots & \hat{\mathbf{x}}_{FQ} \end{matrix} = \begin{matrix} \mathbf{P}_1 \\ \mathbf{P}_2 \\ \vdots \\ \mathbf{P}_F \end{matrix} \quad \mathbf{S}_{i1}_{i=1,M} \quad \mathbf{S}_{i2}_{i=1,M} \quad \cdots \quad \mathbf{S}_{iQ}_{i=1,M} = \hat{\mathbf{P}}\,\hat{\mathbf{S}} \tag{9}$$

where $\hat{\mathbf{W}}=\begin{pmatrix}\mathbf{C}_1^{T} & \mathbf{C}_2^{T} & \cdots & \mathbf{C}_Q^{T}\end{pmatrix}^{T}$. Equation (9) shows how we have reduced the non-rigid problem to a rigid one. To solve this rigid problem, we assume the knowledge of four common reference points in all images and estimate the matrix $\hat{\mathbf{P}}$ and the vector $\hat{\mathbf{S}}$ using the approach given in [8]. The vectors $\{\mathbf{S}_{ij}\}$ are estimated solving by least squares the over-determined linear system given by (5) and the Q equations defined by the $\hat{\mathbf{S}}$ vector. As solution we obtain a projective estimation of the basis points and camera centers. Different techniques can be used to upgrade these projective vectors, from the knowledge of calibration points in the scene, to an Euclidean reference system [4] [8][15].

3   Experiments

At the time of this writing we are carrying out several experiments to test the accuracy of the suggested approach. Several video sequences from flexible shape objects have been recorded. The Lucas-Kanade's tracker implementation given in [16] is used to track and extract the key-point coordinates along the image sequences [6][9] Our goal is to create non-rigid 3D object graphic models from image streams, thus the presence of calibration points on all images is a reasonable assumption. The experimental results will be shown elsewhere.

4   Summary

A method to estimate 3D object non-rigid models from video image sequences has been proposed. We model non-rigid deformations as linear combinations of basis points that allows us to reduce a non-rigid estimation problem to a rigid estimation one using the same cameras but different points. We estimate camera and points in the rigid case making use of the technique prposed in [8]. The final basis point estimation is obtained solving by least square a linear over-determined equation system.

References

1. Bascle, B., and Blake, A.: Separability of pose and expression in facial tracking and animation. In Proc. Int. Conf. Computer Vision. 1998.
2. Bregler, C., Hertzmann, A., Biermann, H.: Recovering non-rigid 3D shape from image streams. In Proc. IEEE Conf. Computer Vision and Pattern Recognition (CVPR'00) (2000).
3. Costeira,J.P., Kanade, T.: A multibody factorization method for independently moving objects. Int. Jour. Computer Vision, 29(3),1998, 159-179.
4. Hartley, R. Zisserman, A.: Multiple View geometry in Computer Vision. Cambridge University Press. 2000.
5. Lanitis, A., Taylor, C.J., Cootes, T.F. and Ahmed, T.: Automatic interpretation of human faces and hand gestures using flexible models. In Int. Workshop on Autom. Face-and-Gesture Recognition, 1995.
6. Lucas, B., Kanade, T.: An Iterative image registration technique with an application to stereo vision. In Proc. 7th Int. Joint Conf. on Artif. Intell., 1981.
7. Rother, C., Carlsson, S.: Linear multi-view reconstruction and camera recovery. In Proc. Int. Conf. Computer Vision (ICCV'01) (2001).
8. Rother, C., Carlsson, S.:   Linear multi-view reconstruction with missing data. In ECCV'02. Lecture Notes in Computer Science, Vol. 2351. Springer-Verlag, (2002).
9. Shi, J., Tomasi, C.: Good Features to Track. In CVPR'94.
10. Sturm,P., Triggs,B: A factorization based algorithm for multi-image projective structure and motion. In ECCV'96, Lecture Notes in Computer Science, Vol. 1064-1065, 1996, 709-719.
11. Tomasi, C., Kanade, T.: Shape and motion from image streams under orthography: A factorization method. Int. J. Computer Vision, 9(2), (1992), 137-154.

12. Torresani, L., Yang, D.B., Alexander, E.J., Bregler, C.: Tracking and modelling non-rigid objects with rank constraints. In IEEE Conf. Computer Vision and Pattern Recognition (ICCV'01) (2001).
13. Triggs, B.: Plane+Parallax, tensors and factorization. In EECV 2000, Lecture Notes in Computer Science, Vol. 1842-1843. Springer-Verlag, (2000).
14. Turk, M., and Pentland, A.: Eigenfaces for recognition. Jour. Cognitive Neurocience, 3(1), 1991, 71-86.
15. Weinshall, D., Anandan, P., Irani, M.: From ordinal to euclidean reconstruction with partial scene calibration. In Workshop SMILE'98. Lecture Notes in Computer Science, Vol 1506, 1998.
16. http://vision.stanford.edu/~birch/klt/

Author Index

Lecture Notes in Computer Science

For information about Vols. 1–2436

please contact your bookseller or Springer-Verlag